We're Outta Here

by David Wooten

Eggman Publishing
Nashville, Tennessee

ISBN: 1-886371-59-8

Cover Design: Charles Hooper

For interviews and other information, call
502-759-5851
800-931-7472

Acknowledgments

Thanks to...Arthur Mills for giving us thoughtful, sincere guidance in the beginning...Hap Harrington for sharing our enthusiasm when we were very unsure of ourselves...All of our friends who fed or gave us a bed along the way and to those that found a way to correspond with us all over the globe...my sister, Jenni, for "catching the moment" the day after the bike trip ended (on the back cover)...Ron Balsbaugh for hiring me upon our return after nineteen months "out of the mainstream"...Richard Courtney and Harold McAlindon for giving this project a chance...Annie Price for your honesty and insight in the editing process...Charles Hooper, Donna Paz, and Dan Loftin for your creative work on the cover and graphic design...and Lin Pendleton for helping to keep everyone organized in the final weeks.

Dedications

*To my wife, Susan...for agreeing to accompany me
in pursuit of a dream and for keeping me laughing
every day along the way. Your unwavering love
was the glue that kept the trip together.*

*To my precious children, Sarah and Rachel....
You have control of your own destiny; do what
you really want to do, do it well and have fun.*

*To my parents and grandparents...for giving me a "can do"
attitude and zest for adventure and for your love and
encouragement of the crazy little things we do.*

*To my inlaws, Bud and Rita...for your deft editing pen and
your totally unselfish support before, during and after the trip.*

Preface

I guess the need to challenge the status quo is at least a small part of everyone. For many, it stays latent for a lifetime, trapped and stifled like a bird in a chimney chute. For others, a chance occurrence sparks the desire, the pent-up burning energy inside that a person perhaps never knew existed, to escape the confines of "what we are supposed to do" or "what everyone else is doing." To feel and listen to the energy is one thing, to act on it is quite another.

My first opportunity to act on one of these impulses happened when I was a first semester junior at the University of South Carolina. It was early November of 1981 and I was in the midst of the most serious month-long relationship I had ever had. On a chilly Sunday night shortly before Thanksgiving, my girlfriend Bobbie walked into my dorm room with a serious look on her face that I hadn't seen before. Within minutes, I found out that she would soon be on her way to the U.S. Virgin Islands on a semester-long exchange program! Upon hearing the heart-wrenching news, my emotions ran the gamut from happiness for her to helplessness and shock for me. My immediate reaction was to try and join her there, but she sadly volunteered that the deadline for applying had already passed. We hugged, the tears flowed and after an hour or so, she went to her third floor room. Immediately after she left, a surge of adrenaline rocketed through my body. The latent urge had been exposed, like a live wire bouncing on the pavement. Somehow, some way, deadline or no deadline, I was going to find a way to go on one of these exchange programs that I had never heard of until that night. Sleep would be sparse over the coming hours and the very next morning I went to work on my new mission.

Two weeks to the day later, I got a call from the U.S.C. Exchange Office. I had been accepted at Sonoma State University in Rohnert Park, California! I was very fortunate indeed, considering the fact that as a second-semester junior, this was the last opportunity for me to do it.

I drove across country to California in a caravan with two other girls seven years my senior who also were going to Sonoma. It was the first time I had been west of the Carolinas in my life and in nine days I tripled the number of states I had been to in my previous twenty years.

The California experience changed my life forever, giving me the confidence, fortitude and perseverance it takes to conquer any surmountable obstacle or challenge. At a very tender age, I realized that nothing was out of reach as long as I planned, prepared, and wanted it badly enough. Thoughts of biking across the country and seeing the rest of the world suddenly emerged as personal goals that seemed quite doable. The first person I actually told about my new dream was my dad, in early April of 1984, about two years after the exchange trip. Although I had been firmly entrenched in the corporate world since my June '83 graduation, I knew it was not an if, but a when, that my goals would be realized. The bird was now completely out of the chimney and flying high above the clouds and the trip was etched in my mind during every bike ride and 10K race that I participated in over the next few years.

On the relationship front, Bobbie and I broke up the first day we saw each other following the exchange semester despite the fact that we had kept in touch regularly through the mail and on the phone for six months. Three years of "wild oats" later, I met the woman that I would later marry while practicing my "Bud curls" at a bar in Nashville. Susan was admittedly not the most adventurous person I had ever met, but charming, beautiful and smart with a real "can do" attitude. We talked at length about the possibility of a sojourn from the "real world" at some point in the early stages of our union, but I don't think she really thought I would follow through with my plan.

To her credit, she bravely stuck to her promise to join me when "the time" came. Returning to our apartment in Morristown, Tennessee from the West Virginia Snowshoe Mountains on New Year's Day 1990, we decided that we could wait no longer if we wanted to take a year and a half sabbatical and attempt to have a couple of kids by the time we were thirty-five. From that fateful moment forward, we had exactly five months to plan, organize and train for the journey of our lives.

"Everything starts as somebody's daydream."
—*Larry Niven*

"Half of life is if."
—*church marquee*

"You may be disappointed if you fail,
but you are doomed if you don't try."
—*Beverly Sills*

"The sweetest part is acting after making a decision."
—*Indigo Girls, "Hammer and a Nail"*

"The most noble human trait is the ability to rise above mere existence
by sacrificing one's self through the years for a goal."
—*Einstein*

"Fly the great big sky
See the great big sea
Kick through continents
Bustin' boundaries
Take it hip to hip, rocket through the wilderness
Around the world, the trip begins with a kiss."
—*B52's, "Roam"*

"Boundaries are set by dictators
created to regulate cattle grazing
and employ tollbooth attendants.
With no regard for mankind's unalienable rights,
among those to treat the world as it was intended,
as a place of curiosity and chance.
To be walked, scaled, rafted, and by all means, trodden.
Not that limits have no place here.
They do.
But they were never meant to be barriers that keep you in,
only starting points that suggest how much farther you could
GO OUT."
—*Nike ad*

Foreword

Since the industrial revolution began, Americans have been guided by the premise that hard work will lead them to a life of self-satisfaction and happiness. In our zeal to "get ahead" and prosper as individuals and as a nation, we have risen to the heights of economic prosperity. The success, unfortunately, has acted as a drug or intoxicant for many, blinding people's perceptions of the definition of a "balanced life," producing tremendous stress and countless premature deaths. I challenge you to remember the last time you heard someone say, "I wish I had spent more time at the office," as they lay on their deathbed.

Americans have allowed their "average vacation days a year" to sink to the lowest number of any industrialized country in the world—ten. An American employee must work thirty years to get as much vacation time as the typical European gets the first year on the job.

Whether we like to admit it or not, and I have been very guilty of it myself, we have allowed the four-letter word, work, to rule our lives and become an end in itself. Managed in concert and harmony with other physical, spiritual and creative outlets, it is necessary and useful, stimulating our minds and giving us options in the form of a paycheck. It is a naive misconception, however, that most Americans are getting enough ahead as they curse the alarm clock every morning of their lives. In fact, only 5 percent of us will reach retirement age financially independent after all those years of sacrifice, sweat, and many times, less than totally satisfying work.

With these rather ominous realizations in mind, at age twenty-nine I decided to set my stubborn work ethic temporarily to the side and concentrate my energies on tackling some dreams that had been dancing in my head for a decade. Although it would mean stepping outside the comfort zone of the life that I had so carefully constructed and so laboriously maintained, I knew that the time would never be better than the present. Even though my desire to travel was strong, leaving behind the perks, accouterments, friends and challenges of the fast-track corporate world was not an easy task. I knew I was giving up a situation that most people would dream to be in and I was reminded of that fact and the "opportunity cost" of my actions with annoying regularity.

As a married man, I had to plan more carefully and thoroughly for the departure because I never knew when I'd have to overcome an objection or do a super sales job at a moment's notice. Susan and I had been bonded in holy matrimony for a grand total of seventeen months when I made good on my previous foreboding promise that some unconventional activities might actually occur in the early stages of our relationship. With a healthy dose of warranted trepidation, she agreed to accompany me on a *three-month, self-contained, bicycle trip across the U. S. and a year of backpacking around the world!* Although she had hardly sat on a bike seat since prepuberty, Susan recognized the importance of the trip to me and didn't want to sit home idly wondering what might have been. By agreeing to leave job, family and friends for such a long period of time, she made a statement of true commitment to our relationship that can't be overstated.

As we began to chart our course for the next fifteen months, we started to appreciate the phenomenal size of the travel industry. As the world's biggest industry with 127 million employees and $1.4 trillion a year in business, it represents 12.3 percent of total consumer spending worldwide. The vast majority of that total is made up of "sightseeing" vacations or "entertainment" holidays focusing on familiar, lifeless, physical structures, or familiar, active, amusement parks. Although fun and certainly not a waste of time, they don't really engage a person's mind or motivate a person to learn how to associate with people of different outlooks, beliefs, customs or nationalities. If the experiences we have while traveling are "too much like home or too comfortable," why go through the inconveniences, fatigue and associated burdens to have them?

As little as a decade ago, such questions were rarely asked, and only a few pioneers broke the paradigms and attempted to maximize the breadth of travel opportunities out there. Today, more than 5000 adventure travel outfitters based in North America alone assist people in getting off the interstates, into the woods, away from the phones and up to their eyeballs in new and exciting experiences.

Affording travel is a matter of priorities—many people who "can't afford a trip" could sell their car and travel for two years. Although I had saved regularly and diligently since the day after college, I was by no means rich when we decided to voluntarily stop getting a paycheck. For some people, it's not the cost of living that's so expensive but the cost of working. Eighty-three percent of the average person's paycheck is taken up by monthly bills, any of which serve to do little more than reduce their options and increase their headaches. With huge lunch tabs, fancy cars, expensive wardrobes, health club memberships, taxes, mortgage payments and half a dozen "gadgets of the month" around to impress the neighbors, it's no wonder that some people lose their flexibility and spontaneity necessary to truly enjoy the world of travel. A conscious effort has to be made continually to prioritize and simplify. Spending more money at home or with a backpack usually builds a thicker wall between a person and what they are really trying to accomplish.

The goal of our trip was to truly become a traveler instead of a tourist and to fully capitalize on this last great source of legal adventure. We would challenge ourselves to see the world as a cultural garden instead of an inconvenience, and approach it with open eyes, an uncluttered mind, a minimum of belongings and a frugal budget. We would be mobile and flexible with a keen desire to mingle and learn from people all over the globe. As in most meaningful pursuits in life, the real satisfaction would not come from crossing the finish line, but in the pendulum of emotions, triumphs and tribulations of the journey itself.

Table of Contents

Australia 91

Asia 121

Europe

Epilogue

Appendix

"Americans have this compulsion to tame the landscape;
we are on our own personal Tour de France."
—*Michael Marsden, professor of popular culture*
Bowling Green University

"The healthy wayfarer sitting beside the road scanning the horizon
open before him, is he not the absolute master of the earth,
the waters and even the sky? What house dweller can vie with him
in power and wealth? His estate has no limits, his empire no law.
No word bends him toward the ground, for the bounty and beauty
of the world are already his."
—*Isabelle Eberhardt*

"The open road is a beckoning, a strangeness,
a place where a man can lose himself."
—*William Least Heat Moon*

"The best moments usually occur when a person's body or mind
is stretched to its limit in a voluntary effort to accomplish
something difficult or worthwhile."
—*Csikszentmihalyi*

"Human beings have very distinct limits in terms of physical capacity,
but are capable of amazing feats of endurance and determination.
No matter how we develop ourselves, we cannot learn to fly
like a bird, nor run like a cheetah, nor punch like a gorilla;
we simply are not capable of it. But people can learn to run
thirty miles without stopping, swim long distances or
do three thousand sit-ups. If you can do one,
you can learn to do three thousand
if you want to badly enough."
—*The Baseball Book*

"I believe the best scenic overlooks aren't marked by signs
that say scenic overlook."
—*Reebok ad*

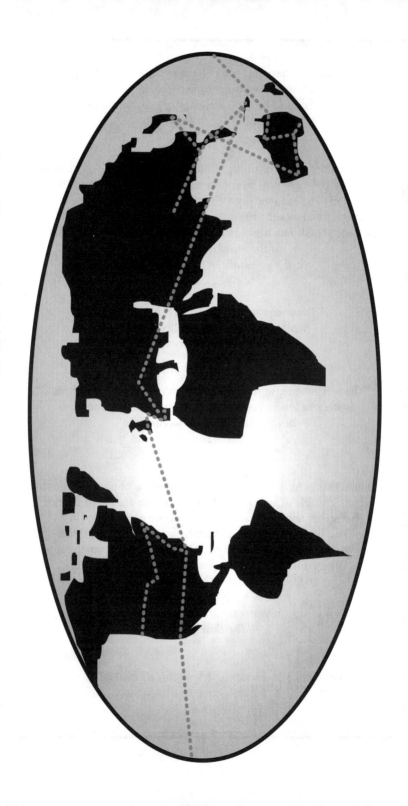

The U.S.

Pre-Trip Planning

January 2–June 8, 1990

The morning of June 3rd, I resigned from my management position with the Pepsi-Cola Company. Although I was convinced it was the right thing to do after weeks of deliberating the pros and cons, it was without a doubt the hardest, most gut-wrenching decision I had ever made. For seven years, I had been a dedicated corporate warrior with the Quaker Oats Company and Pepsi. Now it was time to abruptly put it all aside to live out a dream.

One year before that fateful day, I was promoted to the sleepy little industrial town of Morristown, Tennessee, where Susan and I rented an inexpensive 800 square foot apartment. Since we were in the "serious consideration" phase of "the trip" at that time, I knew that renting was our only option in Morristown. Although our experience there was wonderful, we realized in early January that this would definitely be the appropriate time and place from which to embark. From January through May, we spent almost every hour of spare time we had (Susan also worked full time at a Morristown hospital as an emergency room nurse) poring over countless brochures, pamphlets, books and magazines about bicycling, backpacking and a relatively new phenomena called "adventure travel."

Since I knew we were going to attempt to bicycle across America and backpack around the world, the immediate questions that needed to be answered were not if or what, but how, for how long, and how much (as in spending). As relatively novice cyclists (Susan had actually ridden about fifteen miles on a bike since she was fifteen years old!), our best chance of actually making it across the United States was to travel with other people trying to do the same thing. We checked out several organizations, some for profit and some non-profit, that offered cross-country trip assistance, but only one fit my demanding profile from the beginning. In logging about three hundred miles a year on my bike throughout the previous decade, I had become familiar with Bikecentennial (now called Adventure Cycling Association), a nonprofit organization out of Missoula, Montana that specialized in organizing self-contained (participants carry all gear on their bikes as opposed to "sagwagons") excursions of varying lengths throughout the country. They offered two cross-country options, west-to-east from Washington state to Maine, and east-to-west from Virginia to Washington. We chose west-to-east for several reasons: 1) It covered more states through which we had never traveled. 2) It went with the prevailing winds instead of against them, giving us at least a psychological advantage versus the other way. 3) It crossed the Cascades and Rockies, two mountain ranges we definitely wanted to see. 4) It finished in Maine, on the East Coast, where we could be picked up along with our bikes by my parents at the end of the trip.

For a modest fee of $2,000 a person, Bikecentennial provided groups of ten to twelve cross-country participants with sleeping accommodations and food for the duration of the 90-day trip along with wonderful mile-by-mile maps (one inch equated to four miles) and a group leader who had previously taken a trip of like magnitude. The accommodations were arranged by either the leader or the group members each day, and food was bought just prior to or after arrival at camp each night.

During the weeks leading up to the start of the bike trip, we sold the majority of our furniture, (mostly post-college artifacts that needed to be purged anyway) and boxed everything else up to be stored in Susan's parents' (Bud and Rita) garage in Murfreesboro, Tennessee, about three hours west of Morristown. I gave my company car back to Pepsi and Bud and Rita volunteered to baby-sit our personal car while we were gone.

I second-guessed our decision to leave our very comfortable situation a thousand times the last two months as personal and family expectations rose to a fever pitch. Although we emerge from our years of schooling somewhat prepared to tackle the "real world" of work in America, our impending departure from it was both unconventional and unprecedented among our friends and acquaintances. That made it harder to sidestep promising careers in midstream, even as we knew we were embarking on a true once-in-a-lifetime adventure.

I was born and raised in the Carolinas, the oldest of three children in a family that moved frequently to capitalize on my dad's ever-changing employment prospects in the fledgling computer field. Attending eight schools during my sixteen years of education, I had to learn the meaning of the words flexibility and resiliency or be continually depressed at the prospects of always finding new friends. Looking back on it, I feel that the moves were instrumental in helping me develop the confidence and desire I have today to explore new places and experience new ways of doing things.

Susan, on the other hand, lived in the same comfortable, three-story house in a small town in Wisconsin throughout middle school and high school. Even today, almost two decades after graduation, she can go back to bucolic New Holstein and wave to friends standing in their driveways like she never left. Her background as a registered nurse would pay huge dividends on our trip as we encountered some fairly unsanitary and potentially dangerous health situations. As the oldest of four, she, too, was very independent and strong-willed, but the biggest attribute she brought along was her gift of genuine concern for other people. Although we had our inevitable clashes from time to time, our feelings for one another would actually grow stronger despite the fact that we were together almost twenty-four hours a day for fourteen consecutive months!

With a combined annual income of close to $100,000, it hadn't been difficult for Susan and I to significantly pad the $68,000 in savings that I had accumulated alone prior to our July 1988 marriage. By June of 1990, the month of departure, we had amassed a total nest egg of approximately $125,000 in combined 401K, mutual funds, IRA's and checking accounts. After several weeks of extensive research on the costs of biking and backpacking, I knew that we could live on approximately $100 a day between us for the duration of the trip, leaving us with about $80,000-85,000 in savings to come back to. We planned to live at Susan's parents for the first three or four months after our return while I embarked on a renewed job search. Susan was able to secure a part-time position at a hospital in Murfreesboro prior to our departure, minimizing the pressure on me to find something immediately.

Thanks again to Susan's wonderful parents, managing money while thousands of miles from home was not a difficult undertaking for us. We set up a joint checking account ("David or Susan Wooten, or Rita Klika") before we left with about $5,000 in it, and I presigned enough mutual fund redemption letters to cover the other $40,000 or so that I thought we were going to spend. Whenever the checking account started to get close to $1,000 because of car payments, phone bills, and AMEX bills, (we got cash at AMEX offices or regular bank cash machines around the world using our AMEX card) Rita mailed one of the mutual fund letters and received cash about a week later. (Example: To Whom It May Concern: Please redeem $5,000 of my Fidelity Magellan stock—account #xyx—and send check to David Wooten at xyz address, followed by my signature).

The mail-receiving procedure was also a simple proposition. Before we left home, we chose four "mailstops" to receive correspondence across the United States as well as locations designated overseas in Tokyo, Bangkok, Singapore and Zurich. Although the exact time of arrival was an educated guess on our part, each GPO (General Post Office) kept mail received for a person for up to six months before discarding it. The system really works and it was an emotional lifesaver to have a way to communicate with our loved ones.

After deciding who we were going to trek across America with, we went to work to find the equipment that would give us a chance to make it. The first and only cyclery we visited was Skeddadle's Bike Shop in Murfreesboro, less than a two mile drive from Susan's parents home. Hap Harrington and his wonderful staff were immediately enthralled by our quest and gave us their undivided attention when we walked in their store with a very large shopping list. When we left several hours later, we were proud owners of the following items that would get us started on our cross-country way:

- A pair of 18-speed Cannondale touring bikes with 1/4-inch tires

- Rearview mirrors that velcroed to the handlebar
- Digital odometers
- Bike gloves, an absolute lifesaver from day one to prevent injuries from "road shock," and helmets, which should be required by law in every state
- Three pairs of bike shorts and shirts apiece to get us going
- Two bike bottles each
- Bike pumps that attached to the underside of the center frame
- Extra inner tubes, tires, spokes, and a basic bike repair kit
- Extra handlebar tape to cushion our hands from "road shock"
- Wrap-a-round sunglasses
- Bike shoes

In addition to the items procured at Skeddadle's, we also purchased front handlebar bags that featured a top pouch to keep our maps in place and dry and to store daily "grazing" food, and front and rear panniers, side pouches that held everything we brought along except tents, sleeping bags and inflatable sleeping mats which were secured with a bungee cord behind the seat.

We had the best of intentions to be at our maximum physical preparedness for the ride of our lives (NTR610—the Northern Tier Route commencing on 6/10) by June. A series of "day-at-a-glance," erasable calendars adorned our walls with an intensive training schedule etched in for us to follow. Unfortunately, between work, unexpected parties thrown for our departure, visits with friends, and assorted other procrastinating measures, we had no problem reducing the proposed 150 miles per week regime to about forty. In relatively flat eastern Tennessee, this hardly constituted grueling training. In fact, we managed only a single twenty-mile round trip jaunt with our panniers loaded with the fifty-plus pounds of gear that would soon accompany us for a full ninety days. Since Susan had scarcely ridden a two-wheeler since grade school, the dreaded four letter word, F-E-A-R, rightfully reared its ugly head. Justifiably, she wondered out loud how she was going to scale the Cascades and Rockies by July 4th when she had yet to successfully ascend the hill into our apartment complex without walking!

It was a fair question that I chose to ignore and gloss over with the power of positive thinking. Of course, this whole thing was my idea, so naturally I had no intention of stopping short of the "finish line," even if I had to get off the bike and crawl. Susan, however, had little to no inner motivation, except to "do it for us," feeling it would be detrimental to be apart all summer after less than two years of marriage. Deep inside, we really wondered if that would be enough. One of Susan's journal entries after a short training ride in Morristown captured our mutual concern. . . "I could barely see the '8' mile mark turn over on my odometer because I was looking through eyes full of tears! It was hard to breathe without my lungs feeling as if someone was pulling them up through my throat. At the same time, I was trying hard to hide it all from David."

June 9 & 10: Seattle, WA International Youth Hostel

Three days before the initial leg of the journey, we disassembled our mint condition Cannondales and managed to somehow coerce them into tiny airline bike boxes. Fortunately, by the time we reached Seattle, the cultural melting pot of the northwestern portion of the country, several of our Bikecenntenial comrades had also arrived. We certainly needed their help trying to figure out how to put our new, cherished, life support systems back together properly.

As soon as we landed in Seattle, it felt like we had been out of big-city circulation for a few months too long. A ride with a foreign cabbie from the airport, a confrontation with a rather hostile street person in front of the youth hostel, and being in a true international sleeping environment for the first time certainly kept us on edge for the initial twenty-four hours after arrival. We took a Saturday stroll around the typically soggy city, venturing through the renowned Fish Market and its "flying fish" stall. We also perused several open-air flea markets and got in a warm-up ride on the way to a bike shop for some last-minute extras.

A Sunday evening meeting had been scheduled a few weeks before by our Bikecenntenial leader, Warren, to allow everyone to get acquainted and to review the logistics of what lay in store for us over the course of the summer. At least for the first two weeks or so, Warren was committed to play "roundup" in the back of the pack to make sure that everyone made it safely to camp. We would have breakfast meetings to determine the destination for each day, (Warren or another member of the group would usually call ahead the night before to "book" a campsite) decide whose turn it was to buy groceries and cook for the group, and to review other pertinent details. As we went around the room introducing ourselves and commenting on our cycling prowess, it was obvious that this was a fairly experienced group of bicyclists overall but not a strikingly athletic bunch—Susan and I definitely included. It was clear from the beginning that teamwork, camaraderie and mental toughness would be the key ingredients if we, as a unit, would be able to successfully navigate to the shores of Maine by September 7th.

NTR610

The cast of characters that made up NTR610 were:

Jean—very outspoken accountant (local wine company) from San Francisco in her late thirties who got a paid three-month leave from work by a very understanding boss; married with no children; husband Tom is a lawyer; definitely a person who "seizes the moment" and is not afraid to tackle a dream; husband and in-laws sailed around-the-world about 15 years before.

Jeff—relatively quiet, divorced accountant from Cincinnati who also got a paid three-month leave of absence from Arthur Anderson and Associates; en-

Bar Harbor

Seattle

4,705 miles
coast to coast

joys athletic challenges of all sorts.

Elaine, "Smitty"—pleasant, determined RN from New Hampshire in her late twenties; single.

Peter—Extremely independent, meticulously organized chef for United Airlines in Chicago; married less than a year to Amy whom he missed terribly (he tried to get her to follow his dream but she wouldn't do it); very helpful and action oriented.

Warren "Junior", Bikecentennial leader—Successfully completed cross-country trip the year before from Virginia to Washington as member of another group; had worked part-time since he applied for enhanced role in second year; although not apparent initially, his lack of confidence as a leader was one of the most significant dynamics that affected NTR610; overall, a very nice guy, probably too nice to lead a trip of this mental and physical intensity with a menagerie of extremely strong-willed individuals.

Warren "Senior", "Mr. T" (his last name started with a T but I never knew what it was)—Fifty-nine year old former bike racer who treated every day as if it were a race; since this was not the "Gumball Rally," it was not only inappropriate, but odd and rather amusing; on several occasions, he heated the stove, fixed breakfast and left camp before the break of dawn!

Maria—Twenty-nine year old special education teacher of handicapped children in New Hampshire; went on trans-American trip seven years before as well as a 1500 mile solo jaunt in Canada; a great comrade for Susan, very open about her feelings and energetic; like most everyone else in the group, definitely not afraid to say what was on her mind.

Katie—Probably the quietest member but the most determined to make it every inch of the way without any help from anyone; about the same age as Maria and worked in the same rehab center, veteran of an extended cycling vacation in Ireland; her thighs were like rocks before we even started.

Lee Ann—Chicagoan in her late twenties who worked in the heart of the city; Midwestern tough and an experienced cyclist.

Julie—Along with Susan, the "least likely to succeed" when the summer started; Moody (and not ashamed to admit it), stubborn Jersey girl, inexperienced cyclist and a closet smoker with a heart of gold and a razor sharp wit.

As opposed to a semester-long school project or a summer league baseball team, we all found ourselves in a rather precarious situation. Like it or not, we were married by fate for a long, hot summer as we attempted to stay within two feet of the side of the road without falling off or getting hurt for 4705 miles. It was easy to like everyone at the beginning, but how would we handle the inevitable flare-ups and clashes on the 12 percent grade hills ("grade" in this case is defined as the steepness of a hill, a 5 percent grade is steep enough to merit a warning sign on the highway for truckers to slow down) after eight hours of pebble dodging? Who or what would be the glue that would keep us pushing together instead of apart on the long, winding mountain passes? The most amazing aspect of a trip like this is that any minute of any day could have meant the end for any one of us because of injury, an accident or simply mental fatigue. The unrelenting focus required and the never-ending uncertainty are the reasons why it was important to chronicle some aspect of every day of this trek. There certainly wouldn't be any days we could possibly forget.

Out of the Blocks

June 11: Kitsap, WA Memorial Park (33 cumulative miles)

June 12: Fort Warden State Park (68 miles)

June 13: Bayview, WA State Park (123 miles)

Everyone talks about the rain in the upper Northwest like it is the state animal. We certainly were not spared the whims of the local "beast" on the way to Kitsap Memorial Park as chilly, intermittent showers forced us to try out our waterproof parkas a lot sooner than we had hoped. Through thirty-three miles of rolling hills, narrow, tree-lined, two-lane highways and a heavy dose of the wet stuff, the first day seemed like it would never end. Frustrated and exhausted, Susan lagged in the rear all day with leader, Warren. Quoting her diary, "I was acutely aware of being last out of twelve. I was using all the energy I had just to stay on the bike, let alone pedal it! Warren was hand-feeding me 'gorp' (M & M's, raisins and peanuts) to try and keep me fueled. All the while, I kept thinking, 'Isn't this stuff fattening?'" We pitched our two-person "pup" tent after a group dinner and both collapsed into a well-deserved coma.

June 12

Our 5 a.m. wake-up call was the pesky, obnoxious, black-winged fowl that serves no obvious useful purpose, the all-American crow. Rearranging my aching 6-foot-2-inch frame and changing into my bike gear inside the tent felt akin to escaping from a strait jacket. It would become a very familiar, crack-of-dawn event that never really got much easier.

A hearty breakfast of oatmeal, whole wheat toast, fruit and hot tea smelled and sounded great, but my system was still in an uncomfortable churning mode from the seven hours of exertion the day before. The appetite would come around in spades in due time.

I had a rather inauspicious start, accidentally causing my own flat while hastily trying to pump up my rear tire. Despite the low-hanging clouds that continually teased us with the threat of rain, we found solace in the beauty of the heavily-wooded area. Majestic Douglas firs, spruce, hemlocks and cedar trees blanketed the landscape and permeated the air with the delicious smell of the outdoors.

The whole group suffered varying aches and pains and Susan lagged with Warren again. By the time we mercifully chose our campsite for the night, parts of me, especially my rear torso area, were totally uncomfortable. The stinging stayed with me as I gingerly removed myself from the bike seat, making it next to impossible to walk, sit or lie down. Frustration confrontation number one took place in the woods behind the group picnic table as Susan vented a few "why am I here" selections before we talked it through, vowing to give it our best shot the next day.

June 13

The girls oohed and aahed one last time before we departed Fort Warden Park, the site of the filming of *An Officer and a Gentleman* with his royal studliness, actor Richard Gere. After an early morning ferry ride, we persevered despite an extremely hilly day. The saddlesore had reached excruciating proportions and we weren't even going east yet! I countered the pain with a combination of Vaseline and baby powder, but the only way to put the fire out was to not be on the seat. I could only grit my teeth and hope I could break in the seat, *before* it broke my spirit.

The scenic highlight to this point was Deception Pass, a majestic gorge within the pristine inner island ocean of Desolation Sound. We parked the bikes and snapped pictures in awe of its natural splendor. About 7 p.m., we finally pulled into Bayview, population 8, where we set up camp next to Padilla Bay. The next morning, it would serve as our ceremonial "dipping of the tires" spot (a ritual of cross-country cyclists whereby a person's bike tires are rolled into a large body of water on both coasts) representing the west coast beginning of our trip.

Sore Buns and Ailing Knees

June 14: Rockport, WA State Park (180 miles)

June 15: Diablo, WA Colonial Campground (215 miles)

June 16/17: Winthrop, WA K.O.A. (281 miles)

We awoke to the clamoring of pots and pans as Warren Sr., the elder statesman of our group and the earliest riser, started the gas stove to prepare the oatmeal and coffee. A retired steel worker from Buffalo, New York, Warren, despite pushing sixty years old, was in tremendous physical condition with a penchant for bike racing and high-risk winter sports like paraskiing and helicopter powder skiing. He was the only one in the group over thirty-five, and seemed willing to share his extensive knowledge of cycling mechanics to an overall hesitant bunch in that area.

Before leaving camp, I encountered my second time-consuming, troublesome, mechanical difficulty in four days as my rear tire was dangerously "out of true" (unbalanced and wobbly). Warren Jr. accompanied me back across the bay to Anacortes in a sardine can pickup truck to find a bike shop, where only minor adjustments were required to put us back on the road. By this time, it was 12:30 p.m. and we had fifty-seven miles to traverse before dusk.

Fortunately, it was a predominantly flat day with endless stretches of fertile, commercial fields of strawberries, daffodils and irises. Late in the afternoon, we were able to sprint along an almost car-free road adjacent to the Skagit River, aided by a cool tailwind and the beauty of rose, pink and white rhododendron flowers adorning the edge of the woods.

The state park in Rockport was in a truly awe-inspiring setting with a gorgeous backdrop of snow-capped mountain peaks, an icy, rushing stream and luscious green grass. Susan prepared dinner with Elaine or "Smitty" as she would soon be called. A mouth-watering serving of pasta and spaghetti sauce with sautéed Italian sausage and onion was the perfect wrap- up of our best day yet. Unbeknownst to everyone, however, Susan's knee had begun to hurt.

June 15

Activities that we took for granted only five days before suddenly seemed very cherished to us. Comfortably using the bathroom, breathing deeply, bending over and laughing, among other essential human functions, all required a few extra seconds of thought than usual.

Susan's knee quickly became the most significant "among others" of the entire trip. During a late morning group break, we informally voted that the swelling and bruising had gotten noticeably worse and as a precautionary measure, she should hitch a ride to camp through the eight miles of western Cascade mountains ahead of us. Warren and I tracked down a lady and her sixteen-year-old son at the Seattle Power Company in Newhalem. She took Susan to her house to fill our water jugs and bike bottles because the water lines were down, then gave her and "Bo" (nickname for Susan's bike) a ride in her 4x4, explaining the scenery and workings of the dam along the way. By this time, Susan had become a determined trooper and begrudgingly accepted the well-advised lift, "I struggled with getting the ride from way deep inside," she wrote in her diary. "I felt like I was letting David down—it wasn't until much later that I started to feel bad about letting me down!"

Every inch of those miles into Diablo was sheer torture. Passing through two dangerously dark tunnels, an almost nonexistent shoulder, bumper-to-bumper tourist traffic, and a succession of 8 percent grade hills for good measure, it was our biggest challenge yet, but sadly only a teaser of what was to come during the next two weeks.

We all washed a few pieces of laundry in the arctic Diablo Lake, only fifty feet from our tents. We caught a couple hours of fading sunlight and with the afternoon winds, most of our clothes dried quickly.

June 16/17

Warren and I secured Susan ride number two with the quintessential all-American family. We couldn't have hand-picked a better one if we had scoured the entire state of Washington. They were thrilled to share their rented RV and give her and Julie, who was experiencing similar knee problems, a lift to Winthrop. Eight-year-old James became Susan's buddy from the start, checking out her bruises and bike, and even picking a beautiful assortment of wild flowers at a rest stop.

Warren and I got another late start on the North Cascade Highway, which until 1972 went no further than this picturesque spot at the Diablo Dam. It took a hundred years of lobbying for the miners and cattlemen of the eastern slopes to convince the state legislature to complete the gap in the highway. Even today, because of dangerous weather conditions, it's only open for travel from April to November.

From the campground entrance to the thirty-two mile mark, we inched along a 6 percent upward grade, rising in elevation from 2500 to 5477 feet, almost half a mile! Warren paced himself to keep me in sight and encouraged me to fuel my body every fifteen minutes or so with Powerbars, peanut butter and jelly sandwiches, cookies, and fruit. We began to run out of food near the top and he resorted to bread morsels to "tease me up" in 300-foot increments. I know we stopped over a hundred times as muscles tightened around my ailing wrists, neck, knees and torso. I tried to look only a few feet ahead as I rode, concentrating on reaching and passing a million tiny milestones like cracks in the pavement, a sign on the road, or a pebble. Until we reached the Washington Pass precipice, I could hardly enjoy the increasingly wonderful scenery because I really didn't know if I would make it.

Once at the top, we witnessed a mid-June winter sports fest with cross country and downhill skiers and snow boarders right next to the road. They obviously drove up there!

The last thirty-four miles to camp was a blur as Warren and I wound down the steep eastern slope of desert-like terrain in a little over two hours. The free fall from Washington Pass with a cliff on one side and a wall of rock on the other was rather unnerving to say the least. In mid-run, despite our wobbly legs and tired upper bodies, we had to force our minds to concentrate 110 percent on keeping rigid and staying balanced because it was painfully obvious that a single misplaced stone could send us flying headfirst over the handlebars. At the bottom, we took an emergency stop at the first port-a-potty sighting in miles, but every spider, flying stinging insect and ant in the county had unfortunately beat us to it. This was definitely not a place for the maid service set.

Just prior to Winthrop, a herd of sprawling cattle ambled slowly in the road ahead of us. After witnessing snowbanks only moments before, it felt like a daydream to suddenly be in the presence of farm animals! About 6:30 p.m., as exhausted as humanly possible, we collapsed into camp. The group treated itself to delivered pizza and zonked out at dusk. While Warren and I were careen-

ing down the mountain, Susan had plenty of time to ponder why we were sub-
jecting our bodies to this agony, "I feel so wimpy, so much of a cop-out. Poor
David, he so sweetly looked for a ride for me and now he has to rough it on his
sore knees. Sometimes I wonder what he's out to prove, although I'd much
rather have him this way than without goals, plans and dreams. He's a bit out of
his realm—there isn't a suit, company car or hotel for miles—he's adjusting to
a whole new life. I'll just love him and encourage him. I wouldn't trade our love
for anything."

The initial rest day was an emotional and physical lifesaver for everyone.
Although we had only 281 miles out of 4700+ under our belts, crossing the
Cascades was a significant milestone and confidence booster.

Susan, Julie and I limped around the "wild west" town of Winthrop for a
couple hours as my feet and legs cried for rest. The ambiance of the area really
made us feel as though we were on the set of *Bonanza* or *Gunsmoke*.

As I napped in our very warm tent during the early afternoon, Susan went
with Peter back to town where the conversation drifted from cycling to serious
topics like marriage, sex, relationships and the death of his father. He spoke of
his recent marriage to Amy and the decision to leave after only a year together
to pursue his lifelong dream. A very sensitive and caring individual, he would
prove to be a strong support for our own relationship as we had our ups and
downs throughout the summer.

They stopped at a local tavern after peeking through the door and saw an
Eddie Rabbit look-a-like belt out the song "G-L-O-R-I-A." After a wine cooler
or three, Susan put her vocal chords into action by singing a few old Marshall
Tucker tunes with the band. She's a wonderful closet singer who always says
she wants to be a rock star in her next life.

It was becoming very clear after only a week together that our group did not
contain a shortage of strong, independent personalities. I guess that's what most
people would suspect with an undertaking of this magnitude. Warren Jr. recommended that Susan and Julie play it safe and stay off their bikes and injured
knees over the next three days. Both fought his suggestion vehemently, but
Susan knew that it was best long-term to make sure no further damage was
done, "I can handle the pain, but I'm frustrated because I know nothing about
orthopedics. Am I damaging my knee? We still have such a long way to go. It
took me so long to mentally concede to this whole trip and now, it's physically
that I can't cut it. I feel more like the team mascot than a team member. Please
God, take care of us. . ."

"Powder Butt"

June 18: Omak, WA Fairgrounds (337 miles)

June 19: Jay's Hostel, Republic, WA (414 miles)

June 20: Mo and Charlie's, Colville, WA(474 miles)

The next three days were unexpectedly excruciating. You anticipate and resolve yourself to pain in the Cascades, Rockies, etc. (Mountain Ranges!), but as we learned quickly, "passes" can be almost anywhere and offer a sizable degree of difficulty. Lee Ann came down with the flu and joined Susan and Julie in an RV caravan of vacationers toward Colville. It definitely turned out to be the right decision for the three of them as the rest of us inched our way through and over the steep Loup Loup Pass, Sherman Pass and Wauconda Summit and the generally rolling terrain of eastern Washington. I felt noticeably weakened and affected by the persistent climbing and humid conditions.

Due to the trail of baby powder that fell out of my bike shorts at every bathroom pit stop, I was now known as "Powder Butt." I thought that nickname was particularly appropriate since we were camping in Omak, near an Indian reservation!

Unfortunately, the powder was doing little to soothe my increasingly painful posterior and since rodeo and bingo were the highlights of Omak, there wasn't much around to take my mind off of it.

June 19

One of the many benefits of traveling with Bikecentennial was having access to ten, consecutive, ultra-detailed maps that covered the entire 4705 mile trip. Going over the day's route became a morning ritual and on only a few, rare occasions did we uncover a mistake or directive that was difficult to follow. All towns and villages of population 100 and up were included, along with the myriad of post offices, laundromats, restaurants and bike shops along the way. When we became comfortable discerning the codes and abbreviations, the maps became as important as our sleeping bags.

After a morning spent fixing a mysteriously broker derailleur, (mechanism for shifting gears on a bike that operates by moving the chain from one set of exposed gears to another) I was happy to be on the road again, but admittedly had some serious concerns about doing seventy-seven nasty miles after 10 a.m. It would prove to be worse than I imagined as my body and bike just never got into sync all day long. There were hills everywhere of all varieties that never seemed to end, the drabbest of drab scenery, scorching heat, and an eerie feeling of desolation that I hadn't encountered before.

Some comic relief did intervene around noon, however, as Warren and I sat down for a few smashed and sweaty peanut butter and jelly sandwiches on the side of the road. A stocky, middle-aged guy with a dilapidated pickup slammed on the brakes when he saw us and ran towards us after jumping out of his truck. In his haste, he even forgot to put the truck in park and it started rolling until we yelled his way!

The man's name was Jay and in a most unusual, spasmodic manner, he gave us the complete minute-by-minute account of his "hooking up" with the rest of our group earlier, and why we should stay at his hostel tonight instead of a campground we had already booked. We were taken aback and more than skeptical, but forty grueling miles and more than a few cuss words later, there he was again, giving our girls a lift from a gas station over the last thousand foot peak and the remaining fifteen miles or so to his abode.

I was extremely tempted to take the path of least resistance and join the crowd, but Warren thankfully played with my conscious by strongly dissuading me. I knew at that moment that it would turn out to be one of the most significant decisions of the entire trip.

About 8 o'clock, we staggered into Jay's yard, complete with horse stables and hot tub, as he had promised. My body was completely spent and after eating as much as I could, very gingerly to prevent my stomach from backlashing, I collapsed on one of the two beds made available to us. I was told later that I snored as loud as a 747! Jay gave us all fair warning about the level of difficulty of the day ahead. To our chagrin, this spiel had become a broken record.

June 20

The first eighteen miles to Sherman's Pass (at 5500 feet) got our muscles grinding at the crack of dawn. After 2 1/2 hours of solid climbing and a degree of relief at being near the peak, we were amazed by the ever-increasing eccentricity of Mr. T. As we were guzzling our Gatorade and reflecting on our just-completed accomplishment, the elder cyclist realized he had left his bike pump at the hostel, and without a moment's hesitation, turned around and went back to get it. We tried to reassure Warren that the overzealous Jay would certainly track us down and bring it to him, or at the very worst he would have to "cough up" ten sweatless dollars to replace it, but as always, he didn't listen. This was one of the first examples of dogmatic individuality overriding reasonable, group consensus, and it certainly kept life interesting as we navigated eastward.

The last leg of what felt like a Tour de France stage in the Pyrennes led us to the base of the mile-long gravel driveway of Mo and Charlie. I rode with San Francisco accountant Jean most of the day and I know I confirmed her suspicions that my screws were also very loose as I loudly gasped, groaned and sputtered like a worn-out Pinto. Our gracious hosts piled us in the back of their open bed truck before scaling the twisting, bumpy road to their house overlooking Colville, Washington.

Susan, Julie and Lee Ann greeted us cheerfully and proceeded to catch us up on three days of hospitality unlike anything they had ever experienced. The setting was *Little House on the Prairie*-personified, ecologically balanced and as far removed from urban hustle and bustle as one can imagine. We were escorted first to the main residence, built in the 1930's, where there was a summer bedroom on the porch for mom and dad and lofts for Gabe, age eleven, and Rachel, age six. A warm, cozy feeling was projected in the open, airy room with no television in sight.

The yard contained a guest bunkhouse built a few years before by cyclists passing through, as well as a barn loft, workshop, greenhouse, sauna and small camper trailer named "Cutey-Pie." The girls worked in and cooked meals from the garden all three days on the edge of fields loaded with colorful wild flowers.

We all sat around the dinner table sipping grapefruit juice before digging into the vegetarian lasagna and spinach salad that had been artfully prepared. I felt like my salivary glands had died and gone to heaven.

After dinner, we browsed picture albums filled with candid shots of recent guests as well as the birth of Rachel. The whole scene felt like a flashback to the 1960's when people were really in tune with nature, life, love, nudity and their inner feelings. The openness and total unpretentiousness of the place made it a very difficult one to leave behind.

Mail!, a New Roof and Medical Clearance

June 21: Ione, WA City Park (522 miles)

June 22: Priest River, ID City Park (582 miles)

June 23/24: Sandpoint, ID Bed and Breakfast (614 miles)

Susan was back in the saddle, rejuvenated mentally, but cautiously optimistic physically. It was a predominantly flat day but the pain in her knee really bothered her towards the end and she was relegated to peddling *with one leg* the last four of forty-six miles into Ione City Park! Reflecting later, she said, "By this time, I was really starting to feel like maybe I ought to be taken out back and shot or at least sold to the glue factory. . ." We elevated the wounded limb as quickly as we could and applied some ice that I had picked up at a nearby bar. We were both beginning to really wonder if her knee ailments were going to be fixable in the "heat of the battle."

It was my first night of shared cooking duties and partner Maria walked with me to the local Mom and Pop store where the bare aisles bore a striking resemblance to a bowling alley. We were allotted $5 per person or $60 total out of our Bikecentennial "group funds" (taken out of our $2000 participation fee) to procure dinner, breakfast and lunch for the entire group and carry or cart it back to camp. A rotation was set up so that everyone had to cook an average of once every six days with cleanup duties the day following cooking responsibility. For the most part, the system worked tremendously well.

If a store was not accessible to camp, we prearranged to meet as a group in the nearest town with everyone chipping in and carrying groceries in our already over-stuffed bike bags. I'm sure we looked like a band of gypsies with up to three feet of sleeping bags, spare tires, miniature lawn chairs (Jeff only!), whole wheat bread and boxes of corn flakes stacked on the back of our bikes.

My Chef Tell effort at BBQ chicken over an under-flamed grill took me close to ninety minutes to leave the "wouldn't serve it to your worst enemy" zone, but as darkness fell, the reviews came in surprisingly positive. The gang must have been hungry. Jeff and Smitty celebrated his birthday in a local tavern as we finished dinner, and judging by the laughter coming from their corner, managed to find a very happy hour indeed.

I finally got the dreaded cold that "Typhoid Maria" had been passing around, causing a slight problem in our two-person "Tadpole" tent for Susan. Our sleeping space seemed to get smaller and smaller every night, especially when one or the both of us was sore, sick, irritable or showerless. Since those unpleasantries had been occurring with unfortunate regularity, we unanimously concluded that the attainment of a "bigger house" was a necessity.

June 22

We exited Washington and its barreling lumber trucks on a very enjoyable, predominantly flat day. Susan managed well until Old Town, Idaho, where Warren and I secured her a ride for the final eight miles to a rundown railroad town called Priest River. She was really starting to get down on herself and needed to see a doctor soon to find out what the precise problem was before even more damage was done to her knee. Like most nurses, she is especially stubborn about succumbing to and seeking medical help herself. We camped at a city park that was pretty scummy even by our rapidly declining standards. One clogged toilet, no shower for the second straight night, sticky, humid weather and an impending monsoon helped us finalize our decision to shop for a bigger tent—immediately.

June 23/24

A breezy, sun-kissed morning energized everyone as we set off on a relatively easy thirty-two mile day. As a precautionary measure prior to seeing a doctor in Sandpoint, Susan got a ride with a kind lady that Warren and I befriended at a convenience store the night before. I rode with Jean and Julie and laughed all morning long. The group was starting to get comfortable with each other and that translated into moving from mostly exchanging pleasantries to "spilling guts" about life secrets. The road would have been a very lonely place without the camaraderie. We traveled some very isolated back roads over rolling hills with only the occasional scampering rabbit or squirrel impeding our determined eighteen miles-per-hour pace.

With no preconceived notion of Idaho at all, the city of Sandpoint really blew our minds. It was truly an oasis in the middle of nowhere with a gorgeous mountain backdrop, sparkling lake, sandy beaches and a quaint touristy town center the likes of those usually reserved for a tropical island paradise.

We set up camp in the front yard of a youth hostel across the street from Lake Pend Oreille and went to collect the surprises awaiting us at our first mail stop. "The haul" included some homemade oatmeal-caramel bars from Susan's parents and a half dozen well-timed letters of encouragement from family and friends. We also found and purchased a new house, a.k.a. "the Bullfrog," about 50 percent larger than the previous tent and still only four pounds, a very important consideration.

Susan's knee was diagnosed as "overuse syndrome" by a knee doctor who was an avid long-distance cyclist himself. He recommended heat, a steady diet of Naprosyn and lots of stretching. I was glad that Susan seemed relieved that he didn't suggest catching the next plane home. She could have very easily "called it quits" by this point and really showed some guts and determination for persevering with the Rockies looming ahead. It would have been a much less enjoyable experience without her sarcastic wit and support.

Yaak Attack

June 25: Bull River, MT Campground (660 miles)
June 26: Yaak River, MT (706 miles)
June 27: Yaak, MT Mercantile Store (738 miles)
June 28: Eureka, MT Trailer Park (796 miles)

As we crossed the state line into intimidating Montana (derived from a Spanish word for mountain!) on Highway 200, a road sign proclaiming "Moose Area Next 25 Miles" reaffirmed that we were indeed moving away from civilization again. From day one, all types of water, from the Puget Sound to inlets, rivers, streams, waterfalls and icy lakes, seemed to follow our chosen path, racing alongside as our companion during the day and greeting us at camp at night.

Bull River was our next destination and nothing yet had refreshed quite like the washcloth bath we enjoyed upon arrival. Maria and Julie bravely lowered their whole bodies into the surging waters of the only river that flows upstream in the entire country. After a delicious pork chop dinner prepared by chef Peter, Susan (whose knee did surprisingly well) and I took a leisurely stroll through the heavily-wooded campground where we spotted two male moose and a statuesque bald eagle. We suddenly felt like we were a million miles away from the closest interstate.

One of the many special aspects of a trip like this was that you never knew when one of those memories that would become etched in your mind for a lifetime would actually happen. Yaak, Montana, of all places, emerged as one of them.

June 27

A cool morning ride ended without incident and we all paused for lunch at powerful, deafening Yaak Falls in the wildflower-adorned Cabinet Gorge Mountains. The community of Yaak, population 2, (that we actually saw), contained the only standing buildings in the hundred-mile stretch between Bull River and Eureka. Since we were left with a difficult sixty-five mile ride through desolate mountains the rest of the way to Eureka, we promised to buy groceries at the Yaak General Store in exchange for a free campsite. We honestly had no other choice.

The Dirty Shane Saloon kept our chugging contingency happy for most of the afternoon while testing our prowess with a pool cue. Around 5 p.m., a posse of telephone repair men, who apparently were working and staying behind the General Store as well, meandered through the swinging doors with a primary goal of evaluating the swinging intentions of our group.

Our group convened for dinner around 9 p.m. and the lively chatter reverberated along the banks of the river as the state of Montana welcomed the later and later nightfall. Shortly after the final dish was cleaned and the last tent zipped up, we were startled to attention by the smell of smoke, the crackling of fire and the spastic muttering of loud voices. After close to eight hours "in the sauce" and a fairly weak selection of "things to do next," the telephone repair gang reached a unanimous decision to verbally torment and possibly convert us into toast.

With a roaring, gasoline-fueled bonfire less than fifty feet away and a chorus of choice comments like "let's torch their tents after we get the women," they were unknowingly facing twenty-four startled eyeballs in nervous anticipation of a good old-fashioned western brawl! Since our most dangerous weapons were a Swiss Army Knife and an Allen wrench, our only hope in the event of a skirmish would be to either outrun them or take advantage of their highly inebriated condition. As I peered anxiously threw the maze of mosquitoes outside of our mesh tent window, it felt like a KKK rally gone berserk without the hoods. The threats petered out slowly over the next two hours, as one by one the tormentors retreated wobbly to their spinning campers.

June 28

We all compared notes over breakfast to see if it had all been a dream, since no one actually got out of their tents or spoke during the unexpected festivities of the evening. Ever outspoken Julie couldn't help herself and gave the bad guys a nasty, expletive-filled wake-up call and feminist speech as she stood on their trailer steps. I'm sure they agreed afterwards that it could not have been worth that.

With no shower and no toilet facilities on the premises, we were forced to find ourselves a semi-quiet, secluded spot to take care of business. It was quite an amusing sight spotting the squatting toadstools decorating the wilderness and gave new meaning to the expression "crack of dawn."

Somehow, I ended up riding with Jean the entire way to Eureka. I struggled, spat and cussed as the hills and hairpin curves meandered towards our first pass in over a week. The view from the summit was breathtaking, overlooking the expanse of ponderosa pines, rock formations and little else. I let out a couple of wildly echoing primal screams, but with no houses or cars in sight for forty miles, only the animals would hear my call.

It was a veritable outdoor zoo throughout the day as we spotted a galloping antelope, a creek-side moose and her calf, eight cows roaming quietly in the road, dozens of frisky deer and one very shy bear trying to become invisible. The 3300-foot climb really took its toll on my still anguished rear end and by the ninth and final hour in the saddle, I was relieved to be done, but very concerned about my continuing dismal condition. With the towering Rockies looming in the foreground, I began doubting myself for the first time.

Sometimes we have to almost hit bottom before we'll really listen to what others are saying and Peter came forth as my savior that night. With a lot more biking experience than I had, his simple but effective remedy was to keep the area clean, keep the powder and Vaseline to a minimum and basically let it air out as much as possible. In layman's terms, I had been attracting bacteria from not having a shower or washing my shorts for three-day stretches and then going for the quick fix pain relief instead of finding out the real cause. Except for the occasional normal saddle sore from a long day of climbing, I would take his advice this time and finally fix my problem.

"Going to the Sun"

June 29: Whitefish Lake St. Recreation Area, MT (854 miles)

June 30: Lake McDonald, MT (895 miles)

July 1: St. Mary's Campground, MT (935 miles)

Warren Jr.'s suggestion that we splurge a little of our food stash on a hearty restaurant breakfast met with unanimous approval. We all converged on the folksy Sunshine Café in Eureka, a quaint little eatery in a bright yellow house where the specialty was huckleberry pancakes the size of hubcaps! No one had ever heard of a huckleberry before, and for good reason. They are a relatively scarce, expensive delicacy, rounder, fatter and more flavorful than blueberries, and their patches are closely guarded family secrets!

I drank my first significant helping of coffee in three weeks as my stomach was finally getting stable enough to handle caffeine without causing me to race to a toilet. The java definitely gave me an early morning surge of energy as I left the restaurant like a filly at the Derby.

It was also a triumphant day for Susan, as she was able to ride alongside or draft behind me for almost the entire two-lane, fifty-eight mile stretch along Highway 93 to Whitefish, in spite of the fact that the rolling hills, sharp corners and head wind were rather annoying. The scenery was increasingly breathtaking as the towering Rockies loomed in the distance, awaiting our arrival, but the pre-holiday onslaught of 18-wheelers, RV's and logging traffic forced us to redouble our concentration on the single white line before us. We tried not to think about just how close those outstretched passenger side mirrors came to sending us careening into the gravel.

A bevy of inviting, sparkling lakes had decorated the length of our journey that day, but none were as majestic as the one at the Whitefish State Recreation Park where we settled for the evening. Even in the middle of summer, it was icebox cold, but Katie and Maria were accustomed to the polar temperatures in New Hampshire and thought nothing of taking a dip. Maria had a contagious sense of humor that served her well in her chosen field of teaching handicapped children and also helped keep Susan's spirits up at times when they looked impossible to lift. Susan got compliments from the group about the improvement she was making on the bike and the tone showing on her lower body. She was finally beginning to feel like all the effort might not be for naught after all, "I can see my body starting to change—my calves are very muscular and even the back of my thighs are changing. I thought they were swollen!"

June 30

In my haste to complete the morning ritual of pumping up my bike tires, I caused my second flat tire of the trip before I even left the campground. Jeff had some preventative maintenance of his own to do so he hung around and left with me.

One of the real benefits of traveling with a group cross-country is enjoying the combined knowledge and companionship of a variety of very different individuals, all with a shared purpose and goal. It would have been unimaginable for Susan and I to successfully complete a trip of this magnitude alone after such a modicum of preparation. All factors connected with the trip including lodging, food, bike mechanics and transporting gear were made easier and more enjoyable to varying degrees by the camaraderie that was developed. Riders that we met traveling by themselves or in couples all remarked about the synergism we achieved and were in most cases quite envious of our situation.

The ride to the genesis of "Going-to-the-Sun" Highway was a pleasantly short forty-one miles, and was punctuated by a succession of stops along the way to buy bike accessories or simply relax and enjoy the surroundings, luxuries that had been few and far between to this point. The roasting sun was beginning to take its toll on the few exposed parts of our bodies and SPF 15 sun block became a frequently reapplied life saver. It felt odd being surrounded by camera-happy tourists at a rest stop in West Glacier. Suddenly the thought of traveling by car or RV seemed unappealing as we had come to feel a closeness to nature that is simply not achievable any way except cycling. It really was the best way to get to know our country.

At the campground, I decided to play *Sports Illustrated* photographer with Susan as we took advantage of some toasty afternoon rays, gorgeous glacier-fed McDonald Lake scenery and my most inviting bikini-clad subject. It was one of those priceless interludes that you never seem to make time for on a "regular" vacation.

After dinner, we carefully stowed away scented items like food, deodorant and toothpaste in the padlocked "bear boxes" around our campground. One camper the previous year reportedly got attacked while sleeping because he left a tube of Aquafresh open inside his tent. It was enough of a threat to keep everyone on edge and sleeping lightly throughout a very short night. Actual bear attack fatalities, we found out later, are rare, with the last occurrence happening in 1987 when an amateur photographer pursued and finally provoked a group of grizzlies.

July 1

The morning started around 3:00 when flashing blue lights signified that a tall oak had gotten in the way of a holiday merrymaker trying to enter the campground. We dozed futilely for the next seventy-five minutes or so until a cacophony of alarm clocks sounded. My July 1 journal entry read, "We must be out of our xo!@? minds to intentionally and deliberately awaken at 4 o'clock in the morning after sleeping on the hard ground all night in the bear infested woods and get up, pack up in the dark, get on a human-powered, two-wheeled apparatus and pedal to an elevation of 6664 feet from 3500 feet, covering twenty-five miles with fifty pounds of gear at our sides to boot!" With the added pressure of an 11 a.m. park-enforced deadline to make it to the top and the added adventure of stopping seventy-two times along the most narrow of shoulders with RV's chugging by to shoot awe-inspiring photos, we were certainly in for a biking experience we'd never forget.

From the hint of daybreak to the moment the sun pierced through the lowest of the sun-peaked mountains, our quiet caravan of peddlers was virtually by ourselves with the sweet feeling of anticipation warmed by every layer of clothing in our possession. Skittish mule deer, mountain goats, curious marmots that looked like huge guinea pigs, and even a breakfast-seeking black bear graced our presence as we navigated towards the popular summit.

One of the most appealing aspects of long distance cycling is the fact that you're going slow enough to see, feel and really absorb the sights, sounds and smells around you. We traveled carefully through the numerous tunnels that dripped with condensation, and marveled at the "Weeping Wall," where rainbows reflected brilliantly off the pavement thanks to a mammoth wall of melting snow. The distant sound of rushing streams, chattering flying squirrels, and the whistle of birds echoed through the mountains carpeted with lodgepole pine, aspen and spruce. Despite the traffic, it was refreshing to be on a road conspicuously absent of billboards, motels and chicken shacks.

Warren motivated Susan, encouraging her to fuel her weakening system with nuts, raisins, energy bars and bread. They brought up the rear again, but I had never been as proud as I was seeing her make that last turn before the 500-foot uphill stretch run to the pinnacle of Logan Pass and the Continental Divide. At exactly 10:59 a.m., she successfully crossed the imaginary finish line under the power of her own wobbly knees to a reception and congratulations of Olympic proportions by our "welcoming committee."

Following a well-deserved lunch break at the top, we motored quickly down the other side with intense concentration, dodging camera-toting tourists, impatient parkers and gallons of garbage. With the increase in heat and human commotion, our animal playmates of the morning were nowhere to be found. Unlike the swarms on the road in the afternoon, they seemed to know that there was no reason to scurry spasmodically around because their mountains weren't going anywhere anytime soon.

After the anticipation and satisfaction of conquering "Going to the Sun" Highway, we all faced a trying afternoon when our emotional defenses were at their lowest ebb. Warren had made reservations for us at the Rising Sun Campground, but the owners took one look at our sun-baked, drained and stinking bodies, (three showerless days and counting), and suddenly decided that they had a policy that disallowed cyclists. So, we tacked on another seven miles into a twenty miles per hour head wind and tried the St. Mary's Campground, named after one of the area's most picturesque blue glacier lakes. We got the last site they had and although it wasn't very attractive, it was home for that night. Katie and Jean had a rather intense spat about whether to ride or walk to the grocery store two miles away. With the heat, flying insects everywhere and a rather unkempt bathroom where I dunked my head in the sink to cool off, nobody was exactly in the mood for a big meal anyway. Shortly before dark, as the almost desert-like breeze turned suddenly chilly, Susan, Smitty, Jeff and I took a long lazy walk into town for chocolate milk shakes. It was the first real "treat" we had enjoyed in three weeks and I seriously doubt that we'll ever have one that tastes that satisfying again.

"Oh Canada"

July 2/3: Waterton Park Campground, Alberta (985 miles)

July 4: Wagon Wheel Campground, Alberta (1045 miles)

July 5: Cut Bank, MT (1145 miles)

With all the hoopla about the Glacier National Park area, Warren saved the review of our next trek, over Chief Mountain on the way to Waterton National Park in Alberta, until departure morning. I'm rather thankful that I didn't have time to worry about it beforehand as I was physically and mentally exhausted from the onset and felt as though I had an extra twenty pounds of gear and a flat tire all day long.

After eighteen miles of climbing up a steady 7 to 10 percent grade on a dreary, cloudy day, we reached the Canadian border for the standard interrogation and search procedure. I paced myself with Julie and Maria near the rear of the group most of the day while Susan and her ailing knee struggled with Lee Ann, whose hip caused her to walk her bike up several of the tougher hills. The final five-mile stretch run into Waterton was a true endurance test. Susan's journal entry captured the incredible degree of difficulty, "It was the worst five miles since we left Seattle. I was in the "granny" gear (rarely used lowest of eighteen gears) going downhill into a headwind about to crash because of the driving rain. But it wasn't the speed! I was pedaling just to go downhill as opposed to backwards! It was terribly stressful with all of the Canada Day traffic, etc." That wind would put its stamp on our layover the next day as well.

The first order of business after entering camp was a long-awaited hot shower that I allowed to envelope my body for a solid twenty minutes as every aching tendon and ligament was soothed to the core. We all limped into town to reward ourselves with our first inside dinner of the trip at a pizza parlor and proceeded to engulf six large specials, five pitchers of beer and nine pitchers of water.

After a little shopping in this very pricey resort community, Susan and I converged on the charismatic Thirsty Bear Saloon for some alcoholic refreshment and a game of darts after spotting Smitty and Warren Jr. excitedly waving us towards the place. It was a riot watching Warren let his guard down a bit for the first time as we perused the posters, license plates, bear skins and other assorted memorabilia adorning the log cabin watering hole.

We were awakened early the next morning by the howling of a fierce wind unlike anything I'd ever heard, much less slept through in a canvas tent. In one absolutely hilarious interlude, Susan and I attempted to overcome the frustrating obstacles and make love before anybody got up. Unfortunately, in our half-dazed, one-track-minded promiscuous state, we didn't realize that everyone was up and within ten feet of our dwelling while I tried desperately to enjoy this rare moment of rapturous pleasure and keep the tent from blowing away at the same time! The tent stakes were completely out of the ground and my 200 pound frame was the only thing anchoring us and all our worldly possessions!

We found out later that several people had gotten blown away during the night—literally—including Maria, a solid 140 pounds of muscle, who had bounced across the field like an out-of-control human tumbleweed. Peter had a similar fate and managed to lose his wallet.

The "rest day" around Waterton was hardly relaxing as we fought fifty-plus miles-per-hour winds while walking around town doing laundry and visiting the grocery store. Although it was impossible to partake in any of the highly-acclaimed outdoor activities, the scenery was truly spectacular. After a short nap on my half-inch-thick sleeping mat beneath a food/wind shelter, Smitty and I prepared the tenth different "pasta surprise" concoction of the trip. Over dinner, we all watched a bevy of very excited little kids feed some semi-tame baby deer on the water's edge.

July 4

Just outside of the campground area, we decided to tax our somewhat rested legs early the next morning by climbing a nasty, curvy hill to the Prince of Wales Hotel. The building, perched majestically and visible from miles around, faced the eerie center of the series of mountains from which the icy Chinook winds billow through with chilling regularity.

It was certainly the coldest July 4th we had ever experienced with mid-40° highs, but if someone hadn't told me what day it was, I wouldn't have known. Since it was essentially a holiday everyday for us, it really didn't matter. We managed to stop with almost the whole group intact for a round of hot chocolate, coffee, and goodies stashed for consumption throughout the day. The rest of the day was relatively uneventful with rolling hills, very few cars and lots of low-lying clouds. Once we arrived at the appropriately-named Wagon Wheel Campground in McGrath, everyone administered long overdue cleaning and maintenance on their respective bikes while Susan fixed sloppy joe sandwiches (one of my favorites) for supper.

Peter noticed that my back wheel was a bit wobbly and upon closer inspection, we found a broken spoke. In my extremely limited cycling career, I had never seen or heard of anyone having one of these bike maladies and I certainly had no clue as to the repair procedure. Neither had anyone else except Warren Jr. who did encounter one or two of them during his '89 cross-country jaunt. With the help of the friendly campground owners, we located some improvisational tools and eventually repaired the damage. I vaguely remembered hearing a "phling" noise while bouncing over the half-mile, heavily-pebbled driveway leading to the campsites; that must've been when the damage occurred. Unfortunately, it would become a noise I had to recognize with frustrating regularity.

Although we were tired, it was still very light at 9:30 p.m., and the group, minus Warren Sr., decided to take up the proprietor's offer to ride around town in the back of his horse-drawn coach. Good, clean fun in a good, clean, western Canadian town, these people still lived "life in the slow lane" of a bygone era.

July 5

Our day of reentry into the United States produced one of the most unusual and longest stretches so far. Jean had a flat tire in camp and I volunteered to stay with her to fix it and pull "sweep," (bikers who brought up the rear of a group to make sure everyone made it safely) leaving our site around 9 a.m. on a seventy mile day. It was a prophetic omen as more delays were to come. We quickly caught up with Julie and realized that we were riding into an uncharacteristic morning head wind that was blowing fifteen to twenty knots directly into our faces! We managed to grind along at about five miles per hour on flat roads for the first eighteen miles. We're talking about a bona fide small craft advisory, hold on to your handle bars with both hands, blow your skirt up around your waist sort of breeze! Then. . . just as the wind changed course long enough to give us a slight reprieve, I heard a faint "phling" sound again, except this time it came from the direction of Susan's bike. We got her wheel off without any problem, but since we didn't have a big enough wrench to take the flywheel apart, Warren and I were forced to use the top of a fence post as a brace to remove it. By this time, it was after 1 p.m. with over fifty miles to go, so Warren decided to hightail ahead to try and catch the others at the U.S./Canadian border. I felt pretty uneasy being in the rear alone with Susan the way things were going. It just didn't seem like we were destined to make it.

Mere minutes after Warren pedaled out of sight, Susan's chain became disengaged, falling into her spokes. We tried to play roadside surgeon again. . . but were unable to get it back on track. Something was definitely wrong and we had neither the tools, patience or mechanical expertise to solve the problem. After screaming at each other for more than ten minutes on the extremely desolate highway (Susan wanted to *walk* her bike the twelve miles to the border in the hot sun!), I managed to flag down an Alberta government employee in his bright orange truck. Thankfully, the guy stopped because we would have strangled each other if we had been forced to wait an hour for the next vehicle! It was our first experience on four wheels in several weeks and at seventy miles per hour, it felt like we were breaking the sound barrier!

We got out at Del Bonita and rejoined the rest of the troops for a much-needed cookies and cream cone. With an inoperative bike, Susan was again forced to get a lift to camp, along with Lee Ann who was complaining of a sore knee. While the rest of us continued on the remaining twenty miles "into town" (Cutbank, Montana), the girls waited for the custom agent's shift to end at 4 p.m. Katie, Julie, Warren, Maria and I took turns shielding the merciless wind from one another over that tough remaining stretch. We pulled into camp at 7:30 as a menacing cloud pelted us with sheets of rain.

Jean, Warren Sr. and Peter had been at camp for hours, totally oblivious of our hardships, and were dead set on cramming all twelve of us into a $100 a night hotel across the street. They had been warned about the possibility of a drunken Indian disturbance and didn't relish the thought of soggy tents either. By now, we were used to "roughin' it," almost thriving on it, and the group voted *in favor* of crashing out in the most inhospitable of camp sites, less than a hundred feet from a railroad track!

Susan had already gotten her bike fixed (by a guy she met in the grocery store who volunteered to come to the campsite and fix it!) and had grilled cheese sandwiches and pasta Parmesan waiting on us when we arrived. Standing there filling my hungering cavity in the rain, knowing that there would be no shower and reminiscing about the chain of events of the last twelve hours, it dawned on me that only people who really wanted it could have made it that day. The fact that this trip is not for everyone was never more evident.

Cruisin'

July 6: Chester, MT City Park (1213 miles)

July 7: Chinook, MT City Park (1298 miles)

July 8: Malta, MT Bon Soir Campground (1366 miles)

We needed a "lay-up day" the next day and our prayers were answered. It was such a contrast from the mental and physical marathon of the ride to Cut Bank that it almost felt like a dream. What a difference a tail wind makes! We made it twenty-three miles in the first hour and were in the shower in Chester at 12:30 p.m., covering sixty-eight miles in only four hours!

Chester was also a mail stop, a laundry stop and a pub stop. With an easy morning on the bike, sunny skies, and our "batteries" recharged, we all felt like we might be "over the hump" for the first time. Susan was really bothered by the fact that she got a lift the day before because of her bike troubles and worried that someone was going to buy a stamp for her forehead that read "thanks for the ride!" The good news was that her stamina was improving dramatically and that she really wanted to feel the accomplishment of finishing every day.

July 7

We would average sixty-five miles per day over the next six days, traveling the basically flat, two-lane Highway 2 (known as the "High Line") to Williston, North Dakota. Day one of this welcomed stretch started with another westerly tail wind that was finally living up to pretrip expectations. It carried us over the sixty miles to the booming metropolis of Havre (pop. 10,000) in an unbelievable 2 1/2 hours!

While waiting for the others, Susan and I took a couple of leisurely hours to take care of bike repairs at the first shop we had encountered in two weeks. While the proprietor and his two children repaired freewheels, trued our wheels and synchronized our gears, Susan got her bangs trimmed and then joined me for a totally decadent (and civilized) feast at Pizza Hut. A Dairy Queen, unfortunately, was in the path back to the bike shop and an alien force mysteriously guided a peanut butter cluster blizzard into our hands and down our sweets-starved throats!

The rest of the group glided in about that time, after being held up by a succession of flat tires, and also succumbed to the powerful forces at Dairy Queen. By this time, the skies had opened up, lightning danced across the horizon and my legs were crying for me to either get back on the bike or to be put to rest for the night. It was now after 3:00 p.m. and we still had twenty-five humid miles to travel along a crowded highway in atrocious condition.

The potholes looked like small moon craters and avoiding them and an almost certain nasty spill required a maximum of concentration that I now had little energy to expend. We pedaled with a "get-me-there-now" attitude and except for Susan's flat tire, (repaired with duct tape of all things!) we managed to make it to Chinook in one piece.

July 8

The wind changed direction overnight and turned a probable cakewalk jaunt into a knee grinder. Susan's comment that "everything but my eyelashes and hair hurts" summed up the level of exertion required to make it to Malta. Along the route, the names of the towns sounded more like an around- the-world spin, with Harlem and Zurich sprinkled amidst the more typical Dodson and Wagner. We took time to enjoy the ambiance of the cafes in these little "blink twice and you'll miss it" locales, the kind of stops that 99.9 percent of people on vacation don't have time to experience. It was fun joking around with the bar owners for a few minutes, getting a drink, playing a game of pool or darts and dancing to the jukebox.

At the Bon Soir campground in Malta, I was feeling pretty spunky still and decided to indulge in a little animated Frisbee tossing with a vagabond cyclist named Andy whose friends were assigned to the Havre slammer for public drunkenness. It was a nice diversion from the bike seat, but the reoccurring twinges in my tender knees told me to concentrate on being a hero in only one sport at a time.

The Cafe Crew

July 9: Glasgow, MT RV Park (1441 miles)
July 10: Wolf Point, ND City Park (1499 miles)
July 11: Culbertson, ND City Park (1556 miles)

Just when we were getting a little self-assured and contented, reality would remind us that this trip was certainly no day at the beach. It seemed like every time an unexpected breakdown happened in camp, before we even left, the day would be a long one.

The ride to Glasgow was no exception. The "cafe crew" (Maria, Katie, Julie, Susan and myself) hung around to repair yet another flat for Susan and shortly after hitting the road realized we were dragging. Of course, I was slated to cook that night, a fact that always added pressure in getting to camp at a reasonable hour. We decided to take the scenic, traffic-free alternate route for the first seventeen miles through Bowdoin National Wildlife Refuge, passing dozens of wild horses, deer and a family of antelope indulging in quiet Lake Bowdoin.

Our first mistake of the day was taking a detour along a sandy path in search of the Saco Hot Springs described favorably in Warren's leader notes. (a summary of quips from past Bikecentennial trips that we used on occasion) Between my bike fishtailing in the soft sand and a sudden onslaught of the most ferocious mosquitoes in the Western Hemisphere, I was getting less thrilled about this side adventure by the second. Susan and I engaged in a silly confrontation on the way there because I thought it would be a total waste of time and she had romantic visions of what it would be like. I gave in to take a look and this time anyway, I was "right on the money." It was a totally worthless tourist trap that amounted to nothing more than a highly-publicized hoax. After all the nonsense, it was 1:00 p.m., we were still sixty miles from camp, and I was still supposed to cook.

In the town of Saco, we met Jeff and Smitty who complained of back and head aches and were getting a lift to camp. We fought a tough crosswind the rest of the afternoon as I tried to cheer up an increasingly despondent Susan to no avail. A good Samaritan provided the only positive highlight of the day, picking up my sleeping bag and bringing it to me after it had fallen off the back of my bike!

Just outside of Glasgow with less that fifteen minutes to go to camp, Susan had a blow-out on her rear tire so bad that it punctured the tube and the Kevler tire itself. She was getting pretty vocal about finding the closest airport and letting me "finish this thing on my own," but I managed to soothe the tears and talk her into "sleeping on it" before she did anything rash. A few tidbits from her journal summarized her frustration, "After twelve hours on a bike seat, I've never felt so physically tired. I curse the day I ever agreed to this trip!"

One of the keys to success on an excursion of this magnitude is to not think about it in terms of 90 days, cross-country or to even consider looking at a United States map as a whole, but to concentrate on the satisfaction and accomplishment of conquering every mile and every day. This is obviously easier said than done at times, but the only way to reach a big goal in any endeavor is to first tackle and successfully hurdle a lot of little ones. Today represented the one-third point of the journey—the first milestone of significance. It was hard to believe that we were still in Montana at that juncture but stretching roughly 700 miles from west to east, the state is further across than almost every country in Europe.

July 10

It was a tolerable fifty-mile day with a steady head wind on relatively flat land. After setting up camp at the town recreation park grounds in Wolf Point, we biked in the rain to the Sherman Motor Court dining hall for a celebration feast! I had my first steak since May and got a little tipsy on the flowing wine and daiquiris. Susan and Warren had a squabble before dinner and he made her promise to stick with it for at least ten more days before "throwing in the towel."

After dinner, I again hooked up with Andy and again did something I would regret—shooting hoops with him and two local all-star high school girls. My legs were in excruciating pain immediately afterwards as I gingerly tried to stretch out on the top of my sleeping bag. Susan finished the day by counting her mosquito bites—a total of twenty-one on the lower quarter of her left leg alone! She also noted her bizarre tan lines shaping up because of the unusual cut of our bike wear. What's a girl to do?!

July 11

Even in the boondocks of western no-man's-land with a different zip code every night, the dull creatures of habit within us managed to win the battle over sheer spontaneity most of the time. Regardless of how far away from the norm we get, somehow, some way, our mind and body regulate and adapt. In the mind department, we had ritualized our routine to the point of carefully selecting and bringing our next day's clothing with us to bed at night, planning pit stops along the road ten to twenty miles in advance and doing a little laundry by hand almost every day and drying it on the back of the bike strapped with a bungee. The tent assembly and disassembly process was reduced to a two-minute drill. Our bodies are truly the ultimate machine, giving us back in performance only as much as we fuel it properly and keep it tuned up by using it.

The following day started and ended with kids playing a significant role. We got ready to go as the Wolf Point swim team started their crack-of-dawn practice to the welcomed blare of cranking tunes over the pool loudspeaker. As we finished up a long day in Culbertson, two little towhead elementary kids named Roy and Troy who had the keys to the launderette we had "taken over," gave us the lowdown on their tiny little town. It was like a brief departure into a Norman Rockwell painting or a Peanuts cartoon where grown-ups don't really exist, crime is unheard of, and snails and puppy dog tails are what little boys are really made of. They even went home and got their dog so we could get a picture of them with it before they locked up at 11 o'clock. It was too precious for words.

Tumble Weeds

July 12-13: Williston, ND City Park (1601 miles)

July 14: Stanley, ND Campground (1673 miles)

July 15: Pat's Motel and Campground, Minot, ND (1733 miles)

Past the one-month mark now, the personalities within the group had been firmly established and terms like "group dynamics" and "cyclo-analysis" became the buzzwords of the day, replacing work terms of our previous life like "empowerment" and "key learnings." We had gradually swung our attention and concerns to petty quirks of each other, instead of our swollen knees and muscles, as the road flattened and the Cascades felt like a distant memory. I guess it served the purpose of giving us something to talk about all day since we were now basically riding together instead of sweating and grunting a half mile apart up mountain passes.

I always seemed to get nominated for the role of sounding board and as the only guy in my caravan of sorts (with Susan, Julie, Maria and Katie), I certainly got an earful. I learned intricate details of childhood hardships, hang-ups and dreams that in an office setting would simply never surface.

About five miles from the North Dakota border, we took a break from the sun and heat with a respite in a town that didn't even make our very detailed map. The sign entering Bainville said "population 200" but unless they lived in the basement of the post office or gas station or were stacked up in the grain elevator, I can't fathom where they were. We only saw one person in two hours, a bored looking bartender that resembled the lone survivor from *Night of the Zombies*. It was the quintessential ghost town with tumbling weeds bouncing in front of an old boarded-up financial institution with the word BANK in big letters in the front, nothing more. This obviously used to be a town that functioned, perhaps in the early 1900's when the grain elevator business was good. A few droughts too many had it hanging by the thinnest of threads.

We all converged at the state line for the perfunctory group photo before heading east against an annoying head and cross wind that only got worse as the afternoon progressed. It was akin to listening to the sea from a whelk shell all day, one on each ear, and by the time we arrived in Williston, we felt dazed and wobbly. After seeing one lonely cloud over eight hours, Susan commented that this had to be the place for which "blue skies and amber waves of grain" was intended.

A Democratic fund-raiser was taking place at the park where we set up camp and we were invited to imbibe in a free, delicious, "all you can eat" picnic there. I think I went back for seconds at least ten times! Since a day off was on the horizon, a few of us walked over to a place called the Neighborhood Bar for a little revelry, pool and even a dance or two. After sidestepping cheek-to-cheek to "Wonderful Tonight," one of Susan and my favorite songs, we walked back to our tent beneath a canvass of a billion stars.

In my wildest dreams, I never would have guessed that going to a K-Mart would be considered a "religious experience" by anyone. For Susan and Julie, even though they had no room to carry anything else bigger than an extra sock in their panniers, it was almost just that—a comforting sight and a sign of civilization at long last.

While they got their jollies eyeing merchandise, my thrill for the day was getting some shock-resistant padding installed on my handlebars to help offset some of the road bounce that was making my hands and wrists more numb by the hour. I also decided to break my oath to let my hair and beard grow to wonderfully disgusting lengths and look for a barber. I must have appeared a little unkempt because the hairdresser asked me, Mr. Conservative Corporate Guy in Remission, if I wanted to "keep it spiked!" Just goes to show that appearance is everything!

July 14

Although the Bikecentennial-provided maps were amazingly accurate and an indispensable guide to life on the road, in a few isolated cases, we made a group decision to veer from the route and shave unnecessary miles from our itinerary. On this day, we saved two hours of biking time and still had a challenging seventy-two miles of gusting cross winds and even a few low-grade hills. Susan almost got blown off her bike on numerous occasions!

In Williston, almost everyone purchased Walkman stereos or handlebar bag speakers, and although clearly dangerous, (prohibiting us from hearing car horns, etc.) they were the rave of the moment, offering a nice change of pace and a welcomed alternative to the sound of the howling wind. The morning highlight was a scrumptious breakfast of egg and cheese biscuits at a diner in Ray. Susan accompanied Maria and her five-week-old hacking cough to the Stanley Community Hospital for long-awaited X-rays and diagnosis. As nurse Susan expected, she had a nasty case of pleurisy and was issued some antibiotics, a few pain pills and strict counsel to stay off the bike for at least three days. For Maria, one of the most hard-headed and determined people I knew, that would be next to impossible.

Our campsite was spacious but had grass a foot tall and bugs a plenty. Why did the RV's always get a golf course lawn while tents got the ungrazed cow pasture!

July 15

We took advantage of a tail wind from heaven all morning and coasted the sixty miles into Minot by 12:30 p.m. An extremely wimpy group vote was held and the "stayers" outnumbered the "go-ahead another twenty milers" seven to five.

Warren Jr. let the strong personalities of the group get the best of him and in doing so established a precedent that would eventually threaten to dismantle the whole group. It was sad to say but as everyone's confidence in their physical and mechanical abilities improved, his value as a group leader diminished considerably. Unfortunately, he never really recognized that or adjusted his style of leadership to fit the situation and consequently had a frustrating second half of the summer.

Crosswinds and Grasshoppers

July 16: Rugby, ND C & R Campground (1801 miles)

July 17: Devil's Lake, ND Campground (1890 miles)

July 18: Cooperstown, ND City Park (1972 miles)

July 19: Page, ND Hotel and Cafe (2012 miles)

Susan experienced her second broken spoke of the trip as Julie, Katie and I followed behind, taking turns shielding each other from the wind. Repairing the splintered wheel was a total team effort as each of us had at least one of the special tools required to fix it. If any one of us had not been there, we would have been stuck. Sometimes it's better to be lucky than good.

Grasshoppers also became an unexpected nuisance as they swarmed the ground and air in our paths, clinking our front spokes, getting in our shirts and banking off our goggles. During times of drought in North Dakota, they strip the trees and plants and even chew down the handles of hoes and shovels. It was a futile exercise trying to play dodge ball with the creatures because they were *everywhere*.

Maria, still weakened by the pleurisy, managed to make it part of the way before getting a ride on to Rugby. Jeff and I shopped for dinner and prepared burgers on the grill while the "mother of all storms" heated up on the horizon. We took our positions beside the highway, watching a lightning display that put any fourth of July fireworks demonstration to shame. The sunset was a picture perfect montage of velvet, cantaloupe and mauve and I'm sure the fifty or so onlookers from the campground would have gladly paid admission to see the ever-changing show.

July 17

We capitalized on a seventeen miles per hour tail wind to chalk up a record high eighty-nine mile day! Mr. T had assumed we were staying in Minnetonka at the sixty-mile mark and apparently spent the better part of an hour exercising his liver at a local pub. He couldn't walk a straight line when we found him, but he was coherent enough to realize that going on to Devils Lake would not be a safe move. His penchant for beer seemed to be escalating at about the same rate that he was distancing himself from the group. From day one, he seemed to be more interested in interacting with total strangers than us, now it was a foregone conclusion.

Susan had a rocky start the next morning when she slid out of control on the road leading out of the Devil's Lake Campground, catapulted over the handlebars and landed on her feet, waist high in weeds in a ditch! Somehow she released her feet from the toe clips in time to avert going down with the bike on top of her. Maria and Warren came around the corner just in time to see her airborne!

July 18

Our first stop after that was in Warwick (pop. 27) at an old Mayberry RFD-looking gas station. The owner served us free java while we engaged in small talk, waiting out a passing rain shower. A cooing kitty decided to call it a day on my lap to chuckles from the greasy gallery around me. We paused again in Pekin where an entire neighborhood of kids surrounded us in the park, showing off their bikes and favorite pets. After that, Mr. T. and rejuvenated Maria rode together (very unusual), in what was to become a race to the finish line. Warren was running on empty since he actually started the day from Minnetonka and didn't have the energy to keep up with a steady, hell-bent Maria. "T" was visibly devastated when he got to camp, having "lost a race" with someone who a month earlier wouldn't have stood a chance. He simply wasn't able to alter his "racer's mentality" and enjoy this type of long-distance mental and physical endurance test with a group who didn't always see or do things his way. That night, he undoubtedly began to put his plans in place to chart his own course.

July 19

It would have been impossible to imagine the words, forty miles and easy being in the same sentence back in May, but after six weeks in the saddle, the ride to Page was a three- hour breeze. Our only stop on this enjoyable, sunny and flat ride was in Hope where we savored root beer floats and bowled at the appropriately named Bowling Cafe. With only two lanes, it looked like an addition that someone might have built onto their mansion.

Maria was battling an annoying case of heat rash caused by exposure to the sun and her pleurisy medicine. She had us rolling in laughter on the quiet streets as she covered up every inch of exposed skin on her body, put a bandanna on her face and pretended to be an armed bandit with her loaded squirt gun!

Susan had gotten "into a groove" the past few days and dared to admit that it might be possible to make it all the way, "I can't believe we'll have forty-five days in soon. Our anniversary is in four more days—can't believe that either. How are we going to keep our life exciting so we will stay together after the trip. We can't bike across the country every summer. . ."

Anniversary Celebration

July 20: Morehead St. University Dorm, MN (2070 miles)

July 21: Woodland Trails Campground, MN (2135 miles)

July 22/23: Douglas Lodge, Lake Itasca, MN (2180 miles)

July 24: Knutson State Park, Pennington, MN (2245 miles)

Images of the Road. . . We are leading a life of primitive men and women
of the 1990's. . . gathering food and making our bed wherever we end
the day. . . making the best of the road ahead of us
and the conditions of the moment we face.

A steady morning downpour kept us soggy to the bone until we stopped for a reprieve in Arthur at the thirty-mile mark. To this point, we had been incredibly fortunate in the inclement weather department, and on relatively flat land, the rain really didn't bother me much.

Donning our iridescent yellow rain gear, multipurpose protective helmet, wraparound goggles (if only they had tiny windshield wipers!), and plastic bag-covered shoes, we at least looked impressive slicing through the drenching cloudburst. The quaint little shopping court we stopped at in Arthur reminded me of a scene from the movie *Cocoon*. A mid- morning gathering of retirees was paired up all around us, drinking coffee, "mall walking," shopping, and simply conversing. With our odd conglomeration of soaking gear, I'm sure they thought we were auditioning to be a scuba diver or to work in the Biosphere.

It cleared up in the early afternoon and Warren Jr. joined our group of five as we rode cluster-style all the way into Fargo, the first of only two medium-sized cities on our entire itinerary. Invariably someone had to make a visit to a bike shop whenever we found one on the route, and Fargo was no exception. Unfortunately, it usually took several hours to take care of all the minor repairs and purchase needs of the group, and I always found myself playing the waiting game way beyond the point when "Flash's" (my bike) needs were satisfied.

At breakfast the next morning, it was obvious that several members of the group were battling nasty hangovers after our "one beer" pit stop at the Trader and Trapper lounge the night before. I admired the quantity and frequency of the inebriation interludes and the fact that no one ever seemed to be suffering too badly in the stamina department the morning after.

July 21

Rolling hills, an abundance of pine and spruce trees, corn fields and cool temps welcomed us as we entered Minnesota and the fertile Midwest. Our pretrip foresight of trying to be in the country's least humid area at the hottest time of the summer was starting to pay dividends.

I was in overdrive all day, sprinting in the front of the pack with Jeff and

Smitty and playing "bat the can" along the side of the road with a plastic base-ball bat. Susan, meanwhile, watched Maria and Warren Jr. lock tires and fall in the road (at a slow speed) after he playfully asked Maria for a "push" up the hill! It certainly was nice to be able to play a bit without worrying if we'd make it to camp or not.

We staked our tents at the Woodland Trails Campground where we got more than a little drizzle in the pasta surprise. Julie and I had a hilarious creative session at the spacious welcome center as we prepared for our halfway-point variety show. My Oshgood Slaters-affected right knee was really ailing and I couldn't help but wonder if I was causing long-term damage. Who knows what the breaking point is?

July 22/23

One of those "frozen in time" magic moments happened for Susan and I the following morning. Two white-tailed deer kept pace with us for a thousand yards or so at eighteen miles per hour, cautiously glancing at us from a parallel field before trotting across the road and dropping out of sight. Our quiet, ap-proachable bikes probably seemed more like a companion than a menace to these gracious animals that thrive in the Minnesota timberland. It was appropri-ate that such a special unexpected pleasure fall on the day we had earmarked to ride together and celebrate our second wedding anniversary.

Susan and I separated from the group for the night (for the first and only time of the bike trip) and decided on a log cabin-style room at the Douglas Lodge, circa 1905, for $48. Amenities like a dressing room, fireplace, bathtub and a screened-in porch gave us a chance to stretch out and relax without the threat of interruptions. We bathed together in Skin-So-Soft for an hour or so and melted slowly into a state of oblivion.

No one expressed surprise when Mr. T set out on his own for southern Canada en route to home state New York. As Susan and I slept in at the Lodge, we didn't even have a chance to say good-bye. Despite his mostly intolerant reaction to the group concept, he provided some timely comic relief with his unique ver-nacular of "T-isms": panniers were "pantaleers," bungee cords were "bundy cords," etc. It was sad to hear that he was gone.

Jean, Susan and I decided to rent a canoe and paddle around a lake near the headwaters of the Mississippi River. Warren and Julie did the same, alone, as we all chuckled like high school kids about the prospect of Warren trying to use the moment to kindle a relationship. Katie and Maria opted to try their luck as anglers and after a few hours of sunburn and some serious horsefly swatting, finally came away with a pair of prize walleyes.

Before dinner, Susan sneaked away with "Bad Influence" Julie for a beer and a few ciggy butts. After the first week of the trip, the Jersey rebel and Jeff both ceased trying to hide their smoking, which annoyed Warren substantially.

Another emotional issue surfaced when Peter's wife of less than a year, Amy, showed up at our campground. After an afternoon with her, Peter very unexpectedly announced that he would have to go back to Chicago for an indefinite period of time to "take care of a personal emergency." I had a premonition that it involved a serious problem with their relationship, but the whole story would not come to light until September. That made two guys in one day who went their separate ways, leaving Jeff, Warren and I to carry on now with the seven girls. The emotional roller coaster would escalate from this point on.

We heard some rustling in the middle of the night but went back to sleep in a half daze not thinking much about it. Lee Ann informed us the next morning that we had a raccoon intruder that managed to dig Susan's journal out of a zip-locked bag in one of her panniers secured under our rain- fly! They are incredibly nimble and sly little animals with hands as dexterous as humans. Being a novice tent camper before the trip, I found it increasingly fascinating that our daily lives on the road were so profoundly affected by such a variety of creatures.

July 24

The first day of the second half of the summer started auspiciously sunny as Susan and I tried to keep up with "churn and burn" Jean for the first forty miles to Bemidji. Although my derailleur was malfunctioning, effectively leaving me with four less gears, my legs felt sufficiently revived from the "off day" and my drive and determination had never been stronger.

We took full advantage of Bemidji's broad range of amenities and ended up in and around the town for a total of five hours! With laundry, a camera repair shop visit and extended "Bo" and "Flash" outpatient surgery at the congenial Homeplace Bicycle Shop, the day's agenda was packed. We were beginning to feel like residents by the time 5 o'clock in the afternoon rolled around, but unfortunately there were still twenty-five miles to go. Of course, we couldn't resist a farewell root beer float fix for "extra energy" before departing the site of Paul Bunyan lore and legend.

The stretch to Pennington was not a lot of fun, with mundane, marshland-type surroundings, thick, sticky pavement hindering our progress, and a hot afternoon sun beating down on our backs. Susan was quite vocal about her disapproval of the circumstances but I reassured her that we would get there before dark and we would be able to find the rest of the rapidly diminishing group.

I was thankful that everyone had chosen to take a rest stop at the one and only general store in Pennington so I wouldn't have to eat my words. Lee Ann surprised the group by announcing that she was also leaving, opting to travel a similar Northern trek like Mr. T with a newfound road buddy from Santa Cruz, California. Her secondary motive was to try and convince her boyfriend (living in the Upper Peninsula of Michigan) to drop his work and carry on to the East Coast with her.

We found our sleeping turf for the night only 2 1/2 miles down the road at a picturesque woodsy state park and on-site lake. Right after setting up the tent, I limped down to the edge of the water and joined the rest of the group snapping photos of a sinking red ball slowly descending into the placid water. As we popped the cork on the champagne to celebrate the day of our second anniversary and eat yet another pasta dinner, the fabled Minnesota Mosquito (known to locals as the state bird) and his thousands of third cousins and great aunts joined us with an intensity that literally drove us into our dens. After a thirty-minute spree of giggling in the tents and clapping our pesky intruders to death, we succumbed to the sheer exhaustion of another long, but very satisfying day.

Freak Accident

July 25: Grand Rapids Fairgrounds, MN (2310 miles)

July 26: Palisade City Park, MN (2366 miles)

July 27: Isle Hotel, MN (2431 miles)

Julie and I were on a mission all day as we attempted to beat the others to camp in Grand Rapids, shop, and have a meal prepared before the rest of the group got there. We made it to the city limits of our destination without much of a hitch, but after stopping at a convenience store to get directions to the "Fairgrounds" (our camping spot for the night), a peculiar and potentially fatal incident occurred.

By this juncture of the trip, I was so used to wearing my 7 1/2 ounce Giro Prolight bike helmet that I really didn't feel it on my head. I had taken the helmet off upon entering the store and when we hurriedly got back on our bikes to try and outrun the drizzle that was suddenly coming down, I inadvertently left my "hat" sitting on top of my gear which was bungeed to the back of the bike. I started ahead of Julie by about two bike lengths with no more than a foot to navigate our bikes between the curb and the stream of rush- hour traffic.

In a matter of seconds, I heard a prolonged screeching of bike and car brakes that sounded like an eerie precursor to a loud crash. Julie had run over and destroyed my foam head protector the instant it fell off my bike and landed in her path. I was obviously relieved a crash did not occur and that she wasn't hurt, however, the fate of my bicycle helmet was a bit unsettling since it usually sat on my head! Immediately thereafter, I bought another one of the same material at a local bike shop.

July 26

Mother Nature blanketed us with an intermittent drizzle and downpour the following day for almost the entire fifty-six miles to Palisade. Two perfectly-situated roadside taverns saved us from completely melting away. In the morning, we stopped in Jacobson (pop. 12) at Don's Bar for some coffee, great juke-box tunes, dancing, and overall silliness. We "owned" the place for an hour and

Julie even took Don's place behind the counter in a "she's obviously done this before" show of bartending.

Less than an hour from our final destination, the whole gang hibernated at the Big Sandy Lake Resort where we caught up on postcards, fine-tuned our ever-improving pool games and finished chowing down on anything and everything edible left in our panniers.

I was possessed with a sudden burst of energy the final twelve miles of sunflower and corn fields to Palisade, but unfortunately had to fix a flat en route in the rain. Refuge from the wet ground for the night was found in the form of a picnic shelter where we set our tents up underneath, between, and on top of a few, scattered picnic tables. A toasty fire helped warm our soggy bones and very quickly put us to sleep.

July 27

A steady diet of the wet stuff had gotten us into the daily habit of putting all of our belongings in dual plastic bags inside our panniers and on our back rack as well. Our bodies went from a semimoist, semicomfortable, cement floor sleep to an instantly nasty, gross, sloshy feeling the minute we hit "the muddy trail." By this point in the trip, everything we owned stunk like someone had thrown up on it so it didn't really matter. Our nasal passages were, needless to say, totally desensitized.

We broke up a most unsavory morning with a pleasant coffee break and "chew the fat" session with a gathering of older folks at a tiny breakfast hangout in Aitken (pop. 1770). An attempt was made to dry our damp clothes under a vent on the wall! Maria, Smitty and Susan committed a "TP demeanor," nabbing two rolls of toilet tissue each from the bathroom. It was almost impossible to keep that vital stuff usable with the dampness.

Warren realized that we badly needed a dry, inside, sleeping arrangement. Within minutes of arriving in Isle, we were able to find a nondescript establishment right on Mille Lacs Lake for a mere $6 a head for two rooms. I took the opportunity to thoroughly clean out my disgusting panniers for the first time and even used a hose and soap for proper "defunktafication" of the peanut butter and jelly, crackers, bike tires and grease congregated at the bottom of the compartments.

Restoring Faith in Humanity

July 28: The Mobeck's, Harris, MN (2497 miles)
July 29/30: Apple River C-ground, Somerset, WI (2541 miles)
July 31: Smitty's Campground, Lake City, MN (2617 miles)

Before leaving the "Walleye Capital of the World," I had a chat with the motel owner and was shown pictures of two awesome acts of nature that had wreaked havoc on them over the past decade. A menacing-looking tornado swept across the lake in July '85 and the very next winter a freakish ice avalanche of sorts happened during a spring thaw, driving walls of slush into the defenseless lakeside cabins.

It was odd that such a discussion of nature gone haywire would be followed by a day when the world felt like "Ozzie and Harriet" or "Leave it to Beaver" all over again. Everywhere we went, people were so overwhelmingly friendly, it really made us forget the past and future problems of the planet.

Halfway through the morning, Katie had a flat by the yard of a woman who owned a small campground. While our ever-patient and thrifty comrade repeatedly attempted and failed to patch up the tire for close to an hour (I always went right ahead and replaced the tube, not bothering to patch, since the tubes only cost $2), the lady, whose husband had just recovered from a stroke, made us a fresh pot of coffee and brought out a huge plate of homemade raisin cookies. There's something about being hopeless-looking and sweaty on a fully loaded bike that brings out the best in people!

Just outside of Stark at Big Fish Lake, Jeff, Smitty, Susan and I decided to take a dip in the lake while Warren scoured the streets of the small town looking for a friendly neighbor who would allow us to sleep in their yard for the night. (there were no parks, campgrounds, churches, etc.) We hit "pay dirt" with the Mobeck family, a couple in their mid-fifties who were extremely hospitable, accommodating and even bikers themselves! We had the run of the house and yard for a night and were within easy walking distance of an intensely competitive fast-pitch softball tournament (90+ MPH!). We were told that it was some of the best of its kind anywhere in the country. I certainly couldn't argue with that.

A turning point in the group's respect level for Warren occurred during the evening in an episode with frequently emotional, off-the-wall Julie. She was trying to humor (or shock, I'm not sure) Warren a little bit by asking if we had a bridge coming up on our route anytime soon. Of course he diligently tried to find out (even though the maps weren't *that* detailed), and when he finally questioned Julie about the comment, she said she was contemplating doing the "S" (suicide) word and was just curious.

Instead of taking it as a joke, he got increasingly serious with "we have to talk" comebacks and the next thing I knew Julie, Maria, Susan and Warren were embroiled in one nasty cat-scratching verbal apocalypse. I was trying to mind my own business and get caught up on the sports page but couldn't resist eavesdropping on their collective two month's worth of frustration being unleashed like a fire hose on him. He was completely spent after a turbulent hour or so and decided to ride by himself to Somerset the next day to cool off. Those three never saw eye-to-eye with Warren the rest of the trip, despite the fact that he was by far the most instrumental in getting them to that point.

July 29/30

The few remaining group members, who either still hadn't left to go their separate ways or didn't need time alone, broke camp about 8 o'clock in the morning for a leisurely, tail wind-aided joyride into Wisconsin. We felt naughty straying from the Bikecentennial route, but chopped off fifteen miles and had our tents set up at Apple River Campground by 1:25 in the afternoon.

Susan's best friend from college, Julie, her husband, Brian, and their two kiddies, drove the three hours from Marshfield and met us for burgers at the local Dairy Queen and a couple of "brewskis" at a nearby pub. It really lifted Susan's spirits to see a familiar face from yesteryear and to finally make it to her home state. I knew in her mind and heart that she never really gave herself a chance to make it this far.

The "off day" provided several hours of true relaxation and good, old-fashioned, kick back and get silly fun! We braved the icy Apple River in a chain of inner tubes starting about 11 a.m., but after three hours of sun, a half-dozen Bud Lights and three (walk across the river to the edge and hope everybody waits up) tinkle breaks, I was feeling warm and fuzzy and adequately mushy-headed. I wobbled back to camp for a sandwich and a fifteen minute snooze that could have easily turned into an all-nighter.

July 31

Sunny skies guided our route past the endless cornfields, haystacks and silos along the Wisconsin/Minnesota border. At the seven-mile mark of the day, I had a broken spoke and flagged down Jean to help me out and give me some company. We ended up riding together almost all the way to Lake City, exchanging humorous stories and anecdotes while trying not to be cognizant of the fact that our muscles were being forced to work overtime. It seemed very strange passing the Afton Alps ski resort right in the midst of rolling farm country. It's definitely a far cry from the real Alps!

Susan and Julie, meanwhile, got caught just in front of a historic drawbridge in the quaint little river town of Stillwater. There they stood on their out-of-place, innocent two-wheelers leading a succession of over a dozen vacationing cars and RV's while the lights, bells and arms of the gate took their time letting a boat through. It was a symbol of why we all set out in the first place, to catch a front row glimpse of the real American heartland as it used to be and still is in these hard-to-get-to places.

At our mail stop in Redwing, we picked up a postcard for Maria that we had actually sent to her ourselves in Itasca. It was a picture of three scrappy little raccoons, periodic campsite companions that Maria was particularly amused and annoyed by, with the caption "triple trouble." I wrote a note to Maria from them signed Mip, Bip and Flip. When she and Katie finally drug into camp just before nightfall, it produced a tired laugh.

Bob

August 1: Winona KOA, IA (2674 miles)

August 2: Andy Mtn. C-gr., Harper's Ferry, IA (2749 miles)

August 3: Grassy spot behind cafe, Colesburg, IA, (2826 miles)

August 4: Picnic shelter, Oxford Junction, IA (2896 miles)

Images of the Road...midday horns, miles of corn...wide open spaces,
inquisitive faces...North Dakota plains, Minnesota rain...
flowers on the roadside, sores on my backside.

No matter how routine a day looked as we glanced over our maps with the morning coffee, something unusual or noteworthy always managed to cross our paths or impact our progress. On the first day of August, it was Bob. With forty-five of fifty-seven miles behind us, Susan and I stopped for a seemingly quiet pause at a country store in Goodview. As we mounted our Cannondales for the stretch run, a smiling grandfather figure of seventy or so was also leaving on his green, 1950's-model, five-speed Schwinn Special with a basket on the front. Although we had crossed more than half the United States, his bike looked like it had been through the Tour de France, the Tour de Trump and the streets of Winona a few dozen times to spare!

Bob had retired on March 15th after a lifelong career in a mundane assembly line job with Winona Knitting. He had been tooling around the countryside on his two-wheeler, forty miles a day, every day since. With his blue jean overalls and loafers, it was hilarious watching his tiny frame make a running start before jumping on the bike to get going and then putting on the brakes à la Fred Flintstone when it was time to stop. (In cyclospeak, that would be mount and dismount.) He even volunteered some personal gossip about his "girlfriend" who he said thinks he's a "nut" for biking so much. "She's in her early sixties but acts like she's eighty-something."

August 2

We weren't exactly current events buffs on this journey, but thanks to Jeff's transistor, we managed to catch wind of the shocking news of Saddam's invasion of Kuwait. It would be one of the few doses of reality that penetrated our wall of isolation from the outside world.

Susan and I toiled the seventy-five miles to Harper's Ferry together. We faced a lot of sudden, unexpected hills and our disposition fluctuated accordingly. As we crossed over the Iowa border, the climax of a lot of pent-up frustration came out in a crazy five-mile screaming session along mostly deserted State Road 26. I don't think (and certainly hope) anyone else heard us except Jean who rode past, figuring out real quickly that we needed some time alone to work this one out. Normally laid back and easygoing, I was at a boiling point like I've never reached before. I could almost feel my nostrils flaring! After seven weeks of the closest of contact and a pendulum of emotions, anxieties and experiences, I guess we were entitled to one "blow out."

August 3

Who would've ever imagined hilly terrain and panoramic views in flat Iowa! The scientific explanation for this unexpected shocker is that northeast Iowa somehow escaped the glaciers that leveled the rest of the state centuries ago.

Early in the morning, we took a two-hour break to check out a most unusual tourist attraction, the burial grounds of ancient Indian tribes from hundreds of years B.C. known as the Effigy Mounds. The unique aspect of the grounds is that the burial areas are built in the shapes of birds, bears and other animals of great importance to Indian life. Most impressive is the absolutely huge Great Bear Mound, a whopping seventy feet across the shoulders and forelegs, 137 feet long and 3 1/2 feet high!

We passed through Monona as the ever-present noonday whistle sounded across the fields, letting everyone within miles know it was time to knock off for a while. Searching for edible fare, we noticed a woman from the Monona newspaper darting out of her car to find out just what the nine of us were doing. Obviously, we were a very unusual sight in small-town Iowa or almost anywhere else for that matter. She proceeded to interview us over the next half hour and promised to send along a copy of the article to Bikecentennial.

At 6:15 p.m., with sixty-four miles in, eleven to go, and three huge hills looming ahead with drizzly conditions, a station wagon from heaven (actually the folks from Willy's Tavern in Colesburg), stopped us and offered lifts into town. I was glad for Susan as her knees were sore and swollen and ready for a respite, but after making it this far without a ride, I wasn't even tempted anymore. Katie and I (the only two who kept riding) received a hero's welcome of sorts an hour later at the neighborhood swimming pool where the others had gotten permission to take an outside cold shower. Simple pleasures indeed.

We set up tent behind the Deluxe Cafe and post office and dined and drank at Willy's. About half of the gang fell into their tents sometime in the middle of the rainy night that also featured a fireworks display around us, courtesy of some local teenagers. Jean and Warren stayed up until 3 a.m. trying to identify license plates while a rather complacent sheriff apparently made matters worse with a "kids will be kids" attitude. Thank goodness I had no problem snoozing through these periodic nocturnal sideshows.

August 4

After a long, "all they could make" breakfast at the Deluxe Cafe, we headed in the direction of Oxford Junction. After only fifteen miles on the road, we were distracted by a monumental pit stop in Dyersburg, the actual filming site of the movie *Field of Dreams*. For a baseball aficionado like me, it was indeed heaven in Iowa. It's goofy to think that a fabricated baseball field built in the middle of a corn field could send shivers down a grown man's spine. Inexplicably, this one did. Maybe it was the luscious sunny day with the clearest of azure skies shining down on the perfect Iowa farmhouse, the green sod, the white picket fence and the tall stalks of corn. Or, the exciting realization that our street of dreams had so wonderfully intersected with such an oasis in the middle of the Midwest as this. It was like being transformed to an eight-year-old all over again—wide-eyed, filled with anticipation, like every nerve ending was about to burst. My final and lasting impression was of a little boy of three with batting glove in rear pocket, catching glove on hand and hat on his head being guided off the field by his dad. You could almost see the ghosts of baseball's past marching across the field. . . it was indeed a magical moment.

Although it was a scorching 95° all afternoon, back on the road I felt very comfortable, breezing along the rolling hills in the fifteen to twenty miles per hour range. Jeff and I went ahead to try and locate suitable free camping, literally walking the streets of the tiny community of Oxford Junction. Eventually, we settled on the Legionnaires Park, a very nice, but unfortunately showerless shelter. A few curious drunks from a company picnic wandered in our direction and began imitating "Curious George" around the bikes. One saw Susan's *Field of Dreams* tee shirt and said, "Hey, they made a movie out of that tee shirt!"

The Yeasts

August 5/6: Yeast Residence, Davenport, IA (2947 miles)

August 7: Timber Campground, Cambridge, IL (2997 miles)

August 8: City Hall Chambers, Henry, IL (3053 miles)

The easiest day of the week led us through Donahue, Lowden and Eldridge where we met Marty and Jerry Yeast, our surrogate parents/gracious hosts for the next day-and-a-half. A couple in their fifties with two college-age kids, the Yeasts were fellow Bikecentennial members and Jerry had been a group leader in the past. They led us the last ten miles or so into Davenport, the second "metropolis" of 100,000-plus population so far. Cruising through Eagle Supermarket while waiting for our laundry at Duds and Suds was a major case of

sensory overload—too many choices! Jean went off on side trip number two to
see her folks in Chicago. (In the cross- country Bikecentennial trip, everyone is
allowed two separate, three-day sojourns from the group as long as a person
gets picked up and dropped off at the appropriate predetermined locales.)

What a nice break to be able to spend an entire day in a home, with a couch,
a shower, and a VCR, with real-life parents. We all did some obligatory bike
maintenance and cleaning, then made a run to Target to purchase a few birthday
items for Warren.

After a second consecutive multicourse, close-to-perfection dinner prepared
by Susan and Mrs. Yeast, we brought out the party favors and whooped it up a
bit for Warren. I think he really needed the positive reinforcement he got from
fellow group leader, Jerry, as he was really at a low ebb confidence-wise. He
was finding out the hard way that being a leader is not as easy as it looks.

August 7

The 67th Street Bridge was our gateway from Davenport, Iowa to Rock Island, Illinois, a combination iron rail and expansion bridge that had a tricky,
narrow, bike path. I caught a glimpse of the picturesque Davenport minor league
baseball facility as it beckoned a capacity crowd of cheering spectators on a
lovely sunny day. Our first taste of urban blight and poverty hit us suddenly in
Rock Island with its full compliment of moon crater potholes, catcalls and an
unidentifiable foul odor, probably emanating from a nearby factory.

Passing through Henry County in the early afternoon was a treat as we stopped
to admire the miles of "hog condos" populating the roadside. In this self-pro-
fessed "Hog Capital of the World," the "oinkers" live like King Tut with lush
feeding stalls, roaming and relaxing areas, and what appeared to be sunbathing
pads. If Robin Leach ever did a show for hogs, this would be Monte Carlo!

We knocked off after fifty miles at the pleasant, woodsy, and spacious Timber Campground, just south of the middle of nowhere in Cambridge. The Yeasts
rejoined us for dinner and surprised everyone with a half gallon each of Whitney's
fresh strawberry, butter pecan, and chocolate Swiss almond ice cream. As no
one in this group was worrying about calories, we made sure they didn't have to
take any back.

August 8

In the sudden absence of a substantial biking challenge due to the flat terrain
and our "over the hump" fitness levels, it seemed like everyone was paying an
inordinate amount of attention to the inane idiosyncrasies and quirks of their
fellow group members. Maria and Julie, Susan's two closest biking buddies,
also seemed to get on her nerves at the same time, so. . . when that happened,
the world basically stunk all day. Unfortunately, my mostly unemotional, practical, rationale, matter-of-fact resolutions were not always the therapy she sought.
She explained in her journal that day, "Whenever I have a tough ride or an
unfortunate event, (i.e. broken spoke, flat) all of my frustrations come out in the

form of blame for 'making me take this trip.' I know you didn't make me, but I just want you to know how difficult it is for me." While it was very difficult to carry on a marriage under the constant, watchful eye and ear of eight strangers, I never questioned the overwhelming advantages of doing the trip with them.

Aunt Ida

August 9: Odell City Park, IL (3126 miles)

August 10: Iroquois City Park, IL (3194 miles)

August 11: Buffalo Tall Oaks Campground, IN (3251 miles)

August 12: Lagro, IN, Colene and Aunt Ida's (3313 miles)

To avoid even the possibility of being in the firing zone of rumored fireworks or another vandalism incident in the park, we were encouraged by the authorities to stake our floor spot at Henry's City Hall the night before. Julie and I chatted as we strapped on our bike gear on the sidewalk the next morning. A well-manicured, prim and proper City Council woman of forty-five or so crossed in front of us on her way to work and initiated a little idle conversation. As I was trying to act respectable despite my "Scumby" (Gumby caricature) tee shirt and skintight cycling shorts, Julie very nonchalantly applied her underarm roll-on deodorant, totally oblivious to her own crassness. The woman kept on talking, but undoubtedly had the story of the month for the bridge club meeting! It's amazing how quickly you can get out of sync with social graces and accepted behavior when you live on the streets and in the woods for a summer.

Just before Wenona (not to be confused with Winona), a massive construction area made us wish we had mountain bikes for a while. Sand and mud bogged us down substantially as we walked our bikes between two rows of a corn field!

Julie's second flat of the day occurred after we were detoured off the main road around a ROAD CLOSED sign and through a long stretch of gravel. We realized Julie had a faulty valve, but instead of changing the flat again, I was nominated to be "Hanz and Franz" (à la *Saturday Night Live*) for the next seven miles, flying off my bike (while Susan held it up) at half-mile intervals to "pump up" Julie's sagging tire. It was hilarious, but only because it was the end of the day along a desolate, flat road.

August 10

With flat roads and warm, sun-drenched conditions, it seemed like a group party all day long. The first mini-stop of the morning in Campus introduced us to the entire town of kids aged four to twelve, (there must have been twenty-five in all), all buddies and on bicycles of their own. They followed us to the town tavern where they inquisitively played "Twenty Questions" about our trip and we found cold drinks and air conditioning. I think we made their day and they certainly made ours.

Around lunchtime in Ashkum, everyone descended on the Dairy Queen where Jean "Reckless Makris" returned from her three-day sojourn with long-lost Peter who was back for the duration but offered no tidbits about his sudden departure in Minnesota. About the same time, Julie's brother came to pick her up in his '65 yellow convertible and take her away to points unknown for three days. Julie had repeatedly dreamed aloud of sitting over four wheels again and smiled from ear-to-ear in the company of her beloved sibling.

Late in the afternoon, we came to a bridge that was being systematically demolished by a huge swinging ball at the end of a crane. Warren and I carried the last five bikes across a precariously narrow ledge on the far side of what was left of the bridge. As each one was loaded with forty to sixty pounds of gear, that was no easy trip.

Mitch and Lu, Maria's old riding buddies from her '83 Bikecentennial trip, met us at the city park in Iroquois. They became friends on that ride, broke up with their previous significant others, got married and now had an eight-month-old baby girl, Kayla. We all took turns taking a rather unorthodox, but very necessary and refreshing, "bucket bath" under the lone spigot on the premises before gathering around the picnic tables under the shelter to exchange "war stories" with our new friends. Meanwhile, Susan's state of mind had greatly improved over the past forty-eight hours, "David rode with me again today. He's been so loving—when things are right—it feels so good. He's made me feel less afraid of the future."

August 11

A country road marked "stateline" reminded us that we had entered Indiana, state number nine. Mitch and Lu rode with us to Brook with Kayla neatly tucked and sleeping soundly in a comfy-looking "bugger" connected to her daddy's bike. They can't do as much or for as long as they used to, but nevertheless, they're continuing their favorite sport with child literally "in tow." We enjoyed yet another "heaping helping" of small-town breakfast before waving good-bye to the little family.

After a lot of suggestive selling and kibitzing, we had convinced Warren that he really needed a break from the group and that it was okay to take a three-day leave of his own. He seemed uneasy getting into a loaded, matchbox Toyota with two of his friends from native Indiana, somehow feeling that he was playing hooky from his assigned duties.

The rest of the gang had grand plans for the evening as we looked forward to listening to an on-site country band at the Tall Oaks Campground in Buffalo. Unfortunately, a torrential downpour right in the middle of dinner preparation put everyone in an "eat and retreat" mode instead. It was the absolute worst and most sustained storm of the summer, driving us into our tents at 7:00 for the duration of the night. A light mist permeated the microscopic holes on all sides of our tent for hours on end, making us feel like plants in a greenhouse. I thought it was almost refreshing, but Susan coined it a "hot, sweaty, misty, moisty mess." Despite the garbage bag liners in our panniers, everything got wet.

August 12

Only the initial 25 percent of the sixty-mile ride to Lagro spared us from more wet stuff. We did the group laundry thing in Royal Center after the previous night's drenching and carefully double-bagged all of our belongings this time. Katie found a tractor pulling contest/dirt bike race in mid- afternoon, so at her insistence, we stopped to witness this fiercely competitive, cultural phenomenon of small town rural America—until Mother Nature bogged it down.

The original game plan for the day called for finding a camp site at the (no shower, no shelter) Salamonic State Park, but this ever-creative, finagling bunch had better ideas. Sleeping in a tent in the rain is somewhat tolerable as long as it doesn't become a habit, but cooking, eating, setting up camp *and* sleeping in it is certainly worthy of avoidance.

The gang found refuge at the Lagro Cafe/Grocery Store while Peter and I scoured the town for sympathetic locals. When we returned, empty-handed, we discovered that not one, but two, attractive alternatives had presented themselves: a fair proposal from City Hall and a "too good to be true" one from Colene, a sixtyish lady living with her aunt.

Colene had purchased her mother's childhood brick home and stayed in Lagro between June and October fixing it up while her ninety-three year-old Aunt Ida came up from Florida. The home was actually built in the 1840's and was once used as a hotel for fur traders and Canadian travelers along the Wabash River. Colene was in the process of turning it into a Bed and Breakfast or bike hostel and decided that we would be an ideal group to practice with! Aunt Ida spryly chatted while cleaning her green beans at the kitchen table as Coleen gave us the grand tour of the cluttered, crowded abode loaded with antique artifacts from the surrounding area. It could just as easily be made into a history museum.

The group was nice enough to allow Susan and I to sleep in one of the two upstairs bedrooms, enlarging the smile on my face even more. From floor to ceiling, it contained an amazing array of dolls, including dozens of pictures, images and pieces of memorabilia of Susan's old friend, Raggedy Ann. Tucked safely away from the pelting rain in a dry, comfortable bed with distant train whistles blaring, it was an unexpectedly memorable night indeed.

"Spudd"

August 13: Monroeville, IN, City Shelter (3376 miles)
August 14: Bowling Green, OH, Campground (3469 miles)
August 15: Travel Holiday C-ground, Avery, OH (3539 miles)
August 16/17: "Spudd's" House, Cleveland, OH (3607 miles)

At roughly the two-thirds point of the trip, we took time at the enclosed Monroeville Park Pavilion to reflect a bit about the miles behind us and play a combination game of Pictionary and charades. My toenails even hurt from laughing!

August 14

With a little tail wind and the last of the totally pancake terrain, it was a perfect day to establish a new distance record, ninety-three miles! The morning started with a dense, pea soup fog that reduced visibility to ten feet. I posed for Susan to take my picture as I rode into oblivion along another state line road, this time between Indiana and Ohio. After two weeks of talking about it, Susan and I finally found a cornfield secluded and accessible enough to manage a little "afternoon delight" between the rows of stalks.

Only a pair of dots on the map, Miller City and Cloverdale, came between us and Bowling Green all day. A weary and hungry group rolled into camp about 6:30 p.m. after picking up our postcards and letters from mail stop number four. The opening and reading ritual always seemed to make the aches and pains seem a little less traumatic.

August 15

Bureaucracy slapped us in the face this morning in the form of the banks of Bowling Green, which despite our pleas and begs, simply refused to cash our cashier's checks. (Until that time, I thought they were equivalent to cash.) The excuse was that they were from out-of-state, but I'm sure the real reason was the fact that we looked like street bums to them. In "real life," as the lawyers, nurses, therapists and businesspeople we were, there is little doubt that this would have been a solvable problem. It never ceases to amaze me just how powerful a statement our dress and appearance makes about us. We eventually got a cash advance from our VISA cards and tore up the cashier's checks.

Maria, Julie, Susan, Katie and I paid a long visit to one of the very best bike shops we had frequented yet, owned by a personable guy named Dave. I picked up three spare tubes, some handlebar tape and toe straps before getting started with dinner partner Katie an hour ahead of the others. The two of us "smoked" the asphalt at a steady clip with the aid of a generous tail wind, stopping very briefly three times and covering the entire seventy miles to Avery in five hours.

We passed a number of migrant workers bent over picking cabbage, tomatoes and cucumbers with pails strapped to their backs.

About ten miles from Sandusky and one of the world's largest roller coasters, we had definitely crossed the imaginary line from the Midwest to the East. Motor homes, boats and pop-up campers were everywhere, quite a change from the predominantly city park quietness of the past three weeks. The owner of the campground we stopped at was rather cantankerous, disallowing us to set up camp until "the man with the money," Warren, got there. I had to sit across a busy highway with our bags of Subway sandwiches because he wouldn't let us consume the food on the premises until we forked over the astronomical $8 a tent fee! (We had been accustomed to paying 0-$5 at the most.) We finally were given three tiny sites less than a hundred feet from the highway exhaust fumes.

August 16/17

It was one, long, mentally-exhausting ride into Cleveland. Our host for the next two nights, Jim "Spudd" Sasak, a recent Bikecentennial leader who Warren knew, suggested that we try a more scenic route than our maps recommended and that turned out to be one ill-advised proposition. Construction crews dotted the congested highway almost the entire sixty-plus miles into the city. Crater- sized potholes, bumps in the road that looked like ski moguls, golf ball-sized rocks and sticky asphalt provided an intriguing obstacle course, in addition to the bumper-to- bumper Friday traffic, small animals, construction equipment and pedestrians. On several occasions, we were forced to take sidewalks due to city ordinances restricting bikes on the road.

About twenty-five miles away from inner city Cleveland, "Spudd" met us at McDonald's. He escorted the group in on a rush hour "urban assault" mission unlike anything we had experienced on our mostly back roads journey thus far. Peter bent an axle on the way and we all rested at the downtown Bike City bike shop. To get to "Spudd's" pad, we rode alongside Lake Erie where a smattering of kids on their no-speed bikes tried to keep up with us.

"Spudd" was a character in every sense of the word. As the official President of the Cleveland Chapter of Couch Potatoes of America, he proudly admitted partaking in hours after hours of "guiltless television viewing" and had one in every room of the house to satiate any sudden desires. Ironically, he was actually the antithesis of the stereotypical TV addict with an extremely active lifestyle. He was one of the most visibly hyper adults I'd ever seen and was a bicycling fanatic, routinely riding his bike twenty miles to and from work every day. He had just returned from leading a three-week Bikecentennial trip from Glacier National Park through the mountain ranges of Alberta, Canada, and proudly narrated a slide show at a party he threw for us.

We all converged on the neighborhood bar shortly after our arrival and hoisted numerous Mickey's Beers skyward to the wonders of life on the road.

The Hills of Pennsylvania

August 18: Campground on the Interstate, Austinburg, OH (3660 miles)
August 19: Methodist Church, Cambridge Springs, PA (3713 miles)
August 20: Penn Hiland Campground, Lander, PA (3767 miles)

"Spudd" volunteered to escort us out of town on an overcast Sunday morning. We left in a light drizzle and Warren had his first flat in front of a city park before we could get completely down the street. While everyone pitched in on the repair job, Julie and her coffee buzz stood on top of a makeshift platform and screamed obviously made-up campaign promises to a shocked gathering of open-mouthed kids. Never a dull moment!

Our gracious host led for the first thirty miles and then joined us for lunch at a roadside bar and grill. We had a few uncharacteristic midafternoon "pops" and cranked the tunes, basically taking the place over for an hour or so. Then, it was a farewell group photo session and tearful good-byes to our newfound friend.

August 19

Rolling hills, dreary gray skies and intermittent drizzle and rain kept everyone a little edgy all day. Susan moved into the spoke-breaking lead with an unprecedented two in one day, bringing her total to five. We still hadn't solved the riddle of why the two of us had nine between us and everyone else combined had only one. We did master the art of fixing them, however, conquering her second one with everyone cheering in a record seven minutes, twenty-eight seconds! And she says she's still "not a biker!"

I felt particularly strong and really kicked it into high gear the last twenty miles. It felt wonderful to finally take a sport "to the next level," something, I venture to say, that few nonprofessional athletes ever have the opportunity to do.

Warren earned some serious "brownie points" with the group with his crafty procurement of the Cambridge Springs Methodist Church for shut-eye and cooking, and a nearby high school for showering. A carpeted floor and a roof over my head that wouldn't leak was all I needed to hear.

August 20

Sitting blissfully in the hot tub at Jay's Hostel in Republic, Washington back in June, we met a group of guys traveling east to west who told us that the steepest terrain on this entire trek was in northeastern Pennsylvania. It was hard to imagine then, but on this day we discovered that they were right. I did my best to keep Susan's spirits lifted, but I soon realized that this would be one of those "just pray she doesn't quit before we get there days."

On one particularly ominous 10 percent grade hill on this dreary, misty, cloudy afternoon, I had to concentrate every second of the way to make it to the top. When I looked back down the damp asphalt of the curvy incline, I was shocked to see Susan and "Bo" lying on the side of the road below! I thought for sure she had been hit by a car and I instinctively raced back down the hill to find her slumped over, dirty, greasy and crying just for the heck of it in the gentle rain with cars blowing by within five feet of her at sixty miles per hour! I held her close for several minutes, very relieved that she was in one piece! She had been crying for three solid miles of rolling terrain and when she saw yet another stark contrast in elevation, she abruptly stopped and let the bike hit the ground beside her. Susan's journal entry that night read, "Although I know there's no turning back now, the rain and the hills made it next to impossible today. The sheer physical exertion required to just make it to camp was almost more than I could manage."

The Second Act

August 21: Elk's Lodge, Endicottville, NY (3817 miles)

August 22: Police Station, Danville, NY (3892 miles)

August 23/24: Watkins Glen, NY, Campground (3950 miles)

A succession of early morning mechanical adjustments left me alone with Warren and leaving close to 11 a.m., more than two hours behind the rest of the group. First, Susan tried to true her wheels by herself, an almost impossible task without a bike shop's precision equipment. Then, it was my brakes that needed an adjustment, and finally, Warren had a "shotgun blast" blow out on the steep gravel entrance road to our campground, completely destroying both tube and tire.

The terrain to Endicottville was eerily reminiscent of the rude awakening experienced in the Cascades and Rockies. It more than made up in steepness what it lacked in length. My conditioning and stamina had definitely improved tremendously and I was proud to be beating Warren up most of the hills. (That simply did not happen before.) Around the New York/Pennsylvania state line in Little Valley, we scaled a mountain appropriately coined "Murder Hill" that typified the Allegheny range. The panoramic expanse of green visible from the peak was majestic and awe-inspiring, especially since it meant we would soon be going down again.

Susan rode with consistent Katie and didn't walk up a single hill. After the lows of yesterday, I was a little shocked. Peter and Jean secured us a place to stay near Endicottville at an Elk's Lodge, about a mile from the ski resort town. We took turns engaging in sink baths at the lodge and feasted out as ace cookers Peter and Susan concocted grilled cheese sandwiches and chicken surprise. (That's what it is actually called.)

August 22

A combination of high mileage, consistent 6 to 8 percent grades, head wind, bad roads, heavy traffic and driving rain made this the most challenging day since Chief Mountain Pass on the way into Canada. It was one of those you never forget because you are truly physically and emotionally tested time after time. There were little short hills, short long hills, ten-mile progressive climbs and everything in between.

Barreling through Nunda after lunch, Julie wiped out on a dangerously slick metal bridge built for snow to melt through it in the winter. Jean, Peter, Warren and I were two miles ahead, scaling a hill of course, when a man in a pickup truck slammed on the brakes in front of us, got out and proclaimed that "one of your girls is down on the bridge back there" in choppy, out-of-breath phrases.

I immediately thought it was Susan since she had, jokingly I thought, threatened just that morning to wreck on purpose so she could go home! I don't remember the lightning sprint back to the bridge to see what had happened. It turned out to be Julie, and fortunately, aside from a bump on the head, a bruised psyche and assorted aches and pains, she came out of it okay. She was lucky that she didn't break her arm or get hit by one of the two cars that screeched to a halt less than ten feet away from her.

A combination of the wet bridge, carelessness and the uneven weight distribution on her bike (no front panniers) caused the mishap. To superstitious Julie, however, it was the second act in a macabre play. (The helmet incident in Minnesota was the first.) She refused to get a ride for the remaining fourteen-mile climb to Danville despite her mild state of shock and a driving cold rain. I came out of the interruption strangely energized and led the pack into town, legs pumping like a madman and a "nobody's gonna catch me" kamikaze ATTITUDE.

We threw everything but our bodies into the dryer of the first launderette we saw, and thanks to Jean's efforts, stayed at the local town hall/police station—dry, cozy and dead tired.

August 23/24

The first order of the morning was yet another bike shop visit where I desperately needed to get my wheels precision trued after the numerous flats and broken spokes and Susan needed a derailleur adjustment. The owner was an absent- minded gentleman who walked the one-and-a-quarter miles through his neighborhood to work everyday. He was more amazed than comfortable with our Cannondales, Myata, et al as he had probably done little more than pump up children's tires over the past ten years.

After wasting two precious hours of early morning cool temps by intermittently adjusting and looking perplexed, he finally admitted that his toolbox and expertise weren't equipped to handle our sophisticated demands. At least the bikes were rideable, if not perfect.

Katie, Maria, Susan and I left the shop together and were only at the ten-mile mark in Perkinsville about 1:30 p.m. We were in for another afternoon of merciless grades; at times it felt like we were climbing a tree! Entering the popular Finger Lakes wine region outside of Hammondsport, we took a breather at the Taylor Wine Company, sipped some wine, walked up more hills to the exhibition gallery, and bought a few bottles for the upcoming day off.

Around dusk, several dozen hills later, the sign for Watkins Glen finally came into view and we scaled the last ascent to the State Park Campground. After a few minutes of reminiscing with the rest of the gang and rubbing Ben Gay on our quads, a small prayer was answered in the form of a Domino's delivery truck and five large pizza pies. Warren had them chauffeured up the mountain while he shopped for groceries in the valley. Shortly after 10:00, he arrived with only a flashlight guiding his path to our tents.

The next evening, I again had cooking duties and attempted to prepare burgers on a very uncooperative grill, however, I couldn't stop thinking about the depressing stock market news we had read about that day. As a long-term investor, I wouldn't be concerned about market fluctuations normally, but in a few weeks I was going to have to sell quite a bit of stock to help fund the rest of our trip. I had to keep reassuring myself that it was something I could not control.

Over the Adirondacks

August 25: Cayuga Lake State Park, NY (3999 miles)

August 26: Sleepy Bear Campground, Port Ontario, NY (4077 miles)

August 27: Brown Bear Campground, Boonville, NY (4128 miles)

August 28: Blue Mt. Lake, Lake Durant Pk., NY (4193 miles)

After a week of gloomy, rainy weather and lactic acid build-up in every muscle below our waists, it was a relief to have a normal mileage, predominantly flat and sunny day. With scenic views of Lake Seneca in the background, myriads of vineyards followed us on the left-hand side of the road all the way to the 241-year-old Hazlitt Winery at the twenty-mile mark.

We found the lovely campground at Cayuga Lake State Park and set up in a lush, grassy area. After dinner and nightfall, Susan yanked my shorts to my ankles while I was talking to my parents on the phone with fellow campers around us taking their toddlers to the toilet. That's the last time I turn my back to her!

August 26

I hit a new low this morning by being the first to have two broken spokes simultaneously. It was that kind of day. Seventy-eight hot and sweaty miles that seemed like 178. My legs were mush; it felt like I was riding through a bucket of quicksand. I could've sworn that someone was playing a trick on my bike but I checked it often and it seemed okay. A nagging cold didn't help matters. Susan did extremely well, finishing with the head of the pack. I couldn't pass anybody regardless of how hard I tried.

August 27

Due to a late 7:00 a.m. wake-up call, we had to pack and bungee our belongings in record time to escape a tumultuous downpour by milliseconds. All ten of us took shelter in a hundred-square-foot laundry room while drinking coffee, eating Pop Tarts and waiting for the thunder, lightning and rain to subside. The nutrition level of our breakfasts had steadily declined since the warm and hearty oatmeal with raisins we had everyday out west.

Our first and only significant stop of the day was in Pulaski where we made sandwiches (peanut butter and jelly and tuna) and bought fruit for the duration. The damp fog lifted soon thereafter and left us with a classic afternoon of cool, breezy, sunny weather and a welcomed tail wind. Robogirl Susan was in cruise control, impossible to catch up with at times. She wins the "most improved award" hands down. Nobody else would even get a vote. She saw a pay phone just outside of Boonville and surprised her favorite former boss, Dr. Bill Herndon, in Charlotte. I had encouraged her to call her friends and family for support along the way but today she just wanted to brag a little.

Boonville is a sleepy little community of 3000 whose claim to fame is being a former meeting site for United States Presidents over a century ago. The old house that used to be their lodging quarters is now a landmark restaurant.

We rode three miles outside of town to a wonderfully relaxing place called the Brown Barn, currently owned by a sweet couple in their seventies. It was, in fact, a huge barn, probably ten times bigger than most, full of surprises and oozing with character. The building was still used for a variety of purposes including cyclist haven, antique car holding center, dance hall, basketball court and bar. Susan and I slept upstairs near the basketball court on a wooden platform surrounded by advertising memorabilia of the 1950's (Coca-Cola, milk, etc.) and antiques from the days when the place was actually used for horses.

August 28

My first front wheel broken spoke, another flat for Warren and some brake adjustments kept the two of us inside the barn until almost 10:30 a.m. and necessitated that once again we would be riding together. I really liked riding with Warren by this time in the trip since we were now cruising at a similar pace. It was nice to occasionally concentrate on simply riding and enjoying the sights, smells and sounds of nature around me instead of yakking with the girls.

Less than a mile away from the calm serenity of our resting place in Boonville, we encountered some back- breaking, knee-grinding hills that had us sweating and cussing most of the twenty-five miles to the Farm Restaurant in Old Forge where we met up with the others. We later realized that we had just ridden through a very difficult stretch of the Adirondack Mountains! The traffic on Highway 28 was extremely hectic as Labor Day weekend had apparently started prematurely. At least it was four lanes with a shoulder!

Susan must have ingested an extra bowl of Wheaties at our rest stop because she was absolutely uncatchable traversing the picturesque stretch of gentle rolling hills along the Fulton Chain Lakes called Southern Shores Road. Airy cottages with clever sounding, seductive names like Seventh Heaven, Summerwind and Dreamescape had her dreaming of bare feet, hammocks, lemonade and relaxation. The area reminded me of a modified version of the utopic 17 Mile Drive in California.

The final twenty-five mile stretch run towards Blue Mountain Lake with Katie and Susan was sheer exhilaration. With a breezy tail wind and the sun dancing on the late afternoon asphalt, we shifted to our highest, hardest gear and put the quads in overdrive. I never stopped pumping as we navigated the winding mountain roads, taking in a rush of autumn as summer passed us by.

Broken Axle

August 29: Paradox Lake State C-Ground, NY (4254 miles)

August 30: Rochester, VT, Hostel (4317 miles)

August 31: Rest and Nest C-Grd, E. Thetford, VT (4365 miles)

September 1: Maple Haven C-Ground, N. Woodstock, VT (4428 miles)

It was another one of those difficult mornings when I was convinced that my legs were doing more work than usual. Were my tires rubbing? Did I need to grease something? Could it simply be the 4000-mile wall?

Susan continued on one of her energy peaks, and although it was a bad day for me, I was thrilled that she was finally able to enjoy the scenery and biking without worrying so much about being last or just making it to camp. As her journal entry read, "I was never even short of breath today—after a summer in the saddle, something finally clicked! Maybe it's just the pure high of knowing that there's only nine biking days left! I'm sure it'll be years before I truly appreciate what we've done. I still don't love it. Right now I just want it to be over."

We kept each other company almost the entire ride to Paradox Lake State Campground through New York's version of the Blue Ridge Mountains. Maria and Julie finally arrived around 7:30 p.m. in the back of a pickup, several hours behind everyone else. They had inadvertently gotten thirty miles off course after misinterpreting a confusing directive on the map. It was amazing we never completely lost anyone!

August 30

It was a good thing we were counting down the days in single digits because dear old "Flash" was due for a major overhaul. All morning long my rear wheel was touching part of the frame and my front brakes were rubbing the tires even when they weren't applied. After over a dozen stops and subsequent adjustments by five different people, I finally succumbed to the dangerous last resort of taking the front brake off altogether. Our bike shop visit in Middlebury later in the day couldn't come soon enough.

Just prior to Middlebury, Susan and I managed to create a little spontaneous excitement in the form of passing an eighteen-wheeler going downhill on a four-lane highway at a record speed of forty-five miles per hour! It truly felt like an Olympian moment, especially when another truck, going the other way, sandwiched us between them. At this point of the trip, it didn't seem dangerous or unusual. That was the scary part! Later on, Peter and Jean got a shot of adrenaline for a different reason when a passing truck just missed them on a narrow two-lane road, sounding his horn as they carelessly rode double. It was becoming apparent that confidence was beginning to breed foolishness.

Vermont managed to succeed in charming us as all of our stereotypical notions about it began to unfold. The beautiful rolling hills, old red barns, covered bridges, silos, thin winding roads and crisp late summer air all left an indelible impression as we proceeded to the college town of Middlebury.

The bike shop there proved to be the answer to my bike woes. A pony-tailed, tie-dyed looking guy in his late thirties was sensitive to my concerns and hurried timetable and was one of the very few bike mechanics who truly seemed to appreciate and understand his craft. He shaved my badly out-of-sync brakes down, adjusted them, and trued my equally badly out-of-sync wheels. "Flash" was his old self again and so was I.

For weeks we had teased and taunted ourselves with the reward of visiting a Ben and Jerry's locally founded ice creamery if we made it as far as Middlebury. Despite the ominous Green Mountain Pass ahead with daylight quickly waning, we partook in a decadent feast of various chocolate concoctions, pralines and cream and rum raisin. It seemed appropriate for us to patronize ultra-environmentally conscious B & J's in the midst of our own pilgrimage with nature.

The glaring late afternoon sun and a 14 percent grade hill awaited us mere minutes after the feast-a-thon. Susan took one look at it, got off "Bo" and started pushing immediately. I huffed about halfway up and decided because of the nonexistent shoulder, winding road and heavy traffic to wait up for Susan and try to stay together, figuring it was safer for a car to see two of us than one. After the road leveled off to a continuous, curvy, 7 percent grade, we realized, as we swatted hordes of hungry mosquitoes swarming our sweaty bodies, that this was one scenic passageway indeed. It was also known as Robert Frost Parkway and it wasn't hard to imagine how he wrote some of his most inspired work in these very mountains. The springs, streams and rivers that stayed to our side the entire route to Rochester gave us a much-needed, intermittent blast of clean, cool air. As the setting sun spliced dancing rays through the tall pines, it was hard not to feel totally energized from this picturesque setting, tired muscles, exhaust fumes, mosquitoes and all. It was near nightfall by the time we rolled through the rolled-up streets of Rochester.

August 31

Fresh blueberry pancakes with 95 percent Vermont Maple Syrup got my day off to a carbohydrate-charged start. After a dense early morning fog lifted, we encountered typically rolling terrain and chilly conditions until we stopped at Bethel for lunch. Susan and I ran into Maria and Julie on the one and only main drag in town, chatting with an elderly Rhode Island couple with almost Cajun accents. Maria was obviously in heaven being back on her home turf.

Near South Royalton, we ventured to the Vermont Sugar House where we shipped home syrup and other assorted New England trinkets to close family and friends. Immediately thereafter, we spotted Jean, Peter and Warren sloshing around and soaking up some soothing rays in the river and joined them.

A hilly finish, on none other than "Hill Road," brought us to the Rest and Nest Campground in East Thetford, just short of the New Hampshire border. The owner was the type that went out of his way to make life a little less comforting for his patrons, but at this stage we could've slept in a tree.

September 1

A morning that started with me almost falling asleep as I lounged lazily across a pool table in the shower/rec room of the campground waiting for the women ended up being an all-time "buzzer beater." At the whopping four-mile mark, with group intact about 9:30 a.m. on a potholed, dirt road, I felt the all-too-familiar feel of broken spoke number eight. As I played bike doctor with 4x4's kicking up gravel and dust, I realized another inexplicable malady had befallen "Flash." My rear axle had broken in half! Undoubtedly, the 200 pounds of me and the fifty pounds of gear had finally taken its toll. Seconds later, I was in the front seat of a Chevy truck with a fiftyish woman heading about twenty miles south of the route, in the *opposite direction* of our ultimate destination.

The Mowatt Bike Shop thankfully had six guys on the payroll on this surprisingly busy Saturday before Labor Day. I took a number, but got some prompt attention considering the impromptu circumstances. A young "gearhead" confidently rerigged another axle that didn't exactly fit, but was close enough, I hoped, to get me to the Atlantic Ocean.

Shortly after noon, by myself, with maligned transportation and totally off-course, the odds were not in my favor to beat nightfall. Only after eighty-three days of being in the saddle could I have been as confident as I was about making it. The challenge was on.

After a grinding twenty-three miles on an eerily deserted highway literally in the middle of nowhere, I was stopped in my tracks again by broken spoke number nine. I spent over an hour of precious afternoon light chasing down cars in hopes that one of them had a big enough wrench to get my freewheel off my rear tire so I could get to work and replace the spoke. (Yes, by this time I should've been carrying the "group wrench!") I even walked a half mile or so down to a house where a man sent his ten-year-old boy, a box of miscellaneous tools and a beagle puppy back with me. It was great having some company in my moment of exasperation, but after searching through the box, I was no closer to solving my problem. Finally, on the verge of giving up and sleeping on this roadside picnic table conveniently situated in the front yard of an out-of-town owner, I flagged down a chain-smoking drunk who was fascinated by my predicament and, more importantly, had the tool I so desperately needed.

In the midst of fixing it, I accidentally pierced my rear tire, but my single-minded determination somehow overcame the anguish of the moment. At 3:30 in the afternoon, I was back on the seat with forty-four miles of gradual climbing to go. I could obviously ill-afford another delay of any kind.

In Rominy around 5 p.m., I told the locals that I was biking to North Woodstock *today* and they laughed and said that it simply could not be done before nightfall. They routed me east before heading north, farther in miles, but a bit less hilly than getting on the Kancamangus Pass. After a nonstop, thigh-burning thirty-two miles in 2 1/2 hours, I coasted into my destination, a battle weary, but contentedly happy camper. I had never been so happy to see Susan.

Realizing the Dream

September 2: The Beach Campground, Conway, NH (4471 miles)

September 3: Bear Mt. Campground, S. Waterford, NH (4511 miles)

September 4: Souviez Residence, Dresden, ME (4572 miles)

September 5: Camden Hills St. Park, ME (4624 miles)

September 6: Whispering Pines Campground, E. Orland, ME (4670 miles)

September 7: Cadillac Motor Lodge, Bar Harbour, ME (4705 miles)

Kancamangus Pass did not live up to its billing as the "Going to the Sun Highway of the East," with notable exceptions being the nonexistent shoulder and ungodly traffic. With around ten miles of steady 6 to 8 percent grade climbs followed by a breezy twenty-mile riverside run from the precipice, it actually made for a cushy day.

Julie and I spent most of the afternoon putting the finishing touches on our much-procrastinated assimilation of a Jeopardy game based on real-life trip highlights and lowlights. Susan had visions of a romantic stroll around this last touristy town on our itinerary, so tensions naturally rose due to our dichotomy of ideas of how to best spend the afternoon. She sauntered down to the campground lake for some long overdue solitude. After a rather quiet dinner, I tried to make peace with her with a reverse chocolate Ben and Jerry's. It's amazing how fast you have to make up when you're sleeping in the tiny confines of a seven-by-four-foot tent night after night!

September 3

It was an uncharacteristically leisurely morning as we departed the Beach Campground on our second consecutive "half" day of riding. We took time out to pose creatively around the very last state sign on our maps. Humorously, almost everyone was having mechanical problems with their cameras—I guess the water, dust and constant bumps of the road were finally taking their toll.

The terrain was rolling and uneventful until we found Sweeden Hill about five miles from camp. Out of nowhere we were faced with a monstrous 15 percent grade from an almost dead stop. I used up every morsel of my tasty, morning pancakes and honestly felt like Spiderman scaling the Sears Tower. It was perhaps the ultimate single climbing feat of the summer and only Jeff and I were up to reaching the top without walking on this day.

The South Waterford Bear Mountain Campground was visibly empty on Labor Day night as everyone else in the world, except us it seemed, was going back to work the following morning. The showers were warm and toasty on a Patagonia-perfect, cool night with a gorgeous New England full moon slowly appearing over the gangly fir and spruce trees. It was the kind of night that caused me to reflect on just how special it had been to spend an entire summer outside, becoming immersed with nature instead of being its foe. Our bodies had adjusted to the demands that had been placed on them daily and it would be sad to "turn the machine off" in a sense and return to a more sedentary life. The stark realization that we might never be at this level of conditioning again was satisfying and yet unsettling at the same time. It was definitely a moment that all of us would have loved to freeze for awhile.

September 4

We certainly didn't experience a "cakewalk" into Bar Harbour, Maine. Susan and I chose to stay together to get a reprieve from the group gossip and chatter and managed to reach Dresden after seventy-one long miles intact. It took us most of the summer, but we finally got accustomed to each other's riding styles and learned to handle the pendulum of emotions that could raise their ugly head on literally any given curve, hill or moment.

After lunch, we stopped at the sun-speckled Androscoggin River that looked more like a lake and stole some rare, quiet romantic time. Moments later in Sabbatus, we watched the school children race out after the two o'clock bell, dapper and perfectly coordinated in their respective duds on the first day of class.

At a convenience store in Richmond, we waited for the rest of the gang while asking around about possible places to sleep. As darkness quickly beckoned, we were beginning to wonder if this would be the inevitable night when we were forced to sleep in a parking lot or sitting on our bike seats.

As a last resort, Warren tried to reach a seventy-year- old couple mentioned in his "leader notes" who lived five miles away in Dresden. Once again, fate was on our side as they not only invited us over to camp in their comfortable, grassy yard, but opened up their home to ten sweaty strangers and prepared a feast of spaghetti, garlic bread, salad and chocolate ice cream for us! Doris and Les Souviez were among the warmest people we had met anywhere and in addition to being great cooks, also shared with us the rich history of the area while proudly bragging about their own peripatetic children.

I even managed to secure the reclining easy chair and an orgasmic foot message from Susan while I watched a Clemmens versus Stewart pitcher's duel on the tube—my very first baseball game of the entire summer. After ten hours in the saddle, the pasta, shower and recliner were better than a shopping spree at Nike Town.

September 5

Amidst the unexpected comforts that we lavished in the night before, dear Julie was having a bit of a problem. To the ignorant, baseball-transfixed males in the group, the pails of hot water being shuttled between the kitchen and the bedroom could only mean one thing. Somehow, one of the girls was about to deliver a baby and we never knew it. The truth was that Jules had manifested a nasty blister of sorts on her privates that was causing excruciating pain. Not only extremely embarrassing, it also meant that Miss Determination herself was going to the hospital in the morning instead of on her bicycle seat.

Doris drove her to Damoniscotta to get it checked out and the rest of us biked the twenty-three miles there to meet her for support. It was sort of humorous for everyone, except Julie, as nine misfit, straggly-haired cyclists with tight shorts, helmets and gloves tiptoed nosily around the emergency room like expectant parents. Jules was not a happy patient at all, and we all empathized with her plight.

After a quickie hospital cafeteria lunch, we left our wounded partner in the motherly hands of Doris who would take her on to our campsite in Camden. It was Susan and I alone on Highway 1 the rest of the day with the only significant interlude being a milk shake break at the well-preserved Moody's Diner in Waldoboro. The place was a true 50's living relic, still booming with old jukeboxes and dashing oldies decor.

In Camden, we stopped to peruse the touristy streets and caught our first glimpse of the azure-blue of the Atlantic Ocean! Although celebrations would have to wait until Bar Harbour, I found the perfect accouterment for our much-ballyhooed upcoming end-of-the-trip seafood feast for　Susan—a pair of orange, dangling lobster earrings.

Our stopping point for the night was the very mediocre Camden Hills State Park, which saw fit to segregate us as bikers from the family camping set despite a plethora of vacant lots. We had to walk over a half mile to the nearest toilet/shower area and about as far for water.

During the night, a generation of raccoons paid us a visit, taking over our picnic table, clanging our pots and pans together and tossing silverware and various other dishes within a ten-foot radius. After tiring of that, they decided to rummage through our panniers and with their extremely adept hands, managed to somehow unzip the zippers and sling cameras, wrenches, Band-Aids, money, Blistex, dirty clothes and feminine hygiene products all over the woods. We were awakened around 3:00 a.m. to the sounds of a campsite brawl as our critter conquerors, Jean and Warren, retaliated by chasing our nocturnal invaders all over the lot and throwing whatever they could find at them.

September 6

The first order of the day was conducting an Easter egg hunt to try and find our personal effects scattered everywhere. I guess the raccoons were really trying to teach us a lesson for taking over their living room!

We stayed on scenic Highway 1 all day, edging along the sea-sprayed, two-lane road through coastal crannies like Lincolnville, Newport, Belfast and Searsport. It was fittingly typical weather for Maine, misty, hazy, and chilly, as we navigated to East Orland Whispering Pines Campground.

A very special evening was in store as the proprietors were extremely accommodating in allowing us to use the recreation room adjoining their office to set up the long- awaited Jeopardy game. While Susan helped me get the room in order, the rest of the girls transformed Jules, still suffering from groin discomfort, into Vanna White II. I absolutely lost it when I saw her in her new glory— boobs by Maria (stuffed socks), slicked-back hair by Smitty, earrings by Lee Ann (butterscotch candies), dress by Jean, generous proportions of makeup never seen before and a quirky limp. She looked like a cross-dressing transvestite, but took her role as Alex's (my alias) answer turner very seriously. With beers a flowin' and eighty-nine days of memories on the books, it was a roaring success from start to finish. We gave out tacky prizes to Maria for her trip trivia expertise and celebrated the totally unexpected return of Lee Ann, back with the group after six weeks of riding on her own.

September 7

On the emotional final day, Warren really wanted everyone to ride into the sunset (actually a torrential rainstorm) together, but it would have been totally out of character for this most independent ensemble to do anything *that* contrived, even for just thirty-five miles.

Susan and I stopped in Ellsworth early in the morning, after doing the Seeing Eye dog routine through the dense, wet fog. We wrote postcards—basically exclaiming WE MADE IT!!— knowing that time would not permit us doing that later on. Twinges of nervousness and anticipation echoed through my body as we got closer to the finish line of the longest ride of our lives.

The last eight miles with group intact, and Julie finally back in the saddle, began in a downpour. The terrain was unmercifully hilly—how appropriate that we had to sweat it out to the bittersweet end. As we rolled up Main Street, Bar Harbour, tears welled up in Susan's eyes and I felt a little choked up as well. We both dismounted on the pier at the same time, held each other tightly and relished a monumental moment in our lives. Although we were supposed to dip our tires in the Atlantic to complete the coast-to-coast symbolic gesture, Susan said she was ready to throw the whole bike into the ocean!

The fog and rain prevented us from having a picturesque view of the harbor, but it really didn't matter. Although the journey itself was 99.7 percent of the fun and satisfaction, nothing can make you forget the final scene. The most special chapter of them all was closing and now many more could be written. From this point forward, big challenges would seem normal and normal ones would seem small.

Mom and sister Jenni met us at the post office as we picked up a slew of wonderful congratulatory cards and letters. It was really special to actually see family after weeks of loving encouragement over the phone. We celebrated our 4705 miles of blood, sweat, tears and broken spokes with two pounds of lobster and two dozen champagne toasts at the West End Café. It really doesn't get much better than that.

In reflection, an obvious question one may ask is how we were able to overcome our obvious lack of bicycle acumen and experience to carry a very difficult physical and mental challenge to fruition. With daily temptations to ride to the nearest airport or call a parent or friend to drive us home, why did we persevere and tolerate the pain and risk possible lifelong injury? I believe it was simply the power of the dream, wanting something badly enough to see it through despite inconveniences and headaches and very importantly, the intensity of our love for each other. Although it was never said out loud, Susan and I just didn't want to let the other person down and we both knew long-term that it would be a solidifying bond for our relationship. We were right.

Transformation

We had given ourselves a solid month to circulate among friends and family, relax, sleep late, pay a few bills and gradually change modes from cyclist to backpacker. Perhaps the hardest adjustment was the instant transformation we had to make after living on our bikes for so long. It felt like we could've gone on forever, but we'll never know just how our stamina, and more importantly our interest level, would have held out if we had opted to stay in the saddle.

Driving again, and being in a car for the congested forty-eight hour interstate trip to the North Carolina Outer Banks to visit with my parents was a test of the nerves, especially for my fellow passengers. It felt strange covering so much distance, so fast. The thought that wouldn't leave our minds was the image of those countless, lonely, back roads, small towns and open woods that we knew we were passing at seventy miles per hour. We certainly would never look at them the same way again.

Despite the fact that we knew a fair number of people and had quizzed anyone who was nice enough to listen, we had not encountered a single person who either knew someone in a foreign country or had been to more than a handful. None had attempted international travel outside of plush hotels, air- conditioned taxi cabs and first-class train berths. The fact that we set our sights on "roughing it" through about thirty countries had more than a few of our loved ones seriously questioning our sanity. It was one thing to "grunt and sweat a little" on a bicycle for a summer they figured, but the thought of carrying around nothing more than a 14-by-24–inch backpack, a guidebook and an open mind for a year was a bit much. In the Carolinas and Wisconsin where we grew up, just leaving the state was a rather significant happening.

Putting the final touches on planning our excursion necessitated a number of calls to our extremely knowledgeable and supportive travel agent, Mr. Arthur Mills of Odyssey Travel, Orlando. Arthur specialized in overseas particulars and took special interest in our unique situation, giving us valuable tips on where to go and what to expect from places like Thailand and Nepal. We secured our around-the-world airline tickets and Eurrail Pass through him and heeded his advice on immunizations, visas and other important areas.

"Backpacking" is a rather recent phenomena in the exploding field of travel. Simply put, it is a way of getting from point A to point B that focuses more on where you are going and how and what you are actively doing than what you are wearing and carrying with you. It is travel in its purest form, removing barriers and allowing one to experience, feel and get involved with people and places. It is a state of mind and a way of life focusing on flexibility and the realization that you the traveler will have to adapt to your destination, not the other way around. Unless we are willing and eager to learn and change our ways in the travel experience, why leave the comfort of our remote control and Lazy-Boy in the first place?

After deciding that this type of travel is right for a person, the first item on the shopping list should be…a backpack. Some prefer steel framed versions for support but they are rather large, heavy and bulky and don't fit in an airplane compartment. If you're doing a fair amount of flying and want to keep the pack with you at all times, this could be a negative. I opted for a lighter, smaller option (from Eagle Creek) with a suitcase-type handle. It fit comfortably on our backs after the front strap was locked into place and because of the size, forced us to carry less than the framed model.

There's an old saying in the adventure travel circuit that a person should pack as little as humanly possible and then cut that amount in half! Not only is "stuff" heavy, it slows you down and takes away that all important flexibility.

(to carry the pack around for periods of time if necessary instead of looking for a locker, etc.) Besides, you want to be able to buy clothing that is indigenous to the area you are traveling so a little excess capacity gets used up very quickly. What to carry is a matter of personal preference but I have included a section in the Appendix on "What You Really Need to Bring" that worked well for us.

Where one backpacks to depends on your tolerance for risk-taking and hardship. Surviving a week in Calcutta is not an entirely relaxing experience even in a five-star hotel, so backpacking there could put some people "over the edge." Because of our inexperience in this mode of travel, we opted to begin our journey in Australia where there was no language barrier and the adventure potential was high. Confident and road-weary seventy days later, we were not at all intimidated when we reached the streets of Hong Kong or the jungles of northern Thailand.

One of the most appealing aspects of backpacking is the fact that you are on your own from the second the plane touches down or the bus pulls up in your chosen city or town. The methods of transportation to go short distances vary greatly from country to country and without restricting, cumbersome suitcases, you can take the cheapest, fastest, or most interesting option without anyone else's help. In many parts of Asia, the best option is an animal!

Meeting fellow travelers along the way is also much easier when you are adaptably "living on the cheap." Unlike hotels where people rarely leave their room to exchange pleasantries, let alone interesting travel facts, hostels and "pensiones" (small rooms usually designated for backpackers) are like a travel think tank, overflowing with information and gregarious people of all nationalities. No two hostels or pensiones are exactly alike but with rare exceptions they offer a reasonably clean bed, a cooking facility or basic meal and camaraderie for those who take advantage of it.

Our usual practice throughout the trip was to wait until we arrived in a city before looking for accommodations. It saved time and aggravation of trying to overcome language barriers over the phone while racking up the expense of a call from another country. It also greatly enhanced the adventurous spark and "seat-of-the-pants" spontaneity that helped make the journey so special. If all else failed, we could usually rely on either our Lonely Planet guidebook or one of the other resources in our mobile library to get us started in a given city.

After months of research, preparation and alterations (reference materials we used to decide where to go are in the Appendix.), the final checklist for Phase II was taking shape. After a lot of forethought and valuable consult from Arthur Mills, we chose to visit Australia, Asia and Europe in that order for three to four months apiece. It was critical that we travel in one direction around the globe to capitalize on the around-the-world bargain fare. Although the flight destinations were fixed (Atlanta-Los Angeles-Cairns, Perth-Tokyo-Hong Kong, Singapore-Frankfurt-Atlanta), *when* we arrived and left each stopover was completely flexible (as long as we gave the airlines notice). Except for the dreaded tearful farewells, we were as ready as we'd ever be to take on the world.

Fully loaded

NTR 610 at
Logan Pass,
Montana

Our humble abode
for the summer

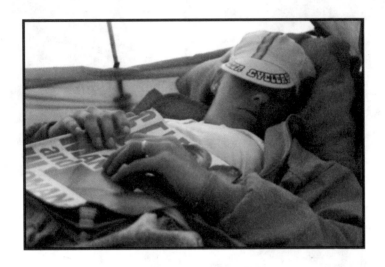

Susan navigating a
winding road in Iowa

A deep breath at the crest of
a steep hill, New York

Ray's crew in front of some termite mounds

A canyon river ride in Australia

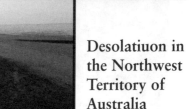

Desolatiuon in the Northwest Territory of Australia

"The Rock"

"We're going where?"

The southwest corner
of Australia gang

Guarding our belongings
at a train station

Whoa!

Along the Annapurnas Trail, Nepal

Sure-footed transportation and inquisitive tribal children north of Chiang Mai, Thailand

"Potty in there? Gag me."

Chaos in Calcutta

Lunch

Tight quarters

Mowing the grass in India

In front of
Hitler's
hideaway,
Austria

Road
crossing in
Ireland

Jac, Susan, Lindsay and David
on our farewell night

"The true adventurer goes forth aimless and uncalculating
to meet an unknown fate."
—*O'Henry*

"So you cut all the tall trees down
You poisoned the sky and the sea
You've taken what's good from the ground
But you left precious little for me

You remember the flood and the fall
We remember the light on the hill
There should be enough for us all
But the dollar is driving us still

River runs red
Black rain falls
Dust in my hand
River runs red
Black rain falls
On my bleeding land"

—*Midnight Oil, "River Runs Red"*

(about "progress" of construction projects
taking place throughout Australia,
many on Aboriginal land)

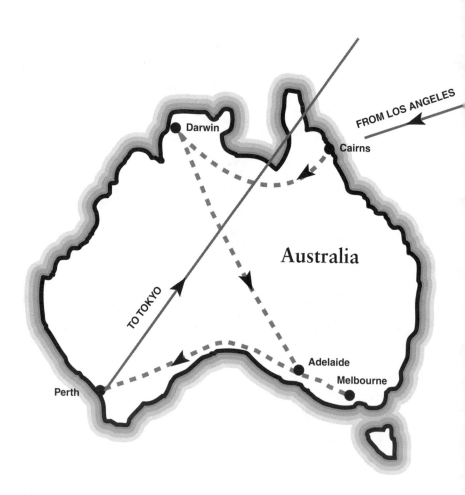

AUSTRALIA

The way the word Australia sounds and rolls off the tongue alone conjures up images of a distant land of mystery, romance and the unknown. To become one of the world's most attractive travel destinations, however, it obviously has to offer much more than a perfect sounding name. It has to be a place that consistently meets and exceeds the expectations of even the most seasoned traveler.

To Work or Not to Work

Our extensive pretrip preparation had included the assimilation of unique facts and figures, secluded destinations, accommodations, eateries and assorted other tidbits about the countries on our must-see list. I had outlined a proposed budget and decided for cash flow as well as cultural stimulation reasons that we should try to locate at a minimum, a few weeks of part-time, albeit without work visa, employment. Australia seemed to be the easiest prospect since we had been there before (on our honeymoon for a single week in '88), the people spoke English and were easygoing sorts, and the fact that there were a lot of folks working illegally there already. The thought of waiting tables or picking fruit didn't sound too daunting while I lay dreaming in my water bed back home, but I would soon learn the difference between the "I can do anything for a while" wistfulness and the unappetizing prospect of being one of the lowest foreign "worker bees" in a country with a 15 percent unemployment rate.

After a lazy first day in Cairns spent wandering aimlessly in a jet-lagged stupor amidst the occasional palm tree and incessant boiling hot temperatures, we decided to follow up on a housing lead (actually a room lead) from Jo, a cocktail waitress at one of the many watering holes in town. We were "greeted" by one of the most hungover-looking humans I had ever had the displeasure of gaining acquaintance. The filthy, unshaven and tattooed man of twenty-five or so pointed apathetically to an almost barren room with a single stained mattress and no windows. At A$70 (Australian currency designation-about US$60) a week, it was cheap all right, especially by Aussie standards, but brought back visions of a pair of summers that I had spent during college enduring a similar living environment. After a decade of decency, I knew in my heart that this just wouldn't be acceptable for more than a couple of nights. I took it as an omen that maybe this work obsession thing would be more trouble than it was worth. I was upset about the thought of not fulfilling the commitment to myself to acquire some type of work while we were overseas, but I knew Susan was dead against it and suddenly it just didn't feel right.

Two Tickets to the Rain Forest

During our walk about town on Sunday, I noticed a faded concert flyer on a telephone pole amidst an array of Greenpeace bulletins, missing dog notices and garage sale announcements. Midnight Oil, one of my very favorite music groups and the toast of Australia, was coming to the nearby Karanda Amphitheater on Tuesday for their first show on native soil in four long years. After a little investigation, I learned that a "handful" of tickets might be available for purchase the next morning in Cairns and to plan on getting in line about 6 a.m. at the City Centre Ticket Office.

After 2 1/2 hours of "concrete camping," I was joined by a friendly, muscular Swedish guy named Sten who was equally amazed at his good fortune of being in exactly the right place at the right time. Shortly thereafter, we were informed that the only way to acquire tickets at this late juncture was to call Persons Music Store in Mareeba about fifty miles away. We got through after numerous attempts and reserved three over the phone that "had to be picked up within two hours."

At home this would have been a rather uneventful directive, but in a foreign country that drives on the "wrong side of the road," the pilgrimage would prove to be the highlight of the day for Susan and I. The only reasonably- priced rental car left at A$46/day was a Moke, a dune buggy-like locomotive with two seats, no doors, no trunk and very little acceleration. With a winding road through a mountain range ahead of us, I knew it would be a challenge to make it. It was a tailor-made situation for my adventure-seeking soul and at precisely 12:46 p.m., we happily forked over A$28 apiece for the tickets. We felt like a cross between Fred Flintstone and a ten-year-old kid in a bumper car at the county fair, but we made it there and back laughing all the way.

The day of the big show, I had to go back to the City Centre again to stand in line for bus tickets. Sten, a bioengineer back in Sweden, was also there and suggested that we meet before the concert for a few cocktails and ride over on the same bus. Armed with a tremendous command of the English language, he was on "holiday" for six weeks in Australia with his wife and year-old son. The two of us conversed for awhile, mostly comparing the likes and differences of our home countries. The most obvious, of course, is the vacation policy in which

Swedes get more time off starting out in a job than an American can hope to achieve in a lifetime of employment. It is unquestionably more expensive in Scandinavia with US$7 (converted to an estimate in the U.S.) a gallon for gas a common sight, but public transport is a more accessible and acceptable alternative for them.

Four alcoholic "iced teas" and a beer at the Backpacker Restaurant set me in crooked motion towards the concert bus. The amphitheater itself was strategically positioned in the middle of a rain forest and the band used the trees as a backdrop for its amazingly energetic, environmentally- accentuated performance. Sten and I purchased a dozen rather strong 4X Aussie beers between us and perched ourselves on a hill with Susan in the middle. With Rum and Coke in a can a very popular choice, the variety of alcoholic options available for concert-goers was much more extensive than at home.

By the time baldheaded lead singer Peter Garrett kicked off the second half of the show with a barrage of environmental references (he is the head of Australia's leading environmental agency), I had that half-floaty, half- invigorated feeling and the crowd was roaring with approval.

He made numerous comments about the destruction of the very rain forests he was performing under, the building of the gaudy, ostentatious and very expensive Mirage Hotel in the Great Barrier Reef coastal community of Port Douglas, and the proposed erection of a "triple, double" chair lift over nearby Barron Falls. With a canopy of stars overhead, there could not have been a more perfect setting for this show.

The heartfelt performance really brought home to me the global significance of the endangered rain forests to our entire ecosystem. An alarming statistic is the fact that the plants in these lush, tropical "bits of Eden," producing over 50 percent of the world's prescription drugs and playing a significant role in cancer and AIDS-fighting research, are becoming extinct at a rate of 50 to 150 each day.

"The Largest Structure Ever Built by Living Creatures"

Our portable alarm clock squealed at the crack of dawn the very next morning as we fought back the cobwebs from the late and loud night before. We had signed up for the slow boat to Green Island, one of the most frequented land masses within the world's largest coral creation, The Great Barrier Reef.

The combination of the typically sweltering heat and the non-wave resistant vessel, mercilessly crawling through the choppy morning waters, had me on the verge of "feeding the fish" for the entire hour-and-a-half. I crouched pitifully with a garbage can within easy reach.

The tiny island was the tropical paradise it was advertised to be with surrounding lagoons and pools as transparent as a fish bowl. Swishing palm trees provided much-needed shelter and a miniature island zoo gave us our first (but certainly not last!) up-close look at the cunning crocodile. We were informed that they are the last living member of the dinosaur era, reinforcing their well-earned reputation as a resilient, adaptable survivor. Susan spent most of the afternoon basking topless while I took a long, leisurely, beachcombing stroll.

Later in the week, we decided to explore the very outer edge of the reef and engage in a little snorkeling. For A$90 apiece, we were fed delicious seafood all day long, given an enlightening reef presentation by marine biologists, entitled to gaze through the underwater observatory and provided snorkeling equipment and instruction. The ride out was on a ultra-modern "Wavepiercer" featuring torpedo-shaped hulls to help provide an uncannily smooth ride. We would learn quickly that while the variety of amenities was nice and easy, it usually was not worth the money and almost always could be done less expensively with more "thrills per minute" another way. Unfortunately, there was no available alternative for this type of tourist occasion unless you knew someone with a very large boat.

Not being a naturally aquatic sort, the snorkeling experience was a bit daunting for me initially. As soon as I started to take Susan's advice to relax and got comfortable inhaling entirely through my mouth, I felt a surge of exhilaration at the thought of entering a totally new domain. It was certainly a natural high to be in the presence of a brand new world of giant clams, flat wing-flapping rays, hundreds of multicolored fish, and of course, the living, breathing coral for which the area is named.

The islands had been built up by the coral, and their plants had grown from either bird droppings or from seeds left from abandoned ships from the eighteenth century. Although the proliferation of tourists and the construction of high-rises on shore took away from the serenity of the entire Barrier Reef area, the "largest structure ever built by living creatures," it is to the locals and tour companies credit that great strides are being taken to preserve its natural state.

A Taste of the Tablelands

One of the first and most important decisions that a traveler must make during his stay in the Land of Oz is his daily "method of movement." There are a bounty of choices from hitchhiking to car rentals to group tours to buses and trains, but none sounded as exciting as the pure adventure of purchasing a beat-up, seventh-hand VW van, piling it full of new friends and hitting the open road. That was our initial intention before we really analyzed exactly how often we would be emptying our poor wallets at the gas pump across such a vast, sparsely-populated continent. At an average price of A$.95/liter (or about A$3.70/

gallon), I figured my tolerance level for the expense and the inevitable break-downs that I would be responsible for would wane rather quickly. So, we decided on the "all of the above" approach instead, allowing the specific circumstances of the moment to dictate our transportation choice.

After a bit of research, taking a guided excursion aboard the Tropics Explorer Bus Tour appeared to be the ideal way to cultivate an appreciation for the northern Queensland Tableland area. Native host Peter treated us to a bevy of enthralling tidbits about the wonderful diversity of this land. In a single day, we learned to identify poisonous stinging plants, ginger roots, strangler fig trees, epiphytes (plants that grow onto other plants), and cascara, a dark, phallic-looking pod that is used as a laxative in some forms. We trudged close to ten miles of hiking trails through the rain forest in search of black, natural pools, icy waterfalls and deep blue crater lakes formed by volcanic eruptions centuries ago. Two-foot long lizards routinely crossed our paths and the threat of leeches felt like it was always there. For an afternoon snack, Peter showed us a tree full of green ants and their lemony-tasting rear torsos that everyone imbibed in with hesitation. As nightfall approached, Peter explained that the ever-present, six-foot tall termite mounds that punctuated the landscape in every direction contained intricately-woven tunnels and continued to grow until the queen was killed.

The next afternoon was spent at the art and craft markets in Kuranda, a town that was literally run by hippies from around the world until the mid-1970's. Our first procurement of gifts and souvenirs was mailed home via sea mail at a cost of A$16 for five pounds. It would take the box close to three months to make it to the States.

The Backpacker Circuit

With the wide range of adventuresome activities available, from Cape York to the north to the Whitsunday Islands in the south, the Cairns area serves as a hub for exploration for itinerant travelers the world over. Youth hostels, backpacker hotels and other budget accommodations dominate the city's lodging options and allowed us to become absorbed into our new way of life rather quickly. Initially, it can be a bit intimidating to be in the presence of seasoned foreign backpackers already accustomed to their temporary lives away from materialism and conformity, but we made a concerted effort to mingle and stay busy from sunrise to sundown.

Susan and I have always prided ourselves for our thrifty spending habits so we had no problem adjusting to the necessity of staying on a tight budget. We regularly visited the grocery store or food markets, a wonderful cultural experience in and of itself, and prepared meals along with our ever-changing group of friends. While out during the day sightseeing or exploring, we carried a day pack full of energy food, suntan lotion, water, guidebooks, maps and other necessities.

The local "backpacker newspapers" are a lifesaver throughout Australia with their dozens of pages of "up-to-the-minute" articles and advertisements touting the various entertainment and travel options. As acting planner and budgeteer, I made an arrangement for us to depart with eighteen other strangers from this rather remote part of the continent by way of a self-contained, four-wheel drive overland camping expedition to Darwin. We felt strongly that no trip to Aussieland would be complete without some firsthand exposure to the legendary outback. Other than the very real possibility that we would be encountering crocodiles and snakes within the next eleven days and the fact that we would be sleeping on the ground every night, we had absolutely no idea what was in store for us.

"Women, Horses and Clouds"

Ray would serve as our surrogate "Crocodile Dundee" driver, storyteller and camp counselor as we headed northwest in hopes of beating the rainy season to Darwin. He was the stereotypically rugged, crass, sarcastic, chauvinistic Australian "bloke" who you definitely wanted on your side in the unpredictable, harsh conditions of the outback, but wouldn't take home to meet your mother if your life depended on it.

Brought up with the Aborigines in the Kimberleys of Western Australia, Ray's family was one of the many immigrant households from England over the past 200 years who came to their sister country in search of land and prosperity. Today about 40 percent of all Australians are either born overseas or have foreign-born parents.

Raised with an Aboriginal tribe until he was thirteen, Ray had no formal schooling to fall back on, but a hundred lifetimes of street smarts and quite the "gift of gab." The "tour guide" type position was the only thing we could imagine him doing given his upbringing, love of this almost inhospitable and unpredictable land and fondness for women of all descriptions and nationalities. One of his many unforgettable comments was his pronouncement of life's most precious entities, "women, horses and clouds." It certainly left little doubt in our minds about his penchant for nature and desires for members of the opposite sex.

Ray had a rather unusual sidekick in "99," a Japanese woman in her early twenties who was so uncomfortable with the English language that Susan had to replace her as his "hostee" to organize pickup procedures of the other backpackers scattered in hostels all over Caines. The fact that he conspicuously used the submissive woman in very chauvinistic fashion on occasion did not go unnoticed by the female contingency in our group and caused a spat to erupt from time to time. In his defense, his Japanese friend was obviously a consenting participant in their relationship. She began to speak better and more frequent English as she became comfortable with us, and seemed to enjoy her unusual, nomadic life with Ray.

Friends for Life

Our introduction into the world of "group dynamics" on the bike trip would serve us well over the next eleven days across barren northeast Australia. With the notable exception of a most cantankerous German couple, we were blessed with the good fortune of being random company to a truly special assembly of people.

In order of nationality with Ray's nicknames, they were:

Tom, a college student from Melbourne, Australia, "Aussie Boy"; six Brits from England, Jacalyn, a single, social worker from a posh, upper-class London background on a six-month working holiday, "Jac"; Derrick, a single laborer from a rural middle-class background on a six-month pleasure holiday; Lindsay, a single lawyer on a six-month working holiday, "Perry" (for Perry Mason, I guess); Jennifer, a recent college grad at Louisiana State University who was born in South Africa, raised in England and had been working at a horse and cattle ranch in Australia for a few weeks, "Springmount Girl" (name of ranch she worked at); Allison, twenty-five year old engaged doctor from London who was on her way to an apprenticeship in New Zealand, "Doc"; Uta, German-born, British-bred, forty-five year-old lady on a six-week holiday away from her kids by herself for the first extended period of time, and Amanda, the most quiet and reserved among the group, hailing from the Isle of White in southern England, also a "Springmount Girl" who worked with Jennifer.

There were also three Canadians: Sheleigh, an eighteen- year-old student on a vacation of unspecified length at the request of her beloved, ailing grandfather who footed her bill, "Pretty Face"; Dewayne, a twenty-four year-old farm hand with a perpetual smile and a kind heart, "Farm Boy", and Sophia, early forties, originally from Hungary and still having some difficulties with the English language.

Our two remaining favorites were Kevin, a lovable, huggable, extremely witty Irish engineer in his late twenties and Danny, a member of the Swiss national armed services (I didn't even know that existed in a neutral country), a bit raw-edged, but an accomplished outdoorsman.

We each took our turns at the "podium" in the front of the bouncing bus, telling a piece of our respective life stories and setting the stage for the 2000-mile journey to Darwin. It was clear right away that this was no ordinary collection of "vagabonds," out of work and carelessly looking for activities to fill their days abroad. The lively interaction of the group would not only help make an arguably mundane trip extremely interesting, but would provide us with a handful of true friends that would play a monumental role in the remainder of our journey.

A Canopy of Stars

On the first night together, Ray inaugurated a ritual that would occur every evening all the way to Darwin. After tossing our backpacks from the storage trailer to the sandy ground below, we all set out into the moonlit night in search of hard-to-find bits and pieces of firewood scattered throughout the landscape. It was unbelievably bright due to the lack of pollution, haze, cloud cover or neighboring communities, and I hoped my shadow would not camouflage my catching a glimpse of an accidentally-aroused, deadly reptile before it was too late. The term "out of our control" had new meaning, as we were at the complete mercy of our eccentric leader and the fate of the "Kangaroo gods." We rolled out two separate "party tarps" that snugly slept the nineteen of us, bundled together in our sleeping bags with a glorious ceiling of the galaxy overhead. The constant threat, feeling, and sometimes reality of "creepy, crawly things" on our bodies never quite dampened the awe of being at one with nature in a way we had never before experienced.

The screeching calls of the wild in concert with Ray's chatter around the blazing breakfast fire were usually enough to nudge our sore and sweaty bodies out of our sacks. If the thought of an ever-so-brief sleep-in crossed our minds, the relentlessly annoying Australian cattle fly proved to be the best wake-up mechanism of all. At the brink of dawn, they smothered in droves and did not let up for a second until we were in the van with windows closed and vehicle moving. Most flies bother you for a few minutes and move on to other targets in the next room or the next county. Nothing was sacred with these pesky creatures as they crawled and buzzed in our ears and on our face, seemingly regenerating at the exact moment we tried to lift a piece of food to our mouth or simply sit and sweat in peace.

Breakfast or "brekkie" as the Aussies and Brits called it, usually found the ever-entertaining Ray singing or cracking crass jokes to anyone who happened to be within earshot. The fare was museli with warm, powdered milk, bananas, (while they lasted!), and lots of toast, strong black coffee and tea prepared on a grate over a blazing open fire. "Brekkie" was my favorite meal of the day because it was essentially an "all you can eat" proposition if you didn't mind warm powdered milk, museli and dry toast. I tried to fill myself up since I inevitably lost my appetite during the course of the day due to the heat, a shortage of replenishment fluids and those steadfast flies.

The most trying aspect of the journey to Darwin, for me, was the omnipresent feeling of thirst that never quite went away. We rationed ourselves to about two liters of water a day at the astronomical A$3.50/liter we were forced to pay the few cattle station shops, road stations and pubs along our route. It was the very end of the dry season and as the days progressed, the dirt roads along the fence lines that we traveled resembled a scene from Oklahoma during the Dust Bowl. There was no way to escape the dust since even our backpacks were covered in it. We bought the precious water ice cold, but by the time a few hours of slow sip rationing ended each liter, it was lukewarm to hot and hardly refreshing.

To recharge our energies, zapped from the hundred degree heat, we sought out creeks, or "billabongs," and swimming holes. Many were absolutely gorgeous with deep green water and cascading waterfalls which we all enjoyed swimming through and standing behind. I was aptly nicknamed "Jungle Dave" by Lindsay after one particularly clumsy attempt at walking through the "mud bog" near a billabong with flip- flops on! Every time I took a step, my flimsy shoes became immersed in the "quicksand" goo, so I quickly bowed out before I completely lost one of my two pairs of footwear. Ray planned our days around cooling off near water and we were extremely thankful he knew instinctively where to find it. The "billabongs" served as our bathing spots, laundromats, drinking water and kitchen sink. The group was extremely conscientious about using environmentally-friendly soap for all of our cleaning needs.

One morning, Susan and I ventured off from the group after "brekkie" for a quiet swim in a nearby creek. As we let the cool, gentle current carry us downstream, we came upon a family of kangaroos feeding in the brush within twenty-five feet of us on the nearby bank. Due to their poor vision and our careful effort to remain as frozen as possible, they couldn't see or hear us and we had a view that was better than a thousand episodes of *The Wild Kingdom*. No camera was needed to etch that memory in our minds.

The deeper we followed the fence line into the outback, the more our lives seemed to intersect with the native fauna going about their daily routines. Another time at daybreak, the entire group witnessed a gathering of wallabies standing on a river's edge inquisitively eyeing our van as we left them behind. Wallabies were generally a smaller, grayer version of the kangaroo and were a permanent and very tame fixture at a camping area near Katherine Gorge. We were able to get as many as ten of them in a single photo around dinner time as they congregated in droves, competing with the birds to literally eat out of our hands. The wallabies managed to virtually eliminate my night's sleep in Katherine by rummaging noisily through every refuse receptacle in a half- mile radius. I was extremely paranoid that they would miscalculate the distance of their nightly leapfrog over our party tarp!

A hyperactive emu, a six-foot-tall bird resembling an ostrich that helped himself to leftovers after dinner, also took a 200-page chunk out of Jac's Australia Lonely Planet guide book during the night. At least he digested the places she had already been!

This part of Australia was fortunate to be in the path of one of the most frequented bird migration routes in the world. Around Katherine and Kakadu National Park (of *Crocodile Dundee* fame), some of the planet's rarest aviary species, in addition to the native hawks and distinctive cockatoos, hovered overhead in anticipation of the imminent wet season.

We hit the Kakadu area at an auspicious time since it is impossible to take the popular 2 1/2 hour Yellow River Cruise after the wet season starts. Our guide, from the Christmas Islands in the Indian Ocean, provided us with a very informative narration of the furred, scaled and feathered wildlife visible along the riverbank.

Halfway through the cruise, the winds picked up to gale force proportions, the skies darkened, lightening crackled with intense energy and our rather unprepared ensemble felt like we were headed for the same fate as the crew from *Gilligan's Island.* Our only hope was that the sly, stalking, man-eating, saltwater crocodiles lurking about in the waters on all sides of our boat would have to settle for fish for dinner instead of us. When the rain (or "angel piss" as Ray called it) started to fall, it was like a million hoses with kinks in them had finally been allowed to spray, and our guide quickly pointed the craft back in the direction of safety. We certainly were granted our wish of seeing some crocs in the wild and several put on quite a show for us on the way in, thrashing into the water towards the boat and eating whole Barramundi (native fish) with a single gulp. It was a bit of a relief to find out that only 2 percent of croc eggs reach maturity,(falling prey to birds, wallabies and other animals in the natural order of the outdoors), until we learned that the majority of the unfortunate 98 percent are devoured by their own parents!

Having lived in this rather dangerous and inhospitable part of the world all his life, it's not surprising that Ray had some of the best camp fire stories imaginable. He went into great detail about his upbringing with the Aborigines, gave his interpretation of current events with a colorful fervor, and kept us on the cusp of an anxiety attack with true-to-life accounts that were a little too relevant to our situation.

One night after dinner, we took turns washing up in a billabong about thirty feet wide and right next to our fire and sleeping area. After Ray and "99" shocked everyone by immodestly bathing nude by flickering fire light right in front of us, our leader got dressed and called our attention to the numerous sets of freshwater crocodile eyes peering right above the water line throughout the creek! It was small consolation to this group of city slickers that these crocs were only "freshies," (freshwater crocs are not man-eaters), and would "never approach a fire anyway."

With this rather ominous backdrop, Ray proceeded to tell us a story about a woman from Daintree, Australia, who was out for a swim with her husband one day in a creek such as this and simply "disappeared into thin air." The man was accused of murder and stood virtually no chance of winning his case unless he could find supporting evidence to prove his innocence. He suspected that a crocodile might have been the culprit since they are known to "get the last person out of the water" and rarely make a sound when attacking because they crush the victim's ribs and all internal organs with one chomp. He ventured back to the sight of the disappearance over the next few weeks with his comrades to shoot, kill and dissect over 1000 crocs. Just when it began to appear as though their efforts were in vain, the victim's arm, with wedding ring intact, was found. He was finally forced to send the animal's entire stomach to Melbourne, more than 1500 miles away, to have it analyzed before the authorities were willing to accept his story!

"Take Only Photos, Leave Only Footprints"

Forgetting the troubles of the moment is one area in which Aussies have always excelled. Whether it is contemplating the plight of the Aborigines, complaining about the 15 percent unemployment rate or celebrating a rugby victory, "drink" or alcohol, particularly in the form of beer, is very easy to come by and could easily be considered the national obsession. Every other building that we encountered on the safari was a pub of some sort and all were quite busy with patrons at any point during the day. The pubs and road stations served as a halfway house for the vagabonds and the homeless with shade and a cold shower for those seeking refuge from the dusty, suffocating heat.

The most memorable watering hole of them all was the oldest in the Northern Territory, the Daly Waters Pub, circa 1893. Dollar bills and coins from hundreds of countries blanketed the walls along with pictures, profane sayings and business cards. The enthusiastic bar staff acted like they didn't get to see "Sheilas" (women) very often, especially not ones that looked like our comrade Sheleigh! After drooling and ogling for the half hour we bellied up to the bar, they made a special trip to our van to present her with a hand-drawn "Perfect 10" award.

"Road trains" were parked in the front of almost every tavern we encountered. That was indeed a scary thought since they routinely blew past us on the dirt roads we traveled, a full fifty feet long with sixty-two wheels and freight train-like momentum. They carried cattle from town to town and did not stop for anything. We were told that it was a lot less costly to disintegrate a stray calf in its path than slam on the brakes, kill a number of cattle on the train, and blow out more tires than they had spares.

The essence of Ray's "most excellent adventure" to most of us was having a "front row" seat in the hostile, inhospitable, but oddly charming and irresistible world that he knew as well as anyone. Tidbits of "street smarts," outback-style, would leave us begging for more, like a three- year-old wanting her mom to read "one more story" before bed.

We followed a snake track sighted on the dirt path from the driver's seat at forty miles per hour, just like the Aborigines did. He noted that cows never go more than ten miles from water and horses never go more than twenty, so when you see one of them, you know you're reasonably close to liquid refreshment. He even slammed on the brakes and flew out of the van to climb a tree in pursuit of a "good-eating," frill-necked lizard. We were shown how to crack a bullwhip and throw a boomerang, one of the Aborigines' many creations.

On one particularly hot, unbearable day, we stopped in the morning to check out snake and cattle tracks and to look at a fossil exhibit literally in the middle of nowhere. Below the 20,000 year-old fossils that used to be a part of a rain forest but now found themselves in a desert, a template placed by *National Geographic* reads, "Take only photos, leave only footprints." This one, simplistic phrase symbolized our newfound appreciation for the outdoors, especially this desolate, drought-stricken land. It is certainly a good slogan for all of us to remember and live by.

"The Rock"

A long weekend of sleeping on a mattress, trying to clean our clothes and gear, reading, shopping and saying tearful good-byes awaited us at the Frogswallow Backpacker Hostel in sweltering Darwin. I can honestly say that it was the hottest, most uncomfortably humid place I'd ever been. For some inexplicable reason, the hostel felt it necessary to add insult to injury and take up pool space with a steaming hot tub. Some of the gang "indulged," but I spent most of the time with a book under the sweeping ceiling fans.

The day before the bus leg of our Australian odyssey was to commence, we frequented the local supermarket, Woolworth's, to stock up on essential road food like peanut butter and jelly, saltines, bread, juices in aseptic containers, Pop Tarts and fruit. The remoteness of Darwin relative to anywhere else in the world helped contribute to the obscene prices like US$3.60 for a rockmelon (cantaloupe) and US$4.50 for a two-liter carton of orange juice. After midnight that evening, a powerful storm, a harbinger of the rainy season, shook the balconies, blew away hanging plants and awoke almost everyone in the hostel. To area residents, it brought back memories of Cyclone Tracy which roared into Darwin on Christmas Day 1974 and leveled the city. Susan said she was glued to me all night, but I barely had a recollection of anything.

We left the driving to Greyhound and hunkered down for the cramped, nineteen-hour ride south with one-third of our safari contingency still intact. Derek and Jac who were toying with the idea of starting a romance, "Doc," in fantasy land about her fiancee back in England, and mellow, easy- going Andy would provide us with more than sufficient comic relief and welcomed financial sharing over the next few days of continuing expensive, adventure travel.

Depending on who you talked to, the 954 mile-long stretch to Alice Springs was coined a variety of monikers, from the standard Stuart Highway, to "The

Bituman" (another name for any blacktop highway), to simply "The Track." It traversed the most sparsely-populated section of land anywhere on the globe with the exception of the polar ice caps. With enough leg room for an under-sized ten-year-old, the bumpy ride to Alice Springs was hardly one of comfort as we played dodge ball with what seemed like half of the buffalo, kangaroos, cows and dingoes in the outback. I always managed to open my eyes just in time to see another "skippy" bouncing on the pavement next to our bus, a split second after he had met his match. Susan, fortunately, refused to look.

At 6:03 a.m., a tired bus and inhabitants squealed into "The Alice" Transit Centre. "Doc," Andy and I rented a Budget camper van for the ensuing four-day jaunt over to Ayers Rock and back for A$133/day of unlimited travel. In a rather touristy desert town of a mere 24,000 inhabitants, literally in the middle of nowhere, this was without question the cheapest way to accomplish our next mission. Before departing around noon, we pooled our resources again at Woolworth's, stocking up on groceries and beer, the favorite indulgence of our "Pommie" (Aussie slang for British people) companions.

In the stifling 110°F sun, our primary concern was finding a swimming pool somewhere in this vast oasis of red desert dust, towering ant and termite mounds, white ghost gum trees and meteor boulders. A long overdue visit to a petrol station led us to an unexpectedly ideal place to cool off the camper and our bodies for the night.

We found fuel (at a gouging A$1.20 a liter!), a very recently filled, ice-cold, swimming pool and free camping accommodations at a single roadhouse just fifty miles shy of "The Rock." There was a competitive battle for tourists going on among the three or four proprietors on the way in to Uluru, a very small community within five miles of the monolith, and they were pulling out all the stops to get travelers to stay and belly up to their always-flowing bar. I did just that a few hours after check-in and learned from the bartender that rain was truly a scarce occurrence in this part of the world. Her son went the first nine years of his life without seeing a raindrop during "a particularly extended drought back in the 1960's." Oddly enough, we felt a few sprinkles on our faces that very night as we slept on the ground, looking for some stars to count overhead.

Having packed the carbohydrates over the preceding twenty-four hours, we were ready to tackle the challenge of climbing the fabled Ayers Rock. As the locals recommended, we got a very early start to try and beat the heat which has a way of making a difficult day either miserable or deadly.

It's hard to fathom that thousands of people venture from all over the world every year to see a rock as the focal point of their travels. That is, until you actually see and climb the natural phenomenon that towers 1143 feet above the scrubbrush-dominated plain and measures 5 1/2 miles in circumference (twice the size of Central London). Perhaps the most amazing fact about "The Rock" is that it is merely the peak of a mountain, and more than half of its total size is buried underground!

We all considered ourselves to be in excellent physical condition prior to

"The Climb," but the ascension is at an extremely steep angle that knotted up every ligament and tendon in my entire lower back after about fifteen minutes. It is inconceivable to me that the Aborigines routinely scaled the monolith without the present-day, tourist-friendly handholds that start at 280 feet. Not only did they climb it, but they also inhabited the dozens of caves around its borders, using them for shelter, tribal ceremonies and burial chambers.

I found the "guest book" sitting on a podium at the pinnacle of the ascent to be extremely out-of-place and almost insulting to its original inhabitants. We paused for a moment at the top to scan the surrounding emptiness that seemed to stretch out to infinity. The twirling smoke emitted by the distant bush fires and an intermittent light drizzle added to the surreal effect that the marvel generated. As "out of the way" as it truly is, there's certainly nothing else like it in the world and I could not have imagined a trip to Australia without experiencing it.

The following day, after a visit and more climbing at a neighboring cluster of round monoliths twenty miles west of Ayers Rock called the Olgas, we were ready for some farewell photos. Known for its penchant of changing color throughout the day depending on the natural lighting, "The Rock" pleased our increasingly giddy group by "metamorphosing" right before our eyes. I caught a lot of good-natured "slack" from the "Pommies" for my simplistic commentary as it changed from golden to purple to brown in hue over the course of the day.

Driving back to Alice Springs, we crossed paths with several groups of present-day Aborigines in the midst of a very sad existence. The only consistent thread in their "new, modernized world" seems to be "drink," (booze) and it has plain and simply taken control of their lives. Packed like sardines in late-model gas guzzler "bombs" with roofs sawed off and windows broken out completely, they are a pitiful sight as they meander along the shoulder of the road from roadhouse to roadhouse in search of handouts beyond what the government already provides for them.

"The Legendary Ghan" passenger train provided a historical means of departure from the "Red Centre" of the continent. Named after hardy Afghan traders and their camel caravans, "The Ghan" was originally the only form of transport available to cover the 975 mile distance down to Adelaide. The ride was substantially riskier back in the early 1900's with the threat of banditry and the prospect of floods until the operators recognized that the original track was built on a flood plain! Nowadays, it's probably the most comfortable way to travel anywhere in the country, and the six of us took advantage of the special extras like videos, refreshment carts and showers that we were not accustomed to every day.

"Diamond in the Rough"

Although it is rarely mentioned when people talk about "must see" stops in Australia, Adelaide is a surprisingly large (close to one million people), culturally diverse and attractive city. It is truly a "diamond in the rough" but has managed to maintain relative anonymity primarily due to its distant proximity to Sydney and the east coast beaches. More in-bound flights have become available in recent years as the biennial Adelaide Arts Festival and Grand Prix have skyrocketed in popularity and the magnificent local wineries have finally been given their due.

Adelaide is the quintessential walking city, fitting our situation perfectly. We followed the trail of the recently completed Grand Prix route along wide avenues flanked by jacaranda trees with beautifully blooming blue flowers. Museums, universities, churches and parks abound throughout the area and we took time to "smell the roses" (literally!) at Rymill Park, the home of one of the world's largest rose gardens.

After bidding Allison farewell as she headed to New Zealand, the remaining trio of Derrick, Jac and Andy decided to culture "us Yanks" at a professional cricket match taking place between South and West Australia. I was determined to be open-minded about the ultraconservative and traditional English pastime, but I couldn't help but compare it to our much faster, and more interesting, alternatives. My enthusiastic commentators made it bearable, although on the excitability scale I'd rank it somewhere between skipping rocks across a lake and ignoring a flashing "Don't Walk" sign.

Susan and I were in the midst of one of our "proximal contact funks" which struck periodically, without warning, throughout the trip. Within earshot of each other almost constantly for six months now, we would have to become more apt at creatively distancing ourselves from one another on occasion to maintain our sanity. Her journal entry read, "David's so intent on 'living on the cheap' that some days I don't care if our money runs out and we get to go home. I can't get home off my mind. Every weekend I think about calling Mom and Dad. I can't believe that Thanksgiving is next week. . ."

A few days of "road tripping" to the Barossa Valley and Kangaroo Island with our British buddies helped lessen Susan's homesickness pangs. In search of the absolute cheapest means of transporting five people to the Barossa Valley, we decided once again to go the rental route. This time it was a luxurious late-1970's model Chrysler with 150,000 miles and a lovely, dirty yellow exterior in dire need of some "bondo."

Even with the obligatory pit stop for lollies (candy in England) to satisfy Jac's cravings, within an hour we were surrounded by totally different scenery more reminiscent of the Sonoma Valley or Finger Lakes region than burly Aussieland. A distinctively German influence pervaded the Barossa Valley in the physical appearance of churches, barns and houses and the namesakes of most of the establishments followed suit.

From a recommendation received in Adelaide, we opted to stay at the Bunkhaus, a hostel exuding a cozy, bucolic charm in a house over a century old. The building we slept in looked like an old one-room house from Abe Lincoln days with a German flair. We fell in love with our humble abode for the next few days, especially the indescribably comfortable peach-colored dunnas that covered every one of the four bunk beds for which the place (I presume) got its name. We half-seriously joked that we should make ourselves get sick so we could stay nestled in these beds all day.

Spoiled with complimentary fresh eggs in the morning and unlimited hot tea all day long, it would've been easy to lie back and tell stories or watch Margaret Thatcher's traumatic resignation on the "tele." Instead we gallivanted across the countryside playing winery hopscotch with giggles per minute increasing steadily as we went. From Penfolds, the largest winery in the Southern Hemisphere, to Rockfords, Krondorf, Seppetfield and tiny, home-spun Bethany, we got royally "pissed" (English for drunk) for one of the few times of the entire journey.

Around midnight, Susan and I slipped away from the gang to secure side-by-side phone booths and call home for Thanksgiving. Tears started flowing next to me as soon as Susan's mom picked up the phone. Although there was not a hint of the holiday "down under," it was wonderful reuniting with both family units simultaneously, even if it was fiberoptically, fifteen hours and 7000 miles away.

Back in Adelaide, thoughts turned to the holiday one month away that almost everyone, everywhere celebrates. With huge blown-up Santas suspended from buildings, beautiful gold and white trees in expensive department store windows, and decorations strung light pole to light pole, the spirit was in the air despite the lack of chilly temperatures and snow. Instead of gloves, mittens and sweaters in the windows, there were short sets, beach towels and sweat socks. It was rather strange indeed.

We descended on the spacious pedestrian mall in the center of town and witnessed a lively street scene echoing seasonal tunes in a hilarious variety of forms. There was a trio of seven-year-old kids playing the flute, duets of teenage girls on the trumpet, dueling banjos, clarinet soloists and processions of singing Santas skipping along the sidewalks.

Susan did make a few creative purchases to augment our 1991 Christmas list (a year away!), and as always, we sent them via sea mail to her parents, Bud and Rita, with strict "Do Not Open" instructions. A taste of home came to us in the presence of Roger and Carol Mitzner from Murfreesboro, Tennessee. Two very special friends of the family, they were in town for work purposes and their twenty-fifth wedding anniversary. Having lived abroad for several years themselves in England and Argentina, they were very interested in our nomadic lifestyle and offered timely encouragement, support and a goodie bag full of necessities like Tampons, toothpaste, dental floss and homemade chocolate chip cookies. Susan about lost it when she opened one of the individually wrapped cookies and found it half eaten with a tiny "love, Dad" note. There is no substitute for having caring family and friends, especially when you're double digit time zones away from home.

Outdoor Zoo

For some inexplicable reason, the native herbivorous, leaping marsupial was called "kangaroo" by the Aborigines, although translated it means "I don't know." Kangaroo Island lived up to its name as we were deciding whether to pay it a visit or not as everyone we asked about the place expressed indifference or apathy towards it. Absolutely no one proclaimed it a "must see," and even our guidebook gave it little positive ink. Throw in a pricey A$26 ferry ride just to get there, and I'm not sure why Jac, Derek and Susan insisted that we give it a try. Despite the collective misgivings and uncertainty about our decision, it would turn out to be one of the most surprisingly enchanting places of our entire trip.

Although the Aborigines named the animal thousands of years prior, discoverer Matthew Flinders actually discovered and named the island in 1802. He found it totally uninhabited by humans but almost overrun with kangaroos and a variety of other animals. Since stone tools have been found in some areas indicating human presence 10,000 years ago, it is almost a certainty that Aborigines once existed on the temperate land mass. The popular theory is that the "Abos" arrived by land bridge when the sea level was much lower, and that their extinction from Kangaroo Island was caused by rising seas sometime after the island was separated from the mainland.

A three-mile walk and twenty-mile bus ride got us to Cape Jarvis, the gateway to Kangaroo Island. We boarded a one-hour ferry called the Philanderer, which headed across the Backstairs Passage to Penneshaw on the smoothest seas imaginable on a chilly, but sunny, November day. After securing another rent-a-wreck for our upcoming tour of the island and checking into the local hostel, we went down to the sparkling, white, sandy beach where Susan sunbathed while I jogged along the shore. Later in the afternoon, I played Ping-Pong with Susan in the recreation/eating area until it was time to witness the nightly fairy penguin parade.

We grabbed our torches (flashlights) and crept down to the rocky cliffs along the ocean's edge. During the day, the adult fairy penguins venture out to sea to breed or "fish" for themselves with their little ones left strategically behind in rock crevices, safely protected from predators and human cameras. At dusk, the animal wanders ashore to their families, waddling recklessly and squawking loudly in a desperate attempt to try and avoid the glaring lights. They are tiny, slow and cuddly cute, but unfortunately wouldn't be too happy in our backpacks.

After renting blankets and tents from the hostel and stocking up on groceries, we were ready to embark on our self-designed, two-day, circular tour of one of the world's few remaining "outdoor zoos." The first and probably most renowned tourist stop was Seal Bay, one of the many national and conservation parks created to preserve the unique habitat living on the island. Due to its aforementioned isolation, the flora and fauna of Kangaroo Island have never been ravaged by dingoes, foxes or rabbits like those throughout the rest of the country.

We strolled through the breeding colony of sea lions whose forebears somehow managed to survive the savagery of sealers who previously hunted in the area. The fifty or so animals we saw were engaged in a variety of entertaining activities like stretching, breast-feeding, swimming and even wrestling. The water was freezing as the next closest land mass south was the South Pole, some 3500 miles away!

The seals seemed innocently playful and tame until we began to leave and Jac and Derrick got unexpectedly cornered by a pair of sassy juveniles who rubbed up against them, hissing and showing their pearly whites. The ranger on duty immediately spotted the confrontation and grabbed his rake to try to divert their attention. After a few anxious moments, our friends were freed from "captivity" after getting a real-life education in wild animal space invasion. A routine lunch stop a few miles away produced an unannounced visitor in the form of a two-foot-long iguana lizard, slashing methodically around us, with tongue extended, looking for a few leftover sandwiches. The girls climbed on top of the picnic tables to escape, but as long as he didn't start flying or something, he was actually a pretty entertaining creature to watch.

Leaving the beach, lagoon and scrub brush for awhile, we decided to venture over to see what "Little Sahara" was all about. Its name implied a desert of some type and that's precisely what was found! Like everywhere else on the island, we discovered that we weren't alone here either as an amazingly laid-back, bearded man sat in the front seat of his car with five camels kneeling on the ground a couple of feet away! A thirty-minute ride across the surrounding dunes on the very tame and rider-friendly animals cost an equally rider-friendly A$5. The owner said that they were capable of carrying 2000 pounds if needed, so we probably felt like bouncing bugs to our humped companions. They had already gone a full nine months since their last formal water feeding, but hydrated themselves in the meantime by munching on leaves along the way. He said he would be taking them back to their home in Alice Springs soon, but we forgot to ask him exactly how he would be accomplishing that.

We stopped to satisfy Jac and Derrick's tea fix at a cozy, little eatery just outside the Flinders Chase National Park. We were saddened to hear that the real owners of the restaurant were going to develop the area the following year and build an eyesore shopping complex similar to the one in Yulara near Ayers Rock. In one of the few, remaining unspoiled areas on earth, there ought to be a law against "progress" such as that.

The park contained our destination for the evening, Rocky River Campground, and arguably the tamest population of kangaroos anywhere on the planet. On the way down to the shelter, we were stopped by a gangly emu who was impersonating a traffic cop. He sauntered over to greet us like he was going to check our licenses, then tried to peck a hole in Derrick's head through a crack in the window! For something that looks as hopelessly innocuous as Big Bird himself, these guys should definitely be taken seriously.

After dinner, it was time to walk deeper into the park towards the Rocky River area to try and find the much more reserved koala. We located the one protected colony of the sleepy-eyed marsupial on the island which contained dozens of them, mostly perched in the upper portions of the eucalyptus trees. All the moisture they ever need is extracted from these trees, hence their Aboriginal name meaning "no water." Although lethargic looking most of the time, the animal can actually run faster with a baby on their backs than humans (without a baby) and can run down a tree faster than they can run up one. Before departing this area, which had the look and feel of a movie set, we also saw assorted flocks of birds such as geese, crimson rosellas, gallahs and cockatoos.

We hurried to try and set up camp before nightfall with the help of a half-dozen kangaroos who were absolutely positive we had food in our pockets. A classic moment occurred when I stepped out of the car after pulling in, looked up and saw two racing roos bounding down the footpath aimed directly at us. Susan sought out the joeys (or baby roos) which were nurtured in their mother's front pouch. The older ones would bravely venture out for awhile, but when they sensed danger, leaped back in headfirst! The blankets weren't quite enough to keep us warm on the chilly floor of our pup tent, but after a day as eventful as this one, it didn't really matter.

A few minutes after packing up the tents the next morning, we traveled the narrow, dusty road to the Remarkable Rocks, an incredible mound of granite that really does look like a "giant's playthings." With the wind howling at gale force along the ocean's edge and the charging sea slapping against the massive structure, it felt like we were truly alone with nature for a few, fleeting moments. In the hustle and bustle of the working world, nature, unfortunately, assumes a very minor role for most people as only 3 percent of our adult lives are actually spent outdoors.

Cruising back to the north side of the island, we entered Western River Cove, an off-the-beaten-path jewel. The traffic (our car!) was held up for five solid minutes in the area as a herd of sheep stood in the middle of the road curiously eyeing this alien machine that had so rudely disturbed their morning walk. The cove was a page out of the "beautiful beaches of the world" handbook with awe-inspiring, turquoise waters in a half-moon shaped formation surrounded by cliffs and rocks and families of sea gulls. It was definitely a place worth stashing in the memory bank for romantic recall at a later time.

The return ferry to Adelaide was the antithesis of the one we had experienced three days prior as the choppy waters had everyone sliding from side to side. I tried to sit with my eyes transfixed on disappearing Kangaroo Island while my body ached with seasickness. The next time I would make it a point to remember the Dramamine.

To save ourselves a night of accommodation, we booked a pair of 8 p.m. seats on the Greyhound bound for Melbourne. Jac and Derrick went the hitch-hike route, but miraculously, we all reunited at the same hostel again a few days later. Susan and I used the "free day" in Adelaide to finish up our Christmas cards and get caught up on two weeks of back issues of *USA Today*'s abridged international edition at the library. I tried not to look at the bleak economic and employment outlook that had suddenly manifested after Saddam's invasion back in August. I felt a twinge of quiet gratitude that we left the working world at the precise time we did because it would obviously be harder to justify leaving when times were bad.

Runner-Up City

We would soon become accustomed to being besieged by hostel and motel proprietors as we stumbled groggily off night buses and trains around the globe. Melbourne gave us our initial introduction into this bizarre world of fast-talking, pamphlet-waving, desperate-looking, money-hungry people pulling on our bodies and literally begging for our patronage. The only defense consisted of being as prepared as possible beforehand, with exact names of preferred accommodations and places to absolutely avoid. Guide books and word-of-mouth proved to be the most reliable information sources.

In desperate need of a good night's sleep after a pair of evenings of constant interruption, we splurged for a A$28, unusually clean, award-winning place called the Traveler's Inn with a smorgasbord of amenities including a roof garden, on-site launderette, guest lounge, cooking facilities and an announcement board that was second to none. After a 24-hour recuperation period there, it was back to the type of "grin and bear it" place that was easier on the wallet and usually more entertaining as well.

Due to a surprising absence of vacancies in our price range, we were forced to settle for accommodations that were even a notch below our extremely compromising standards. The St. Kilda Coffee Palace was in dire need of a total overhaul as it immediately earned the dubious distinction of "pig sty of the month." Our double-bedded room was a mere 6 feet by 12 feet, slightly larger than a maximum security prison cell. There were plaster marks on the wall, graffiti on the bed slats, thick mold on the peach shower curtains, bare light bulbs, broken mirrors, filthy windows looking out into an alley and cigarette smoke billowing out of the dining area. It was only a place to sleep, however, and actually fit in quite nicely with the urban feel of St. Kilda.

The super-efficient, cheap and punctual tram was an instrumental factor in

Melbourne's drive to host the 1996 Summer Olympic Games. Losing out to Atlanta did not sit well with the super-competitive, sometimes snooty and class-conscious locals who have been suffering from an inferiority complex with Sydney for decades. In an obvious display of "sour grapes," they sarcastically dubbed them the "Coca-Cola Games" because of the financial involvement of the world's largest soft drink company headquartered in Atlanta. Tee shirts proclaiming "Where the hell is Atlanta anyway?" could be found in places throughout the city, but primarily among the stalls of the expansive Victoria Market.

The market spread out across several city blocks and was abuzz with activity from sunup to sundown as vendors bellowed incomprehensibly at the browsing public. Christmas shoppers mingled about the bins of tacky tee shirts and watches, Ninja Turtle trinkets, Aussie memorabilia and irresistible fresh fruit. Our well-balanced lunch consisted of cherries, apples, strawberries and raw beans.

We dutifully paid homage to the best museums that the "cultural, financial, and commercial hub of Australia" had to offer. An exhibit at the Victoria Museum reminded us of the country's isolation and the extremely brief time period that they have been modernized on the level of the United States or England. As recently as 1975, an Australian had to book overseas calls in advance and talk for a three-minute minimum at a rate equal to 5 percent of a week's salary!

A notice at the Traveler's Inn had suggested a trip to the Court of Appeals where actual parliamentary court sessions could be witnessed. At the bailiff's request, we walked in on what felt like the set of a seedy made-for-TV movie. A seventeen-year-old drug dealing ex-prostitute was on the witness stand trying desperately to convict her live-in lover of "bashing" (beating up) and raping her, while he was conversely hoping to assess her with an attempted murder charge. She was a horrible excuse for a witness, and in the midst of an uncomfortably revealing cross-examination, ran out of the courtroom, crying, yelling and totally disconcerted. After repeated attempts to persuade her to return, her doctor came in and acknowledged that she was legitimately ill and would not be able to continue on that day.

The court room itself was impressively majestic with its huge, intimidating judge's chair, public gallery, defense and prosecutors table and jury stand all crafted from beautiful cherry wood. The lawyers and judge wore the formal black gowns and wigs on top of their heads which somehow enhanced the theatrics of the proceedings.

Like entranced soap opera buffs, we revisited the scene of the action the next day. Unfortunately, the continuation of the drama was short-lived as the seriously affected teenager "fainted" on her way to get some water! At recess, the witty, cross-examining attorney paid us a visit to inquire about our motivation for being there—relative?, friend?, etc. When we explained that we were curious Americans trying to learn something, he lowered his voice and asked us if we thought she was telling the truth! He was thrilled to hear us say that we thought she was lying through her teeth.

Melbourne's reputation for capricious weather conditions was borne out all week long as it was never possible to predict the temperature swings and precipitation interludes when the day started. It was windy and almost cold our last night in town for our reunion with Jac and Derrick, and after bar hopping a bit, we decided to stay indoors and settle in at a place where Jac was to meet a few local friends. While downing a Foster's lager or four, one of the most outrageous bands I had ever seen began entertaining the predominantly black-clad gathering. Decent guitar and harmonica players in their twenties cranked out the tunes while a septuagenarian drunken sot played a pool stick and a thirty-five year-old lead singer bounced around with a "horsey stick" between his legs. They butchered take-offs of barely recognizable songs, interspersing profanity and references to sex for maximum shock, spit beer on themselves and into the audience constantly, and even pulled out their privates and rapped them against the microphone. Although sick and musically inept, it was extremely cultural and entertaining as long as you didn't have to see it more than once.

On the way back to the hostel, we got an unexpected grand finale and appropriate send-off from our very strange visit to Melbourne when we saw an elderly drunk leave an adult book store clad in only a tee shirt that had been washed one too many times. Catcalls reverberated off the run-down buildings, but there was so much weirdness going on, there was no way to tell for whom they were intended. It was definitely time for a change of scenery.

A bus tour designed especially for backpackers had been recently created that followed the coastline along the Great Ocean Road to Adelaide, a stretch that was wonderfully reminiscent of the coast of California. It was a three-day trip, but had the same number of people as our outback safari with the same type of vehicle and a bus driver of the same name. That's about where the similarities ended.

This was basically a 250 miles-a-day "get there tour," with a few scenic rest stops thrown in to break the monotony. It was blustery and misting rain a good portion of the way, but this was undoubtedly more enjoyable and informative than the standard coach ride. Shortly after departure, we stopped to watch a few wet-suited surfers riding the waves at Belle Beach, one of the world's most popular destinations for the sport and the site of many championships.

A series of unique, natural cliff formations had been created by the ebb and flow of the pounding surf over the centuries. The most spectacular of those were the "Twelve Apostles," "London Bridge," and "Melba Gulley," and we spent a few minutes at each surveying the areas and playing shutterbug. It was about time to send another batch of unprocessed rolls of film home to Bud and Rita for development. We occasionally treated ourselves with a visit to the one-hour photo lab to make sure the camera was still working properly, but the vast majority of the ninety or so rolls of thirty-six exposures taken throughout the entire trip were not seen until we were back home.

If an opinion poll were ever taken among backpackers traveling for six months or longer, I'm sure the concept of "sleeping in three to seven different places on as many different surfaces in a week" would probably score high marks in both the positive and negative columns. Even the most hard-core traveler needs a quiet place now and then to "recharge the batteries" and worry about something besides finding his next dozing quarters. Without consciously designating it as such, the East Park Lodge had become our "recharging" spot in South Australia. For the third time in three weeks, we found ourselves checking into the roomy, comfortable establishment run by a pleasant, but virtually non-English-speaking Indian couple. The first person I spotted in the familiar eating area among several familiar faces was outback safari chum Andy who was about to concede a fruitless search for employment in the ever-worsening Adelaide job market. Unlike Americans who face a nearly insurmountable task of getting a legitimate work visa in Australia, all interested individuals from the other Commonwealth countries (England, New Zealand and Canada) may obtain a six-month work visa with a minimal amount of red tape. The likelihood of securing gainful employment obviously varies greatly depending on skills needed in a particular area and the aggressiveness and perseverance of the individual. With a grocery store stock manager background, Andy would stand a better chance of making money at the local casino.

Robbed!

Money would also be the central theme of our final morning in Adelaide for a very different reason. The night before leaving on the thirty-seven hour Trans-Australian Railway journey to Perth, we ran a few preparatory errands which included making a A$500 withdrawal from one of the local AMEX machines. It was a bit more than usual because we weren't sure if or when the next machine would be available.

With our money pouch full of cash and our hearts feeling a twinge of sadness, we arose one last time at East Park Lodge. It had become a "home away from home" as we had become friends or acquaintances with close to half of the transient guests there. We always made it a point to go to the washroom separately so one of us could guard our valuables even though our door was closed. For some inexplicable reason, we carelessly made an exception that morning. In the token five minutes it took Susan to put her contacts in and for me to brush my teeth thirty feet from our room with the door *closed, but unlocked*, someone opportunistically went in and lifted our cash stash, rail tickets, credit cards and driver's licenses.

The moment of frantic realization produced that familiar, but absolutely paralyzing feeling of hopelessness and despair that happens every time you misplace an irreplaceable object or get pulled over by a highway patrolman. Amazed, aghast, violated and shocked, my first impulse was to start banging on doors in the hallway. In retrospect, the best move would have been to immediately block all exits and call the police to come by for a thorough search.

The night before, an older gentleman of sixty or so checked into the room next to us. Although a potential grandfather to almost everyone there, his age wasn't the first thing that caught my attention—it was his necktie. Ten dollar-a-night youth hostels rarely, if ever, attract businessmen for obvious reasons. Why was this guy staying there?

After my brief, spastic and fruitless search, I bolted downstairs to alert the owners to be on the lookout for anyone leaving in a hurry and to call the police. Valuable time was lost trying to get my message across to the flustered Indian proprietors.

I secluded myself in a phone booth that was virtually soundproof and had no windows. While canceling our credit cards and calling the train station to see if we could still catch the only departure of the week to Perth with our ticket stolen, Susan was playing master detective with the older man in the room next door. Although scheduled to check out in two days, he was suddenly in a hurry to pack his belongings and find the front door—hint number one. She interrogated the suspicious character with vague accusations to which he angrily responded with sarcastic comments and references to his "strong religious beliefs"—hint number two. They carried on a verbal spat all the way out the front door where he was met by a pair of guys in a silver BMW—hint number three!

Unfortunately, I learned of his narrow escape after I got out of the phone booth, and about the same time the police showed up to file a report. The credit cards and train ticket would be easily replaced, but the freshly dispensed cash was a total wash. We had no proof of money or a thief so we had simply learned a very expensive lesson in the unpredictable game of backpacking. You expect to have problems in India, Thailand or Italy, but in the peaceful serenity of Adelaide (even the name sounds safe!), we were lullabied into a false sense of security and caught completely by surprise. Nine months later, my driver's license was found by an Adelaide postman who mailed it back to the States. What were the odds of that happening?!

Perth

We had a lot of time on our hands to analyze, replay and reflect on that forgettable morning throughout the one-and-a- half day long desert ride to Perth. The hardest part to swallow was that it could have been avoided and the guy could and should have been apprehended. It was small consolation at the time that almost every traveler we met had a similar story, but at least it kept us from pointing fingers at each other too much.

The only way a person could travel a more desolate area than the Nullabor desert plain would be to hop on the next shuttle to the moon. It is the most uninhabitable area of the entire state of Western Australia, covering an area greater than the combined surfaces of Texas, Japan, New Zealand and the United Kingdom (1.6 million square miles), but claiming a population equivalent to a few city blocks in Tokyo or New York City (1.5 million people). Seventy percent of those live in Perth alone! If the state didn't have the good fortune of being situated in the heart of some of the world's most fertile excavation sites for precious metals and minerals, the area may have been left to the Aborigines and never developed.

Our train took its one and only respite in the gold mining town of Kalgoorlie, about 400 miles east of Perth. The initial gold rushes took place around this area in the 1880's, but a long period of agricultural emphasis pervaded until the present generation. Since the 1960's, rich deposits of iron ore, nickel, bauxite, diamonds and gold from all over the state have added significant contributions to the coffers and helped label isolated Perth as the "millionaire city."

On the train, we befriended a pair of energetic girls named Trixie and Bridgette, who hailed from Switzerland and England, respectively. The four of us were once again "attacked" by overzealous hostel employees the moment we stepped unsteadily off the train. We tried to ignore them, calling around town to check on vacancies, however, nothing was available at that moment. By a narrow margin, going with the only remaining arrogant, pushy, hostel operator won out over setting up camp in the train station.

With nagging colds and fragile nerves, we hit the streets of our last major Australian destination in search of the post office (another mail stop!) and a resurgent positive attitude. The cards, letters and packages lifted our spirits tremendously, as always, but with Christmas right around the corner, Susan had a relapse of "acute homesickness." We challenged ourselves to find some "mates" to enjoy the holiday with so the isolation wouldn't seem quite as dramatic.

The downstairs "special couples" room that "Mr. Pushy" gave us had an aseptic, prison-like feel to it with barren mattresses, gaudy pictures on paint-chipped walls, and the stale aroma of cigarette butts. Fighting train lag and a three time-zone shift, we longed for sleep but ended up lying there, itching from who knows what, and chatting restlessly for close to two hours. Shadows of undetermined insects danced across the walls while we tried to close our eyes and will our way to morning. Shortly after midnight, a guy started banging on our window, asking us to open the side door in front of our room. I incoherently informed him that "I just sleep here" and he mumbled a few choice obscenities on his way around the building. Then, suddenly, I felt something piercing the fabric in a rather sensitive area between my legs. Upon closer inspection, it was a thin but very sharp, metal rod, exposed and very dangerous! While Susan was laughing so hard she couldn't talk, I put my jeans back on, grabbed every layer of protective anything I could find and finally dozed off for good.

Moving over to the very popular Francis Street youth hostel would set the stage for a memorable final two weeks on the "west coast." Registered, "official" youth hostels like this one can be found in almost every country throughout the backpacking world. We carried the familiar 4- by 10-inch hostel reference book among our veritable library of organized reference materials that we consulted for our lodging and entertainment needs. They were not, however, the accommodation of choice among the experienced traveler set in Australia.

Unlike the "anything goes," "come as you please," independently-owned backpacker hostels that were sprouting up like Western Australia wild flowers, the official Australian Youth Hostel variety kept strict mealtime hours and curfews and required all guests to complete a cleaning "chore" every day. It's not surprising that many folks had a hard time stomaching the thought of scrubbing toilets or vacuuming carpets when they were already paying for a bed.

In Perth, we found a rare exception to the rule. The Francis Street Youth Hostel was the "in" place to be thanks to its ideal location and a helpful, fair and friendly staff. They were mostly travelers themselves who fell in love with the balmy temps and thriving nightlife and couldn't bear to leave. Like the East Park Lodge in Adelaide, it was comfortable and clean and filled with interesting, gregarious people.

In 1987, Perth and its surrounding environs sailed into the international limelight as the America's Cup was challenged in the turbulent, choppy waters near Freemantle. Ancestors of the folks in "Freo" 150 years back received similar attention as the picturesque, rocky coastline became the first Australian port to welcome European tourists. Today, the concentration of recently constructed tourist facilities, hotels and restaurants blend in tastefully with many restored, historic buildings along the waterfront.

It was a lazy day of browsing the Sunday open markets and gearing up mentally for our imminent five-day swing into southwestern Australia, as well as our New Year's Eve departure to Tokyo and beyond. As usual, I focused on the practical task of information gathering (guidebooks, talking to fellow travelers, etc. about what we were getting into), while Susan took time to reflect on family and friends, creature comforts, and the uncertainty of what lay ahead for us. Her journal entry that day read: "All my friends seem so far away...they are, I know, but I feel like I have so many letters to write. I wrote Ann (sister) the other day. Have to write and thank Santa Klika for the goodies (sent a package). I hope home knows how much they mean to me. All I want is a big bed and a warm dunna (comforter)—peach or sea green in color. I've forgotten what it's like to wake up next to David instead of four feet above him. I miss getting dressed up once in a while. I miss a nice bath and my terry cloth robe. I miss the telephone! I miss cooking and night stands and little lamps instead of big, overhead bulbs. Trouble is, it's only going to get worse. Tokyo? India!? Will I survive? Will I leave on a jet plane. . . sooner than expected? Good night, America. I love you."

The Southwest Corner

A single notice on the youth hostel "ride board" placed by Melbourne native, Peter, got things started, and within twenty-four hours there were seven travelers ready to join him on a little impromptu 1200-mile excursion to the extreme southwest corner of the continent. The group picked Susan and I up at the Perth Immunization Center where we got precautionary shots of polio, cholera and typhoid in anticipation of our Far East plunge in a few weeks. Besides Peter and a Californian named Mike we had met at the hostel, we were joined by new friends Bridgette and Trixie from the train and newcomers Maggie and James who hailed from England. With a tank full of petrol and a couple slabs (cases) of beer in yet another rented Budget van, we were ready for the great unknown.

I sat "shotgun" with Peter, on "holiday" for two weeks on the west coast, and the conversation quickly moved from "Aussie and American differences" to common interests like concerts, women and traveling. We were in desperate need of a cassette player for the week, but managed to keep the laughter rolling thanks to the very animated group. We stopped in the tiny coastal community of Dunsborough for the night, and stayed up late spotting constellations, playing Black Jack and putting a major dent in the suds.

Unusual, orange-flowered wattle trees dotted the otherwise barren landscape as we traveled back inland a bit on the second day. Hundreds of brown sheep (from dirt I presume) lay on the brown grass around the trees, looking out-of-place and very unhealthy. Around lunchtime, we took a lengthy trek past a light-house to an absolutely gorgeous scenic overlook where whales and dolphins have been known to populate the waters. The calm seas were a rich, deep, blue color that looked as though they had been painted on the world's largest canvas.

A stop at a winery near the Margaret River later on yielded our drink of choice for the evening. After an unsavory rooburger (kangaroo sandwich) at an Augusta "dive," we created a party at our caravan park with four other back-packers. We also learned very quickly about Trixie's incredible affinity for Cheetos and cookies which she hilariously whined for in her very broken English tongue. Before bed, the whole gang went down to a pay phone to sing "Happy Birthday" to Susan's sister, Kathy, about 7000 miles away.

One of our biggest annoyances in this part of the country was the cloud of locusts that swarmed the van as we motored down the road. Hordes of the little buggers pelted the windscreen (windshield) as we all took turns at the wheel, gradually turning the off-white vehicle to an unsightly brown color.

Besides drinking and socializing, it was soon discovered that the quartet of guys had a common interest in the links as well. A visit to the Augusta Golf Club was an absolute must, despite the fact that it had sandy greens and a Brit-ish Open feel with narrow fairways and lots of nasty-looking rough. The name alone made it worthy of a photograph and a few minutes of daydreaming.

It always amazed me how easily it was to befriend a group of total strangers from all over the world and become a synchronized partying unit within forty-eight hours. I felt fortunate to meet James, a twenty-four year old businessman from England who had already lived and worked in Philadelphia for two years. He was the first new male friend since June that I felt like I had a significant amount of interests in common. He was my more reserved and calculating alter ego and a good balance to hellish Peter and laid-back Mike. Susan, meanwhile, became instant "buds" with Trixie, a totally naive, but very good-natured, Swiss girl of twenty-seven whose misinterpretation and mispronunciation of the English language kept the rambunctious guys entertained throughout the day. She chased me around the van when I got too sarcastic with her, but it was all in good fun. I'm certain she loved the attention and we never stopped laughing.

The elevated, old, coastal town of Albany was enthralling at dusk with great views of bays and inlets leading to the sea. We were extremely fortunate to stumble across the truly special Backpackers Hostel there, maybe the best in the entire country. With a huge kitchen, spacious dining area, pool table, video room, more than adequate "roaming room," three Christmas trees, hospitable (ex- backpacker) hosts and a great mix of guests, it was definitely in a class of its own.

Previously shy Maggie stole the spotlight towards the end of the five-day stint as she told everyone of her love for Esperence, another quiet coastal community at the extreme, southern point of our journey. This was actually her fourth trip to this extremely hard-to-get-to locale so the memories of previous rendez-vous on its rocky shores were naturally quite vivid. She was the most experienced traveler we had met to date in terms of backpacking time away from her home country with four years and counting. Having survived a rape in Pakistan and more than her share of close calls along the way, almost always traveling solo, she was persistent, determined and fun-loving, three essential qualities to have on the open road.

Naturally sculpted out of granite, Wave Rock in Hyden is estimated to be 2700 million years old. The forty-five foot high formation, eroded ever so slowly by water and wind, is streaked with water stains varying in color from deep gray to red to a sandy tint. Instead of marveling at this truly unfathomable feat of nature, Susan and I found ourselves embroiled in an extremely unsettling argument. In retrospect, it was easy to see that it was caused primarily by the almost constant contact that we had with one another over the weeks and months, but at the time, reckless emotion and a healthy dose of holiday homesickness overrode reasonable thought processes. My Christmas wish for the year ahead was to simply avoid confrontations like that one altogether.

Another live experimentation in Group Dynamics 101 was behind us and once again it ranked as one of the highlights of our trip. The trauma of spending *the* holiday season of the year on the other side of the world was lessened considerably by the camaraderie we now shared with six very special people.

Christmas On the Beach

The surprisingly trendy nightlife in Perth gave us an excuse to get dressed up as there were a number of places to go, all within a mile or so walk of our temporary home. Susan assembled the best clothes in her backpack, a purple dress, black shirt, khaki skirt and aqua top for a rare ironing occasion and laid them on a nearby chair and table. Unbeknownst to her, bleach and cleaning materials had been spilled in the area where she had placed precious garments, resulting in a loud shriek of anguish and obviously ruined clothes.

Not long afterwards, we made our Christmas calls home to our respective families. The gift-giving mood was relatively somber with the Gulf War on the verge of becoming a reality, but the love and support could be felt across the oceans. I left Susan talking on the phone while I ran a quick errand and when I returned, she was sitting Indian-style on the ground with her head in her hands leaning up against a concrete column, sobbing like I'd never seen before. She looked like an orphan in the midst of the seasonal fanfare happening around her. As I held her, she said she hated it when sometimes we weren't enough for each other. I know this moment reinforced to me just how important it is to stay close to family and friends because one person really can do only so much.

To lighten the mood a bit, we joined our surrogate family of hostel revelers at Cottosoloe Beach for a Christmas Day unlike any we had ever experienced. Instead of football games in the snow, we witnessed a group of Aussies with Santa hats playing cricket in the sand. With no facilities around to whip up a meal of turkey, dressing and green bean casserole, we packed the eskies (coolers) full of "brewskis," alcoholic ciders (Susan's new favorite), and the occasional soft drink. Baby carriages and picnic baskets were decorated with a Yuletide flair as party goers of all ages enjoyed the soothing ocean breeze.

Back at the hostelfront that evening, we were all invited to the second annual BBQ of steak, sausages, a variety of salads and spiked "party punch." Last year's gathering apparently drew as many cops as participants so we weren't surprised that the punch turned out be pretty weak stuff. Of the forty-five people in attendance, at least fifteen were Japanese guys and gals who kept conspicuously close together throughout their stay on Francis Street. Since we were in the midst of reading and preparing for our imminent visit to their country, we made a strong effort to penetrate their "click" and find out more about them. They were shy and introverted more than unfriendly, and were very uncomfortable with their command of the English language. We found that a little patience and attention helped us bridge the culture gap, and that learning would be particularly important to remember once we arrived on Japanese soil.

The final few days in Perth were spent in preparation for the challenges that lay ahead for us in the Far East. Another round of immunizations gave us some much needed peace of mind as we embarked on the likes of Thailand, Nepal, India and Malaysia over the coming months. Just hearing the words typhoid, hepatitis, polio, malaria and cholera is enough to make a person faint; I couldn't imagine what it would be like to be stricken with one of them in exactly the wrong place at the wrong time. We bought some new supplies like locks and chains that we would use to safeguard our backpacks on future overnight trains. There was film to send home, haircuts to get, visas to check on and last-minute presents to buy. It was a time for reading, reflection and an assessment of past accomplishments and future goals. It was also a time of a renewed sense of anxious anticipation. We were on our way to Tokyo.

Asia

Japan
New Year's Eve

Qantas flight 79 settled onto the subfreezing, overcast runway of Tokyo's Narita Airport at dawn. It would be a day to remember as we entered non-English speaking territory for the first time in our lives. Heeding the advice of our guidebooks, we immediately headed for the airport's Japanese Tourist Center which we expected to see open at 9 a.m. To our dismay, New Year's Day started a five-day holiday period in Japan, so the Center, as well as all of the youth hostels in the metropolis of thirty million, was closed! There were no signs anywhere with a word of English on them, only hundreds of strange symbols. There were no natives that could understand our dilemma despite their sincere efforts to try. It felt like we were the only back-packers in the world who didn't get the message that this was the wrong time to come to Japan. I spent several thousand yen (at exchange rate of 133 yen = US$1) calling about twenty-five hotels and ryokans (Japanese inns) that were posted on a bulletin board outside of the Tourist Center and in our guide book. After over an hour of frustration, The Kimi Ryokan in Ikebukuro was the only one that seemed to understand my English, and thankfully, they also had a vacancy if we were able to make it within two hours!

Now we truly understood the meaning of the words *foreign country*! Clutching our Japanese phrase books and a few remaining remnants of patience, we set out for our strange-sounding destination that would become our "home away from home," off and on, for the next 5 1/2 weeks. As we stumbled our way through instructions to go from the Narita Airport to the Narita Train Station via Keisei bus, then to the Nappori Station and onward to Ikebukuro by train, it was easy to see why the preferred mode of transport of businessmen and up-scale tourists alike is the "US$100 cab ride" we had heard so much about. If we hadn't crossed paths with a gentle old man who showed us how to convert hundred yen coins into tickets at one of the many machines with those incomprehensible characters, it's hard to say where we would've ended up.

We were the only non-Japanese passengers present on either the bus or the trains and Susan's blonde hair was like a neon sign announcing our Western heritage. The first thing we noticed about the locals was their impeccable neatness in appearance and the amazing sameness of the "salarymen's" attire— gray slacks and coat, white shirts, boring ties and black lace-up shoes. The women and their children were decked out in perfectly matching designer outfits with accessories of every description. It would be the only country where we actually felt self-conscious about our casual traveler's garb because the natives never seemed to "dress down" and there were hardly any backpackers anywhere.

After checking into the Kimi, we set out for an exploratory three-hour walk amidst the tiny, narrow streets of Ikebukuro. The presence of numerous vending machines in front of almost every establishment said a lot about the people and their living situation. Since thousands occupy each city block, it is obviously a very effective way for companies to sell products like soft drinks, cigarettes and candy, which we were used to seeing in them, as well as batteries, soft porn magazines, beer, floppy disks and videos. It's hard to imagine these items being sold this way to the general public in America's larger cities! Theft in Japan is almost unheard of and honesty is truly a sacred virtue. How they keep underage kids from buying beer, I never figured out. There were doors on the ATM machines (for privacy, I guess), bicycles narrowly missing us at every turn, and a strange preponderance of white cars. We found out later that up until recently it was the only color that was really accepted in the country. They are also more valuable, getting US$2000+ more in trade than other colors while appealing to the conservative nature of the people who still are not encouraged to express individuality.

Buying a few, cheap, winter necessities, like a hat, gloves and a scarf, was a must as gray, wet and 30 to 40°F was about as good as it would get. I splurged a bit at a department store for a 3800 yen (about US$30) "world watch" that was artfully wrapped by three eager, teenage, female assistants. My change was handed back to me on an elegant tray followed by a bow and a sweet, smiling "domo arogato" (thank-you) from all three in unison. These rare visits to upscale shops on the trip always left us feeling a little "out of place" due to the laughable limitations of our wardrobe.

Two favorite traditions of New Year's Eve in Japan are to place bamboo stalks at the entrance of one's abode or workplace, and to tie bits of paper to trees, supposedly washing away any bad luck from the previous year. Around 4 o'clock in the afternoon, we decided to get an early dinner at a dark, quaint establishment near the Kimi, proudly displaying its bamboo and bits of paper among other holiday decorations. Plastic molds and prices of the selections available were seen in the window at most Japanese restaurants (thank goodness!), and this place was no exception. After taking a seat, I went outside and showed the waiter what we wanted! To our surprise, the man sitting next to us drinking a beer started a conversation in English and became an interpreter for the waiter and ourselves! He was from Malaysia and a friend of the waiter who brought us a complimentary beer because of the holiday. We had some roasted/ salted green peas (comparable to beer nuts) as a "munchie" with the Kirin suds, and ate the entire meal of rice, shrimp and veggies with chopsticks. The candlelight atmosphere, soft Japanese music, great company and food, and a very reasonable check made it an afternoon to cherish. We marveled at the displays of genuine kindness we had received throughout the day and wondered if we'd have the same warm feelings about the country the day of departure.

"The Asylum"

It had been months since we had the good fortune of sleeping in a room with a double bed and we made the most of it with a sixteen-hour sleep-a-thon, melting into oblivion in seconds on the comfy futon mattress, on the floor with a big dunna quilt. With no heat and no windows, we felt like bears in hibernation!

The Kimi was impeccably neat with dark, hardwood floors and a reading/ TV/breakfast room that served as the social hangout. Although the place would be the most expensive dwelling we would stay anywhere overseas at 6000 yen (US$45), it was a real bargain by Japanese standards. The coin-operated room heater cost an extra hundred yen an hour, requiring us to sleep in our clothes! Obviously, we tried to minimize the time we were in the room, but not in the bed, to save money. Susan thought I went a little overboard, "You were so cheap! I was freezing, dreading the moment when getting out of bed was necessary."

In keeping with Japanese customs, shoes were not allowed anywhere in the establishment, but slippers were required in the toilet or bathing area. Instead of showers, we lathered up outside of a tub and rinsed ourselves with a small nozzle before climbing into a large tub of lukewarm water that had been used by everyone else that day! As long as you didn't think about it too long, the experience was fairly tolerable. For the first few days at the Kimi, I found myself second-guessing every step and action. It would take some time getting used to this "custom thing."

The majority of the Western travelers that were in Japan this time of year were either teaching English or trying to find a job doing so. Although the Japanese people are required to study English for ten years with up to 1400 hours of instruction, a large percentage of the teachers can't carry on a conversation in the language. It is merely taught as a field of academic study, so while they are sure to have memorized written English grammatical "necessities" such as dangling participles, even giving verbal directions to go to the bathroom was a stretch. While learning to speak English becomes of paramount importance for the high-flying Japanese executive, it has also become trendy for a family to have their children go through tutorial classes at a very young age, despite the accompanying exorbitant cost.

Conversations in the smoke-filled TV room at the Kimi typically revolved around the inevitable and rapidly approaching Gulf War, the recent displacement of Margaret Thatcher, the Roppongi (Tokyo suburb) nightlife scene and the almighty job search. Although the attainment of an English- teaching position was utopia for many, others opted for positions as models or waiters. The most desperate set got involved in almost assuredly illegal activities that centered around the import/export business or drugs. The residents of the Kimi were as eccentric a mix as you could possibly imagine. It was a constantly changing crowd of nomadic "philosophers" of every physical description from India, England, Australia, New Zealand and Canada, and occasionally the United States. We started calling the place the "asylum" because of the bona fide "nut cases" who seemed to be running from the realities of life in their own countries and trying to hide in the nameless urban sanctuary of Tokyo. We immersed ourselves in their deep, "off-the-wall" bantering from time to time for sport, and engaged in more than a few hotly- contested games of Scrabble.

I have never experienced as many headaches as I did in Tokyo. A feeling of claustrophobia and stress followed us around on most days as we ventured from the tiny confines of our humble 10- by 10-foot sleeping quarters to the crowded TV room to the jam-packed narrow alleys, thoroughfares and subways. After a few days in the city, we were introduced to a place that would serve as our saving refuge from the concrete rat race we had become immersed in.

One Lucky was one of a select few "gaijin" (literally "outside person" or foreigner) bars that really catered to the pent-up whims of the Westerner. Owned and operated by a friendly Japanese man who takes the picture of every customer before they leave to proudly display in a scrapbook that's passed around the bar, the tiny drinking hole was the walking definition of comfort zone. Regulars brought their own cassettes to listen to while there, and left them in a colossal tape case built within the walls for future enjoyment. The meals were hot, filling, and completely devoid of noodles, rice or fish heads, and there were no chop sticks on the premises. The couches and chairs were deep and comfortable and always filled with original, enthusiastic chatter. Some of our very best memories of bar life past, present or future were spent sipping a Kirin in the chairs of our "Cheers of the Orient."

300 Cities of 100,000

On one day during the entire year, the Emperor of Japan and his family make a public appearance before the people of his country, albeit behind a shield of bulletproof glass. We were very fortunate to accidentally time our visit to coincide with this monumental occurrence and all the pomp and circumstance surrounding it.

Walking towards the Palace on a drizzly, overcast morning with throngs of stern-faced security guards and secret service agents everywhere, the first entity that came to mind was the old Communist Bloc regime. We tiptoed inch by inch through a tightly monitored, roped-off passageway that consisted of 99.9 percent equally stern-faced natives. Except for the constant waving of the red and white Japanese flags that were distributed, it seemed like the world's longest funeral procession.

We finally got within eyesight strain of the impervious glass box that the regal quartet would walk into to address the crowd. At 6 feet 2 inches, quite normal by American standards, I suddenly realized that I was the tallest individual anywhere as far as the eye could see. The little old Japanese ladies around me got a big chuckle while I held their umbrellas up and covered twelve people at one time! When the moment we had been waiting for finally happened, the sea of short, black-haired locals let out a strange, muffled, hissing sound while whipping their flags around over their heads faster than a hummingbird stuck in neutral. After no more than a two-minute spiel, interrupted every twenty seconds by a disciplined round of applause, the show was over and we were jostling for position *again*, this time to exit.

Another advantage of being in Tokyo during the New Year's week holiday was to be able to join in with the crowds visiting the various shrines and Buddhas in the immediate area. While many of the temples and statues themselves were quite impressive, the most intriguing part was watching the "Buddha on the Brain" natives actively engage in their various rituals and ceremonies. In Kamakura at the great bronze Daibutsu outdoor statue (in 1495, a tidal wave knocked down the temple that encased it) measuring 42 feet high and weighing 210,000 pounds, gaping onlookers splashed water all over their bodies, prayed, and threw coins towards the Buddha. At others, they wiped smoke from an altar all over their bodies, clapped twice, and bowed their heads in prayer.

Since we were literally surrounded by people constantly, there were ample opportunities for us to take some precious photos of the beloved Japanese children. They were coifed and outfitted more carefully than their ultra fashion-conscious parents even when they weren't wearing the traditionally formal kimonos. They seemed to have a smile from ear-to-ear all the time.

Unlike most of the major cities of the world, Tokyo was devoid of the defining, distinguishing skyscraper or structure like the Sears Tower, the Golden Gate Bridge or the Empire State Building. Since the vast majority of the buildings in the city are ten stories or less, however, sixty-story Sunshine City seemed more impressive than any of the above. The fastest elevator in the world got us to the summit in a mere thirty-five seconds, and the view at the top, even in the smog, fog and drizzle, was mind-boggling. Concrete and rooftops dominated the landscape as far as the eye could see on every side! For the first time, it was possible to imagine that three hundred cities of 100,000 do exist amid the sprawl of this overcrowded megalopolis.

The Japanese are as competitive as we are when it comes to having the biggest, the most and the prettiest of everything, so they have to be a little miffed that almost two Sunshine Cities could fit into the Sears Tower. It didn't surprise us at all to read about a long-range plan to construct the world's tallest structure just off shore from Tokyo. Tentative completion date for the building that is slated to pierce the stratosphere for *five miles* is 2025!

Although a city bus tour helped us meet some very interesting people and cover a lot of ground quickly, my preferred method of trying to understand a culture was to go the ambulatory route. Since we had a few days to spare waiting on our Japan Rail Passes to arrive at one of the Tokyo AMEX offices (they had been ordered on our last day in Australia), we tried to immerse ourselves into the everyday pulse of the city as much as possible.

Paradoxes began to emerge out of the woodwork almost immediately. The English language is seen on billboards and signs almost everywhere, the Beatles and Eagles are heard blaring from speakers outside and within the friendly confines of McDonalds and KFC, and the fashions among young people are thoroughly westernized, yet it is almost impossible to meet anyone who can say more than "hello" and "bye-bye" in English. I never figured out any practical application for knowing how to diagram a sentence when you don't know what the words mean, but as we repeatedly observed, Japan isn't about practical. It's about tradition, image and impression, and the English language is used as a decoration to give the country the appearance that it's vigorously integrating the world's most spoken language into its culture.

That first eagerly anticipated visit to one of the many McDonald's scattered throughout the city produced the taste and feeling of the place we remembered so well, but the size/price ratio of the offerings was definitely out of whack. Half the size at twice the price equated to a major league rip-off that would keep us away in the future, except to patronize the free, clean, Western-style toilet facilities and to get a quick fix of "Let It Be" and "Hotel California" over the loud speakers.

While imported fast food was ruled out quickly as a dining option, the local "mom and pop" type Japanese eatery was a real bargain in every sense of the word. The typical dinner of noodle soup, shrimp and eggs on rice and stomach-warming "all-u-can-drink" green tea was filling, delicious and only 1100 yen (US$8) for two. They even gave us hot towels instead of napkins.

Walking the streets of Tokyo after nightfall was eminently safer and less threatening than even a medium-sized city in the United States, but it was important to pay attention to one's surroundings for a very different reason. As I stood talking on a pay phone to my parents around midnight one evening amidst the revving gears of screaming motorcycles, a peculiar, but oddly familiar, sound could be heard to my left. A glance over my shoulder revealed several men in suits giggling uncontrollably as one of their cohorts "lost his cookies" all over the sidewalk. This would be a sight that we saw often and heard about even more. The "platform pizzas," as they were affectionately called, were left by Japanese businessmen as they ended days of hard work followed by nights of harder drinking.

Despite this rather crass behavior, the Japanese people as a whole are extremely clean and sanitary. They wear "surgery" face masks when the slightest hint of a cold approaches and keep their little shops absolutely spotless. As we walked to the 7-11 in the wee hours of the morning for our Corn Flakes, milk and juice, the very first people we would see were chipper, grandmotherly ladies, cleaning the streets with broom, dustpan and huge smiles beaming on their tiny faces.(Imagine that scene in New York City!)

Our last day in Tokyo before heading north was spent with a trio of girls (two Aussie, one Canadian) who were teaching English a few hours away. We ventured to the "hip and grunge" section of the city around Shibuya where religious fanatics sought converts, kid guitar bands sought groupies, and jeans, cigs and the Beatles were definitely the rage. It was like a huge street festival for everyone who didn't want anything to do with "normal" Japanese culture and those that wanted to see people with guts enough to admit it. I got a little caught up in the madness and sampled some Octopus balls?!?!. . . and a chocolate-covered banana from a street vendor, followed by a decadent double scoop of ice cream. It was a treat to be able to share this "walk on the Japanese wild side" with Westerners like ourselves.

Escaping "the Jungle"

We could almost feel the stress leaving our bodies as the northbound Asakusa line to Nikko left the concrete and entered the forgotten world of nature. Despite the noticeably cooler temps and snow-covered terrain, this popular getaway spot for Tokyoites was just the tonic we needed after ten days of aggravating subway navigation, shoving crowds and cramped living quarters.

Upon arriving in Nikko, our igloo, disguised as a youth hostel, was a bone-chilling, twenty-minute walk from the station, forcing us to put on every layer of clothing we could find in our backpacks. The place had a ski lodge feel to it, and the friendly owner/resident showed us to our room with bunk bed and a 200 yen an hour heater. We were invited to a delicious dinner of green tea, roasted chicken, tofu, spinach soup, rice and mandarin oranges with the family since we were the lone guests in the seventy-bed establishment. We had been buying these small, seedless oranges everywhere we could find them in Tokyo so it was a real treat to get them unexpectedly! The atmosphere was pleasant and quiet with the only sounds being the clanking of chopsticks, an occasional gush of conversation from the family's preschool children and the distant voice of Angela Lansbury (*Murder She Wrote!*), dubbed in Japanese on the tube. Too cold to take our clothes off to brave a cold shower, we huddled under our dunna with windburned cheeks and chapped lips to plot out the day ahead.

Japan was the only country we visited that possessed a conspicuous absence of adventure travelers for a few very good reasons. For starters, it was extremely cold in January there and the "pack light" nature of our mode of travel didn't mesh well with subfreezing tundra. In addition, there simply weren't that many "adventure travel" things to do, at least in the sense we were used to. Nikko's claim to fame above everything else was an abundance of some of the country's, and for that matter the world's, most ornate and beautiful shrines and temples. Not being a regular church-going person at home, the obsession the locals obviously felt towards these buildings and places of worship was incredibly interesting to me. Distinguishing between shrines and temples was an important first step in appreciating our day in Nikko. Shrines are locations for the worship of the gods of Shinto, a religion asserting that mountains, trees, the skies and all other things in the natural world are endowed with their own gods. A double "T" shaped "torii gate" marks the entrance to a Shinto shrine. Temples, on the other hand, are sites for the worship of the Buddha. They usually contain "rock gardens," skillfully crafted from rocks and sand to represent symbolic images.

We bought a group ticket that covered the observation of a number of the most beloved shrines and temples, some dating back 1200 years. While the intricate detail of the structures was fabulous, shimmering from the snow-dusted backdrop and bright, sunny, azure skies, just being outside amidst the cedar trees, cold, rushing streams, and distant volcanic peaks made the day special.

We headed back through Tokyo to pick up our Japan Rail Passes that had finally made it from Perth. (about a week late to the AMEX office because the Australian travel agent forgot to put our name on the outside of the envelope) Buying a Japan Rail Pass after arrival into the country was not permitted and at about US$325 per person for up to two weeks travel, it was much cheaper than piecing together segments along the way.

One of the very few predetermined "musts" of our entire jaunt overseas was a ride on the famous "bullet train" (Shinkansen) of Japan. Traveling at speeds of up to 150 miles per hour, it offers an amazingly quiet ride in addition to an unfathomable safety record. Since its debut in 1985, over *two billion* passengers have traveled along its tracks without a single fatality.

It was dark upon our arrival in Gotemba, somewhere in the foothills at the base of Mt. Fuji. We had been on seven different trains already during the day and a fifteen-minute bus ride brought us within walking distance (we hoped!) of a warm shower and a bed. The next half hour or so felt like the scary part of Hansel and Gretel as we shivered along a narrow, tree-lined, deserted road, dogs howling on both sides, deep into a very dark woods with nothing more than a pen flashlight for guidance. After a little over two miles, not quite sure if we were on the right track or not, we saw the faint front porch light of a hostel at the end of a 800- foot, gravel pathway. A sweet, elderly Japanese lady welcomed us to her establishment with bows and smiles and settled us in within minutes. An unusual-looking, heated table (designed to sit around with legs underneath) provided the only warmth in the building aside from the relaxing shower we were led to down the hall.

The best view we were to get of Mt. Fuji happened very unexpectedly the next morning as an opening through the trees framed an almost crystal-clear sighting of the majestic, revered peak. It was yet another one of those special moments that somehow never happen on that week-long vacation when time is so limited.

After several unsuccessful attempts to beat the fog and cloud cover for a better view of Fuji, we decided to head towards Kyoto. As nightfall approached, we got the ominous news that the stock market had plummeted to around 2450, oil prices had shot up and the Gulf War seemed imminent. The Bush-mandated "January 15th deadline" for Saddam to pull out of Kuwait was set to coincide with our arrival in Hiroshima.

Our week-long colds and hacking coughs (caused by too much time exposed with too little clothing no doubt) had reached the stage where we were considering using those little surgical masks. The fact that every other person on the train to Kyoto smoked didn't help the hack or the breathing. We eventually found some "miracle" cough syrup with all sorts of strange herbs that brought us back to normalcy.

The most impressive collection of shrines, temples, and gardens we saw anywhere in Japan were in Kyoto, however, the highlight of our 2 1/2 day stopover there was the home visit we arranged through the Kyoto City Information Office. The first step was a thorough interview and general character check by the lady in charge of assigning the requested visit. Our jeans, rather plain-looking sweaters and tennis shoes made our selling job quite a bit tougher than I thought it would be. Due to the stringency of the process, we were prepared for the worst but figured that any firsthand contact into the life of a local would be well worth the effort.

Our meeting was finally arranged, and about 1 p.m. or so a petite lady in her early forties named Yoko met us at the train station in nearby Yamashita. She took us along with her two boys of six and nine back to her modest, corporate apartment with a small living room, kitchen, playroom, very small bathroom and, I presume, a bedroom or two. What unfolded over the next seven hours was our own first hand look at a microcosm of Japanese life. Surprisingly, Yoko was just as interested in knowing about us as we were about her. It was like cramming three years worth of pen pal letters into a single afternoon.

While we sipped green tea and helped our energetic new friend through her best attempts at English, the very independent boys plunged into a few dozen games of Nintendo in the adjoining room. One of the first things Susan did at Yoko's request was to bring out her family pictures that she carried in her wallet. She couldn't stop commenting about how happy everyone looked and stroked our egos by repeatedly calling us "the movie star couple." We found it peculiar that despite the obvious doting affection shown towards her children, there was not a single picture anywhere in the house with people in it. Japanese knick-knacks were the only decorations visible.

The topic of marriage and her husband naturally came up and the information Yoko volunteered was totally in sync with our stereotypical notions. They met through a corporate matchmaker when he was about thirty, almost "over the hill" by Japanese standards, and beginning to raise concerns within his apparently very marriage-conscious company. In Japan, it is believed that a married "salaryman" is more productive than a single individual because of the stability that matrimony represents. Many Japanese organizations still attempt to enforce the "cradle to grave" mentality of lifelong employment and service, a notion that seems increasingly foreign to American companies and employees.

After three months of rather uncomfortable courtship, Yoko and her husband were married about ten years ago. Her wedding pictures illustrated an obviously expensive affair, but the photo album and pictures, strangely enough, were the quality of a teenage scrapbook. In a culture so obsessed with taking pictures, I found this very odd. Yoko told us that the reason Japanese people take so many pictures is so they have an excuse to get together "the next time" to look at them and take some more! We were informed that Yoko's husband, who she now calls "you" (translated), never took off his tie and suit coat throughout the entire honeymoon on the island of Okinawa!

"You's" pet name for Yoko is "something not very nice." He spends 95 percent of the time away from home on business about 500 miles away, and "the only time he shows any affection is when he drinks a lot." She told us that it was "okay" to have him gone and that she really couldn't say that she loved him. The children definitely were her first, second and third priorities and she didn't seem to be bothered by her lack of closeness to her distant spouse.

The boys took turns sitting on Susan's lap all the way to the Daigoji Temple, Yoko's favorite. She proudly showed us the spacious, wooded area of several older temples on this typically dreary, drizzly, January day. A home-cooked dinner was graciously offered and we would have insulted her if we had turned it down. We played with the boys while trying to converse across the room heated by a single kerosene unit. Sitting Indian style on the floor, we ate her delicious meal of Japanese sukiyaki. The cabbage, green onion, tofu, beef and noodles filled the void along with a Vodka drink in a can known as shochi.

The morning of our departure from Kyoto, we attended Catholic mass, delivered in Latin, and every woman in attendance wore a veil. We certainly felt the need for an extra prayer or two as we were on our way to Hiroshima with the Gulf War about to begin.

"No War, No Bombs"

It is eerie and ironic that a city within a country so obsessed with cleanliness and litter that they literally sweep the dirt in their parks would be the one that is leveled to the ground by the most destructive bomb known to man. Fifty years after the fact, it would be easy to pass through the youthful and vigorous metropolitan area of Hiroshima without the slightest inkling that one of the worst disasters in history happened there—unless you accidentally stumbled across the Peace Park area.

We felt understandably vulnerable and a bit queasy walking towards the A-Bomb Dome, the only ruined building still allowed to stand after World War II. The once proud governmental building was charred and empty and the skeletal remains of the dome itself looked like a rounded spider's web. A few hundred yards away, we witnessed peaceful demonstrators singing "we shall overcome" (translated) and a children's memorial with 1000 origami (paper folding) cranes strung together in all shapes and sizes. The only English words amidst the mound of brilliantly colorful art constructed by children were the neatly scripted, "No War, No Bombs." It was enough to send shivers down the spine of even the most callous individual. Passing the Flame of Peace and the Flame of Prayer, we entered the Peace Memorial Museum. A decade of signatures and reflections of visitors included a note from former anti-war activist Jane Fonda and her former husband Tom Hayden.

The museum offered an incredibly moving pictorial of the entire ordeal. With memorabilia ranging from the United States Government memo giving permission to use the bomb, to pictures drawn by survivors of the horrors that they lived through with accompanying poignant bylines, it is a place that every leader of the world should be required to visit at least once. A ninety-minute movie detailing the bomb and the destruction that it caused is shown before a person leaves to make sure that everyone is totally affected. Stepping outside into the bustling, modern thoroughfares of Hiroshima afterwards, we felt like we had just left a gripping horror movie. Unfortunately, this was real.

Embassy warnings were now posted for every airport we were hoping to travel to over the next five months. Since Japan's constitution now states that they are never to be involved in a war unless they are forced to defend their own country, we realized that we were safer there than anywhere else in the Far East, or probably the world for that matter.

One night, while seated in a restaurant in Hiroshima, we watched video footage of those first memorable moments of the Gulf War. Since we couldn't understand the Japanese newscaster's interpretation of this historic moment, and there was not an English-speaking person to be found, we were forced to fill in the blanks on our own. It looked like the fireworks display of the century as the darts of light torpedoed across the charcoal Middle Eastern sky.

How odd it was that we were sheltered from the war unfolding before our eyes because of the horrific finale of another one a half a century before. With uncertainty abounding as to the seriousness of this war or the length of the battle just commenced, we were immediately advised by the American Embassy, as well as our very concerned families, to stay exactly where we were for the time being. The situation basically left us with two choices: to throw caution to the wind and make our move onward to Hong Kong, or to pursue the already considered contingency plan of attempting to find temporary employment teaching English. The latter won out despite some serious reservations from Susan. Bigger obstacles than we bargained for loomed ahead.

Back to Tokyo

The harbinger of our upcoming job search should have been the fact that it took us an incredible seven hours of navigating the subway maze to locate one solitary pair of respectable men's dress shoes. The cultural size phenomena was never more evident as clerk after clerk simply smiled and giggled as I tried to communicate my simple need. As we combed practically every store in the city, we were reminded that *everything* is of diminutive proportions there including bathrooms, restaurants, cars, hi-fi equipment, food portions, bus seats, envelopes, doorways and soft drink cans.

Our return to the Kimi was strangely comforting at first as we reunited with a few previous acquaintances and met some new friends in the TV room and at One Lucky. Scanning the want ads of the *Japan Times*, the only newspaper written in English, and questioning our fellow tenants for possibilities, I began constructing the game plan for landing an English tutor or teacher position. From day one, it was obvious that Susan's heart was not into the whole idea at all. She complained of being cold constantly, (it was, although I rarely admitted it) never embraced my pretrip goal of finding temporary employment somewhere along the way for "cultural stimulation," and rightly resisted the fact that we weren't prepared wardrobe-wise to seriously interview. We faced the daunting challenge of competing against hundreds of people committed to staying in Japan for a year or more with a proper interview and work wardrobe, briefcase, telephone, mailing address, etc.

My "office" was the inside of a telephone booth. For the first two weeks, I made close to 200 phone calls and used up six-and-a-half 1000 yen (US$8 apiece) phone cards. Susan's mother express mailed a suit to me after a few days of borrowing clothes from other guys at the Kimi.

We were able to attain as many interviews over the telephone as we could physically get to, despite the harder than anticipated language barrier. The problem was finding where the interviewers were and trying to coerce an on-the-spot decision once there. Intensifying our anxieties about locating the interviewer was the realization that being even a minute late basically sealed one's fate with the ultra-punctual Japanese. It was definitely an employer's market in January 1991 because of the worldwide employment crisis and the relatively lucrative reputation of the English teaching job. This made it easy for them to demand a bona fide work visa which could only be obtained after an employer committed to hire you for twenty or more hours per week.

We even investigated the possibility of renting an apartment and went out to size up a few. With all of the "gaijin" around, it was definitely a landlord's market with a 500-square-foot pad going for about $120,000 yen a month (about US$1000). They were actually measured in numbers of tatami mats instead of feet, meters, rooms, etc.! A non-refundable deposit of up to three month's rent called "key money" was also required for the privilege of living in one of these oversized bath tubs with no furniture and one space heater!

My first and only real paying English teaching "gig" took place on the fourth floor of a nondescript gray building with a shy, eight-year-old Japanese boy who was dropped off by his mother after school. I mulled through a box of Japanese/English flash cards and tried to create a game plan for "entertaining the boy" and keeping him interested for two hours. He arrived expressionless with his smiling mother and bubbly three-year-old sister and sat down on the couch next to me, never looking up or saying anything. He uncompassionately answered about ten of sixty flash cards correctly, then started nodding off to sleep. Despite my valiant efforts, I couldn't fully revive him until the mother and teacher arrived. The mother laughed, paid me 2500 yen, and acted as if nothing was wrong. The whole experience reinforced the notion that it's the act of looking like their kids are learning English, not the results, that really matter the most.

The final day of reckoning happened when Susan and I were both hired to work at a company called the Berkeley House. After an intense oral exam, we were "selected" over several more experienced individuals that actually had teaching credentials. The only explanation we got for this surprising decision was the fact that we were "teachable" as opposed to "know-it-alls." A brief look at the fine print of the contract was all it took for me to make the final decision to abandon the whole idea. We were looking at close to a month of training at minimal pay along with a two-month penalty for staying less than twelve months. Our three-to-four month "make a quick yen" scheme just wasn't going to work with the set of circumstances that existed in Japan at that time. Two years earlier, we were told, anybody who could speak English was hired and put to work immediately with no contract, no training and no visa. It took me eighteen days to find out for sure that those days were definitely a thing of the past.

The decision to pursue employment in Japan was one of the few major fundamental differences that Susan and I had on the trip. As she eloquently explained in her journal, "I almost left you over this English teaching thing! You were obsessed—I was adamantly opposed! It took you eighteen of the longest days in our marriage to figure that out. I had visions of your stuff packed in the garage at home with you coming back to pick them up long after I'd returned to America! I was going to find an airline ticket home with or without you. I went to bed angry for the first time in our married life and you went to One Lucky. After several hours apart to calm down, a love letter from you to me set us in the direction of a much warmer and less stressful country."

Hong Kong

The first chilling reminder of wartime in progress was the team of machine-gun-toting guards crouched and slithering around the understandably edgy crowd in the customs line. Paranoia was in the air as every click of a camera carried the potential of setting off an accidental spraying of bullets through the corridors of Hong Kong International Airport. Our inbound airline of choice was Cathay Pacific, the same one that announced on that day that it would use its planes to ship medical supplies between Hong Kong and Great Britain, with its name "covered up" on the outside!

"Copy Watch"

With the notable exception of major purchases like cars and houses or within the structured environment of an auction, Americans don't generally get a lot of opportunities to perfect the art of haggling. Many people are so uncomfortable with the thought of negotiating purchases that they take the easy route and avoid it altogether. Within minutes after landing in Hong Kong, we got our first introduction into the Asian world of incessant bargaining, a new way of life that we would come to enjoy immensely. The airport shuttle dropped us off on Nathan Road, the hub of life in Kowloon, the sister island to Hong Kong itself. Instructed by our guidebooks and friends to go straight to Chungking Mansion "where all the backpackers stay," we were dutifully en route when we were aggressively sidetracked by a rather spastic guest house owner speedtalking the virtues of his conglomeration of living quarters over the more famous one. Flexible as always, our interest was piqued enough to give it a look despite the fact that it was a little out of the way and our backpacks were gaining weight by the minute. The place was a microscopic thirty square feet in total, but was clean and tidy, had an in-room shower and toilet (luxury!), narrow bunk beds and a five-inch screen television set. We talked him down from HK$150 to HK$110 a night (about US$13) in our debut wrangling exercise and felt ready to take on the streets of the city!

The ambiance of the twenty-story building we were holed up in for the next few days left much to be desired. There were shifty beggars at every turn, heaps of scattered garbage that threatened to break the stink-o-meter, a constant barrage of yelling, clattering noises and dogs barking, and the overall "Cell Block D" look of our short-term home away from home. In Hong Kong backpackerland, we would learn gradually, it was utopia and we were thankful to have found it.

By day, the stark contrasts of water, skyscrapers and mountains merge into one to make Hong Kong one of the most alluring cities in the world. As night falls, the neon of the city streets takes over, unveiling a fascinatingly intricate montage of sound, sights and smells. A canopy of storefront and advertisement lights border Nathan Street for as long as the eye can see. Huge signs in Chinese and English dominate one's field of vision in the gaudy glow like a scene from a disco horror movie. In what has to be the counterfeit capital of the world, we were approached by mumbling "copy watch" (counterfeit watch) merchants incessantly. I'm sure there wasn't a jail in the city large enough to hold all of the perpetrators if a crackdown was ever attempted. We both enjoyed engaging in a little street talk among the hawkers and the store owners, nabbing a few early Christmas presents for a bargain in the process.

Hong Kong is a perpetual gastronomic celebration, from the crab-claw soup boiling amidst the strolling masses to the miles of herbs or dried fish hanging adeptly from the canvas- canopied stalls to the meticulously-prepared delights of some of the planet's most admired five-star restaurants. Over 30,000 eating places of widely varying descriptions decorate the confines of the city—one for every 200 citizens!

As I get older, morning has become an increasingly favorite part of my day. There's something special about being the first one on the boat or the first one on the street wherever you are, but especially in a city like Hong Kong, so intimately connected and defined by trade and commerce. While most people were still fighting with the alarm clock, we were in the midst of the bustling preparation for the day ahead. The ceaseless chatter of spoons, hammers and drills start at the crack of dawn and the smells of incense and oil permeate the air. There is an alley coined Egg Street where more eggs and chickens are congregated per square foot than anywhere I had ever seen. Another area is known as Cloth Alley, where any size, shape and color of fabric imaginable is bought and sold. Medicine shops were omnipresent with their homemade remedies, syrups and pills of every description. Another street seemed to specialize in dried, preserved food including shrimp, squid, octopus, oysters, mushrooms and numerous kinds of fish. Shark's fin appeared to be the most expensive and desired. In contrast to Japan where we generally liked the taste and the cost of the native food offerings, Hong Kong fare, in our humble opinions, was indiscernible, inedible and overpriced. For the first time in eight months, Western fast food turned out to be our best option.

In Search of Fresh Air

The two-hour bus trek to the Northern Territories and the Chinese border commenced as we boarded a double-decker, the size of a small house, at the Jordan Ferry Terminal. Our second floor front row seats provided us with an adrenaline surging, bird's eye view of the cars, bikes and pedestrians around us.

The prevailing smoggy conditions lessened the desired view of the ship-dotted harbor behind us, but did not obscure the rows and rows of forty-story residential complexes that dominated the landscape. Bamboo was commonly used as a scaffold on the outside of these buildings, creating the surreal effect of a giant tic-tac-toe board on each facade. Lines and lines of drying clothes swayed in the breeze, reinforcing the fact that electric dryers are still a luxury afforded by only the upper income bracket in Asia.

The fifteenth-century, walled village of Kam Tin, near the border, came highly recommended in our guide book. (A list of the guidebooks we used in each country is included in the Appendix.) As promised, we were greeted by a pair of old, hunchback-looking ladies with floppy hats and gold teeth who literally came out of the woodwork of this unique residential area. These "hakka ladies" had to be related to the witches in *The Wizard of Oz*! They hurriedly pulled small corncob pipes out of their pockets, begging "picture" as they motioned for one of us to pose with them. For their efforts, we laid HK$2.40 in coins in one lady's hand and watched them humorously scramble among themselves, chattering a mile a minute while dividing up the loot!

Our last full day in Hong Kong was cloudy again and Susan was in one of those tense, "whatever you say, I don't want any part of it" moods. I was determined to make the journey over to Lantau Island, and after a late start, we had a relaxing eight hours away from the horns and the hawkers. The long, slow, ferry ride to the island allowed me some daydreaming, "clear my head" time as gale-force winds made it impossible to do anything but think.

A kamikaze bus ride along mountain cliffs followed the mellow boat trip, providing some breathtaking views of the valley despite the haziness. The world's largest outdoor Buddha, weighing in at 250 tons, rested peacefully at the top, making the one we had seen in Kamakura, Japan look like its midget brother. We perused the ornate temples of the monastery, caught the 4 p.m. prayer of the monks and joined them for a vegetarian dinner shortly afterwards. Besides the tofu and rice, I have no idea what I ate, but it certainly looked green and healthy.

If Hong Kong could be summed up in one word, it would have to be money. From the tailored suit leaflets passed out every ten feet to the "copy watch" merchants to the relentless pressure applied by the licensed and unlicensed street traders, it is a city on a frenzied mission to sell. In 1997, the British "territory" will revert to communist Chinese sovereignty. That "expiration date" has spurred the sense of urgency of a national two-minute drill. We felt fortunate to taste a morsel of its multifaceted personality under British rule, just in case it changes dramatically in the future.

Thailand

Stress for the vagabond traveler in Asia manifests itself in a variety of ways. Will there be live insects or rodents sharing the space we decided to call home for the night? If so, will we actually see them? Will there be more than a trickle of cold water rolling out of the shower head? Where, not if, would the next incident of pickpocketing or burglary take place? Are our backs and knees permanently damaged by the constant strain of lugging fifty-pound backpacks around? Will those preventive-measure shots we took for diseases such as cholera, typhoid and meningitis actually work if pressed into action? Will our marriage ultimately be stronger or weaker after spending virtually twenty-four hours a day together for fifteen months? Did anybody actually clean that chicken? What if the sea mail boat sinks? Will those people ever stop staring? Will our fifteen rolls of priceless film be suitable for development after we're forced to put them through a metal detector everybody says is "bad news?!"

By this time in the trip, I had already lost count of the various types of transportation we had used to get from place to place. As we moved west into the heart of the continent, the quality of the vehicle and the number of passengers crammed into it often turned simple rides into harrowing adventures.

Arriving in Bangkok in late afternoon, we had two choices of transportation to get to one of the travelers' meccas in the free world, Koh San Road. Neither the boring cab ride in the 250 baht (25 baht = US$1) range nor the local bus line, renowned as a favorite hangout for razor-slashing, travel-bag bandits, were particularly inviting, but with its paltry one baht fare, at least the bus would give us a slice of some instant culture.

We decided to take a joyride with barely a clue as to where we were going. The vehicle was packed with a thick concentration of people from all walks of life: school kids in full uniform, baldheaded, orange robe-clad Buddhist monks, gorgeous-complexioned businesswomen outfitted in beautifully colorful dresses and, of course, beatniks that looked like travel-bag bandits. The only thing we were sure of was the absence of fellow Westerners.

Back on land, we trudged through the thick concentration of sidewalk vendors, children, bums and more gorgeous women with beautiful dresses. After a long walk and then a few minutes of negotiation with a tuk tuk (a small, motorized vehicle used to transport passengers, sort of a cross between a motorcycle and a go-cart) "middleman," we boarded the equivalent of a three-wheeled motorcycle with a roof, for the ride of the *hour!*

Because of my height, the low ceiling of the tuk tuk and the bags in our laps, I could barely see anything other than the tires and exhaust fumes of passing cars. With no emissions control on the vehicles and roads jammed to the max almost twenty-four hours a day, exhaust fumes would remain our constant companion.

To say the streets of Bangkok are a death trap is the understatement of the century! Motorcycles and tuk tuks are literally everywhere, squeezing between cars at traffic lights like lizards on fire. We saw a family of four on one small motorcycle with an infant traveling under the father's arm like a sack of bread and the other on the back of the second adult passenger. Those same women in dresses nonchalantly straddle their shirtless male counterparts, barely touching the driver's sweaty back as both legs and high heels dangle on one side.

Khao San Road

Khao San Road was an itinerant traveler's mecca. It looked like an alien space ship had just descended from the backpacker heavens and arbitrarily deposited hundreds of them on this one, single, chaotic street in the middle of southeast Asia. Every square inch of the road, restaurant fronts and guest houses were teeming with long- and short-term vagabonds of every description. Nose and belly button rings, tattoos and dreadlocks were the norm. There were mostly long, scraggly-haired guys and more than a few completely bald women.

Motorcycles, tuk tuks, cabs and ice cream vendors jockeyed for position among the dozens of roving vendors who pedaled everything from indigenous silk scarves (100 baht), to fake designer shirts (150-200 baht), to chicken, shish kabobs, fresh fruit or corn-on-a-stick (10 baht each), to the omnipresent, mind-numbing selections of tee shirts. Elementary school age con artist brothers and sisters posed as deaf and dumb runaways from Cambodia, flashing "help me" cards in English in a most unusual begging effort.

It took us only a few seconds to get caught up in the frenetic atmosphere after dumping off our bags in our 130 baht (about US$5), roadside, air-conditionerless "suite" in the Buddy Guest House. Several different songs blared simultaneously, literally twenty hours a day from the "pirate stands," where cassettes of choice could be had for a mere 25 baht! Coupled with the revving motorcycles, the obnoxious sound of the ice cream man, the constant blaring of horns and the cacophony of fifteen different languages spoken within earshot of our window, it made for a very short and restless first night of sleep.

"Venice of the Orient"

It was truly impossible to imagine that this overcrowded, polluted, constant-state-of-gridlock city was once held in high enough esteem to be called the "Venice of the Orient." We wanted to seek out the reasons why it was given that distinction to begin with, and to see firsthand if shades of a once-glorious past still could be found.

The canals or "klongs" of the city thrived with a life of their own, seemingly far removed from the exhaust-fumed hustle and bustle. Express river "taxis" carried locals and tourists alike from dock to dock along the Chao Phraya River, stopping in a revved idle for, at most, fifteen seconds of loading and unloading time. A young assistant would whistle differently for each command, to slow down, speed up, stop "on a dime" or whatever. The ride was brisk with waves, created by countless other boats motoring around us, splashing over the sides. In sync with every other mode of transportation we encountered in Thailand, it was for the light-of-foot, easygoing, and flexible traveler.

The river is the lifeblood of countless people living in extreme poverty. Children do "cannon balls" off the docks, brush their teeth, bathe, wash their clothes and routinely drink the oil, gas, sludge and trash-contaminated waters. Fish, despite the noise and turmoil, are caught and eaten. The waves that provided a cooling mechanism for us in the humid heat cascade over the locals front porches and into their open doors. With small smiles and faint waves, they seemed oblivious to the luxuries not far from them that they would never experience. It is easy to envision a more peaceful foregone era when this area might have been as pristine as a mountain stream. Today, it is grossly overused, underprotected, and in danger of extinction if precautions aren't undertaken over the next two decades.

One of the most traditional and overtly touristy activities to partake in around Bangkok is a morning among the Floating Markets. "Vendor boats" approached our canoe- shaped vessel on all sides, offering straw hats, bananas and papaya for a pittance. The deeper into the river village we went, the more jungle, banana trees and poverty we saw. Shacks were teetering on the verge of crumbling, held together by little more than match sticks.

Although the Vietnam War had ended sixteen years before, it was impossible to avoid being touched by some of the counterculture it created in and around this city. Judging by the length of some of the unwashed beards and dreadlocks and the spaced-out expressions commonly seen on Khao San Road, many war evaders and post-service wanderers converged into this melting pot of a sister country where sin and sex were cheap and easy to find. The gateway to trouble usually started and ended around Pat Pong Road.

An estimated 250,000 women or 10 percent of Bangkok's adult female population ply their trade as ladies of the evening. The area became a favorite of GI's during the war, and today attracts mostly Europeans who partake in package tours for the primary purpose of finding love in all the wrong places. Although the likelihood of contracting an antibiotic-resistant strain of VD or AIDS is extremely high, Pat Pong is full of curious sightseers and negotiating customers from sundown to sunrise.

Its seedy side notwithstanding, Bangkok is better known for being the spiritual center of a very religious country. Theravada Buddhism is the professed religion of an estimated 95 percent of all Thais and strongly influences daily life. Our educational process began at the Grand Palace, a mere half-mile from our noisy abode. A nine-year-old boy/monk/tour guide convinced us to hire his services for the bargain price of 120 baht.

The palace was in the midst of a huge 200,000 square feet area and was surrounded by walls built in 1783. The intricate architecture was remarkably lavish with its carvings, murals and judicious use of mother-of-pearl. A gigantic, gold-plated reclining Buddha, forty-six feet long and fifteen feet high with inlaid mother-of-pearl soles, was the temple's centerpiece. As we gawked in amazement at the beauty, we were surprised to feel a number of fingers, besides our own, caressing our backs! It was actually a pair of friendly novice monks giving us a sample massage with the hope of landing a baht paying customer.

Based on the number of "rules" dictated by the Buddha, I would surmise that the monk population led a pretty sheltered life. We were informed by our short, loquacious guide that "normal people" have five rules, novice monks have ten and the full-fledged monks, like him, have 213 rules to live by! The Buddha didn't make any rules for women, so there are no women monks—maybe that explains the Pat Pong Road phenomena!

Errand days, backpacker-style, were anything but boring, especially in a place like Bangkok. We bellied up to the pharmacy counter to purchase thirteen weeks of malaria pills to go with the forty-four week ration of THE pill, which Susan brought from home. Our laundry was expertly handled by a team of primary school girls who somehow managed to wash and dry, then find, fold and sort our belongings out of the approximately thirty intermixed loads handled a day. It always amazed me how they went to the trouble of tying a little green string on every single one of our pieces of undergarments, tank tops and tee shirts, never losing one of ours or giving us somebody else's.

The GPO (General Post Office) was definitely a visit to look forward to since it always meant freeing ourselves of excess weight to send home (usually presents, souvenirs, etc.) and usually meant hearing from a few friends or loved ones. Several pieces of correspondence, including a three-page letter from Lindsay, one of our outback pals, helped us recover from the shock of the chaotic, unorganized, bureaucratic mail system. She had fallen madly in love with an Aussie beau during her six months of lawyer work in the Sydney area. We looked forward to staying with her in her London flat on the last lap of our journey in August.

After a five baht Pepsi poured into a goldfish bag with a straw sticking out, we were refreshed and ready to take on the Khao San Road travel bureau. Susan begrudgingly allowed me to schedule a previously unplanned six-week side trip to India and Nepal, immediately after a northern Thailand excursion to the Chiang Mai area.

Susan's fears of Calcutta were reinforced that night as we chatted with a British girl at the Buddy Café. The heavy bandage on her left hand was the end result of a horrific accident that had taken place earlier in the day when her ring finger got caught in a fence and ultimately had to be amputated! We sat in shock as the heavily medicated fellow traveler went into vivid detail about her ordeal, and then proceeded to share a story about someone else she knew who was dangling her hand outside of a train window in India and had a finger cut off by a ring bandit! Now that's an image we wouldn't forget anytime soon.

Chiang Mai departure day started predawn at the incredibly congested Bangkok bus station. Surrounded by dozens of pathetic-looking beggars at the station, we felt absolutely depressed boarding our air-conditioned coach with leg room and a hostess serving soft drinks every two hours! The only problem was the constant heart palpitations caused by our maniac driver who used the passing lane of the extremely narrow and crowded two-lane road more than his own. The bamboo shacks along the way, held together by dried mud and a prayer, made the back roads of rural Mississippi look like Rodeo Drive.

Susan and I were greeted shortly after nightfall by two employees from the SSS Guest House where we had reservations for a couple of days. As we bounced around in the back of their pickup, we thought out loud about how we had been forced to develop very keen instincts about people on the trip because of the reality of meeting dozens of total strangers, in some very strange places, every single day. It was a learned skill that would most assuredly come in handy when we finally got home.

Elephants, Rafts and Roosters

Over breakfast, we booked a four-day walking trek through the jungles of the "Golden Triangle" (the intersection of Thailand, Burma and Laos) with two Brits, three Dutch, a guide named "Bat" (pronounced "baht") and his seventeen-year-old assistant. We had visions of spending a day in a cleaner, gentler, quieter city to bridge the gap between Bangkok and nature, but it didn't quite work out that way. Chiang Mai was simply a smaller version of its more famous southern cousin.

Elephants are and probably always will be the preferred mode of travel in this very tropical part of the world known for opium, opium bandits and not much else. Because of the very real possibility of encountering bandits along the way (Our guide book explicitly said to *not* go on a trek in this area!), we were required to leave our passports and money in a safety deposit box in town. Again, the trust factor rears its ugly head. . .

The pathway from dirt road to jungle was across a rickety, noisy, bamboo bridge. The surroundings were beautiful in a very raw sort of way, and the elephants fit in the same way cars do at home. After a lunch of cold rice, fried egg, cucumber and fresh pineapple while lounging and conversing by the river, we were greeted by several teenage natives who spoke only the tribal languages of the tiny villages we would pass through and sleep in over the next few days. Bat served as the interpreter for us, the native boys and the pachyderms, who also lazed around in anticipation of our afternoon ride. When it was time to get started, we climbed aboard a bamboo platform, stepped across the elephant's head and sat in a porch swing type of seat on the animal's back. We were led along a narrow, brush path strewn with trees and branches by the teenagers with "boom boxes" on their shoulders blaring screeching Thai music. The animals were deterred from independence by a few magic Thai words which caused them to jog forward about three steps and then come to a complete stop. Slingshots were loaded with rocks and aimed at the elephant's rear ends at all times in case one of them stopped too long or strayed from the path. The animals were amazingly surefooted considering the nonexistent margin of error, never missing a step as they navigated over rocky, uneven terrain and through numerous water bogs. Thank goodness we didn't run into any quicksand! They nabbed leaves from overhanging branches as they went, using their trunks to drag the food into their mouths.

Our destination that afternoon was a small village consisting of twenty-five or so families known as the Meo Tribe. Droves of small children came out of the fields and huts to sheepishly stare at us. A few managed a sweet "hello." Most of them were naked except for colorful, but faded little handmade jackets. They warmed up quickly and started showing off for us. Two babies per person were carried around in slingshot shoulder harness contraptions, one in front, one in back. Kids as young as six-years-old assumed the baby-sitter/caretaker role. As in most tribes, Bat explained to us that the women were the workhorses, rising at 4:30 in the morning to make breakfast, spending the day in the fields with the children and preparing supper and bedtime. Some breast-fed as they worked or walked around!

The guys had it considerably easier, looking for fish, building huts, chopping wood for fires, and of course, smoking large quantities of opium. The term "opium den" must have originated in one of these little villages.

The most unnecessary contraption I could think of in this area had to be an alarm clock. The gnawing sound of dogfights and a family of restless roosters began their familiar war chant about 3:30 a.m., every morning, right underneath us, as we lay in the very primitive, but nonetheless tolerable, straw and bamboo huts, built on stilts about ten feet off the ground. Toiletries and other essentials were visible throughout the straw roof that covered our heads. Breakfast each morning consisted of toast, pineapple marmalade and hot tea, definitely the staple we looked forward to the most.

Day two was strenuously hilly and the girl from the Netherlands, Jose, almost passed out. I thought Susan was going to have to use her CPR skills! The paths again were very narrow and the flies and mosquitoes were relentless. Everyone had blood dripping from their shoulders from the bites. All we had were orange slices and water to carry us through until early in the afternoon when we at long last made it to the village of the White Karen Tribe.

It felt like we were entering a page right out of *National Geographic*. Children again were everywhere, beautiful but dirty, with little cream-colored dresses with colored fringe, bead necklaces and bracelets, probably given to them by other travelers. A little girl with a piece of string looped through her ear as an earring innocently approached Susan and asked in sign language if she and I were a couple since our rings matched! (Susan brought an inexpensive wedding band for the trip and left her regular band and diamond ring at home.) The girls were unbelievably playful, carefully touching our few pieces of jewelry like they were gold nuggets.

We talked to the bubbly wife of the family (through Bat our interpreter) about our differences in mating habits, marriage customs and the upbringing of children. She explained that the women marry at age seventeen, aren't allowed to ever get a divorce, and usually had four offspring by the time they were twenty-five!

The men of the tribe, on the other hand, were curious about something very different—how much and what type of tobacco our group brought with us. Not totally satisfied with the offerings, they decided to mix in some wood chips and roll up some Cheech and Chong-style mega-stoogies in banana leaves!

As nightfall approached and the women and children got ready for bed, the "Jungle Whiskey," tasting more and more like tequila, was passed around to anyone in the mood to partake. After close to an hour of wood chips and chemistry experiment fluid, the inevitable topic came up and off we went to watch the favorite pastime of the tribesman—opium smoking. Just being in the hazy, candlelit, opium den watching a guy named Mr. O explain and demonstrate the technique of imbibing was worth the paltry cost of the whole trek. No one partook except the demonstrator, who must have inhaled sixty times! It had become his constant state of being.

Later that night in a half stupor, I thought our sleeping hut was going up in flames when I smelt smoke and saw the shadows of crackling fire. Although I figured out pretty quickly that the fire was intentionally set, for warmth most likely, knowing the condition of fire manager Mr. O was so unsettling, I couldn't think about going back to sleep. The dogs, pigs and roosters were waiting in the wings anyway if I got *too* comfortable.

The areas around the villages were like a scene from *The Killing Fields* with rice patties and bamboo huts as far as the eye could see. It was amazing to be in the midst of seemingly happy and well-fed tribal people in the 1990's, devoid of any contact with the information highway or any sort of capitalism except for their occasional contact with people like ourselves. We didn't even notice the lack of electricity until somebody mentioned it.

Tuk Tuk Yuk

After the trek in the Golden Triangle and a rafting trip in Kanchanaburi, we returned to Bangkok, six million strong and even grimier than when we left it. We spent the better part of a five-day layover going through the bureaucratic red tape of securing an Indian visa. It was actually necessary to "apply" for one at the Indian Embassy, wait three days, and then go back with fingers crossed, hoping that a technicality wasn't standing in our way. For some reason, several

British travelers we had met were having difficulty getting approval, and considering we had already spent a lot of incremental money on flights, I was more than a little impatient to get the verdict. Thankfully, there wasn't a problem, and Susan decided to celebrate in a very unusual manner while I was buzzing around in tuk tuk "yuk" running errands that afternoon.

I returned to find her sitting on our bed reading with her sun-bleached dishwater-colored hair in forty-six tightly-manipulated braids! It was the perfect style for the sticky, humid weather, and along with our new accumulation of tie-dyed garb, really made us feel connected to the Khao San Road scene. Her new "do" was artistically intertwined by a young teenage Thai girl while she sat in a chair on the sidewalk. The total tab was 100 baht.

We were told that the national sports pastime in Thailand is kick boxing and since the arena was only a fifteen-minute walk from our temporary living quarters, it seemed worth a look for only 130 baht each. The walk took us through some fascinating urban scenes: multitudes of street vendors, temples in every nook and cranny, teeming traffic, and of course, animals of every description all around. The bouts were definitely worth our ninety minutes of time and they were actually only a small segment of the overall spectacle. It was fun to watch the ritualistic ceremony between boxer and trainer before the match and between rounds, mostly consisting of some heavy duty rubdowns. Crazy, bone-jarring, Thai music, that seemed to heighten the frenzy of the fights and the spectators, played at record high decibels. We sat amidst the biggest gambling ring I had ever seen anywhere. A handful of the two dozen or so active gambling men and one hilarious, chain-smoking lady stole the show as they frantically paced, shouted at each other, shouted at the boxers and exchanged some significant quantities of baht.

Our final plan of action in Bangkok was answering the cries of the shopping gods who were very concerned that we'd leave without taking half of the city with us. Susan did a tremendous job of negotiating her way to a silk outfit in a conversation that went something like this, "1200 baht, okay, 950 special discount for you, com'on I lose money at 800, okay, 750, com'on madame 700, okay, 600, no lower." (She got it for 600 baht!) I was considering a lousy tee shirt for 102 baht when a lady grabbed my arm (in a friendly way) and wouldn't let it go! The pirated cassette tapes at 25 baht each were being sold by the thousands and we couldn't resist picking out fifteen or so.

We came, we saw and we miraculously made it through our two visits to the "City of Angels" without witnessing or being a part of a single tuk tuk-induced fender bender. It's a city that somehow manages to survive and prosper despite living conditions that would keep Greenpeace busy until the end of time. As we prepared to board Air India for the "City of Joy," we knew that it could and would get worse.

"Nothing attracts a crowd like a crowd."
—*Soul Asylum, "Black Soul"*

The Traveler's Proverb: "Someone did it cheaper than you did.
The beach is always better on the other side.
Eight hours is twelve to fourteen in India."
—*Anonymous*

"Road food is always neutral in color and taste.
It only turns exciting a couple of hours later."
—*Thomas Cobb*

India: "An Assault on All Your Senses"

Calcutta. The name alone conjures up images of one of the most severely-impoverished areas in the entire world. Although we had months to prepare ourselves for the visual shock of what it would offer, we never could have anticipated the all-encompassing effect it had on us every minute of the day. The city and the country for that matter truly are an "assault on all of your senses."

Baksheesh, Betel Nut and Bowels

The airport bore a striking resemblance to a dilapidated train station during the gangster era of the 1920's and 1930's. As usual, the first order of business was finding the place where we could procure enough local currency to get us started before we could find a better exchange rate elsewhere. While standing in a very long line that was going nowhere fast, I befriended a couple of guys having some loud jokes at the expense of chapter one of Indian bureaucracy at its worst. Nick was an Aussie laborer while Jamie hailed from New Zealand where he worked at a ski resort and did other odd jobs. The four of us hit it off so well that we decided immediately to share a 60 rupee (20 rupee = US$1) cab into town and look for lodging together.

The bubble-roofed, yellow, black and rusty cabs looked like cloned replicas from *Bonnie and Clyde.* Our driver was quiet, cool and a bit mysterious and brought along his ten-year-old son for companionship. The "rush hour" traffic was extremely diverse as bicycles, cows, taxis, London-inspired double-decker buses, cycle rickshaws, dogs, human-powered rickshaws and an occasional car vied for position all over the road. With the dusty, smoggy twilight as our backdrop, we got our first glimpse of this real-life apocalypse in action with its crumbling buildings, people dressed in rags ambling about the streets, perpetually potholed pavement, rubble, trash and sewage. Even the constantly blaring horns sounded as though they were in need of repair!

Darkness came en route to Sudder Street, the Khao San Road equivalent of Calcutta only in the sense that it was the place where backpackers congregated, ate and slept. This was a different breed of backpacker, however, and a street scene unlike any we'd see anywhere else in the world. The travelers around us fit in fairly inconspicuously with their "haven't been washed in six months" dreadlocks, multiple nose and eyebrow rings and tattered clothing. Extreme poverty screamed from the faces of the locals occupying cloth "lean-to" living quarters only inches from the leaded gas car exhaust emitted from the mufflerless vehicles.

After a rather lengthy search for accommodations through the dusty, odorous back alleys around Sudder Street, Nick, Jamie, Susan and I settled on the Paragon Hotel. There was one room available for the four of us, and although the place made a Turkish prison seem cozy by comparison, we figured anything was better than the street or the train station for one night. Especially here. Around the corner from the "registration area" was a man puking his guts out into a water fountain. A tiny woman with her seemingly lifeless weeks-old baby cradled in her arms came rushing after us begging for a single rupee (about five cents). Our cement room had two single beds lined up about two inches apart and a filthy floor mattress. There was nothing in the room except these three surfaces to sleep on, no table, no pictures, no alarm clock, no closet and definitely no bathroom. The windows were adorned with metal bars, and the door had a huge padlock on it to keep unwanted visitors from stealing the beds, I guess. We tried to ignore the huge cockroach that scampered across the door handle!

The two cement "bathrooms" in the hall, shared by all thirty or so guests, had a hole in the ground for a toilet and a single cascade of cold water for a shower. This was about the time we really started to appreciate the little creature comforts of life, like air for example.

A few minutes after we finished unpacking in this humble accommodation, the first of several power outages occurred. There was never a very good explanation for why the electrical power for a good portion of the city of Calcutta would shut down for an hour or so at least two or three times a day. At least the hotels had the foresight to distribute candles at check-in and had power generators ready to kick in at all times.

It was even eerier to walk around Calcutta during a power outage. Backpackers roamed the streets toting their candles and every third business or so had generator-supplied lighting. One such one-man operation supplied us with our first taste of food in what seemed like days. Having just left Bangkok and its delicious and safe streetside chicken kabob and corn-on-the-cob vendors, I was unjustifiably confident that my stomach and digestive system could now handle Indian street fare just as easily. While my three comrades took the safe meatless route, I opted for the "chicken" parathra, a fajita-looking item that appeared to have a chance to fill me up. It didn't dawn on me until a day and a half later that the meat protruding out of the fajita was actually red, and chicken was about the only animal we didn't see throughout the streets of Calcutta!

Sometime around 2 a.m., I started to get feverish with a hacking cough while feeling more than a little restless in my sleep sheet. Several hours later, I woke up nurse Susan and her ever-ready medical kit. At six o'clock my fever was 101 degrees, and over the next twenty-four hours, I would consume four liters of water (thanks only to Susan's constant prodding), swallow about fifteen Tylenol, and wear out the path between our "honeymoon suite" and the hole in the floor of the bathroom about fifty feet away. In the midst of one of the sickest days of my life, I could hear the intermittent howling of others who were undoubtedly suffering a similar fate. As my fever rose to 103 degrees, Susan was panicked about my lack of improvement and got out the map of the city to locate the American Embassy, just in case. (We had just finished reading City of Joy which provided a detailed account of how innocent foreigners that visit Indian hospitals end up being kidnapped, killed and sold as skeletons for science classes back in America!)

Although extremely drained and dazed from a day and a half in bed, my fever started to fall during the next morning. I was able to eat very little during our remaining days in Calcutta and throughout the three weeks in India because of this initial scare, the ever-present and very unpleasant odor in most restaurants, and because of the fact that I honestly didn't care much for the taste of the local cuisine. I would eventually lose nineteen pounds in India.

While I was on my "death bed" relegated to our 8-by-8–foot cell, the "Three Musketeers" explored the city. Susan was a magnet for men, women and children alike, attracting stares and comments wherever she walked. We never figured out if it was her smile, blond hair, the bare legs or the dreadlocks that attracted the most attention, but she certainly had more than her fair share. Jamie and Nick started telling the crowds getting in their way that she was an Egyptian princess and that seemed to lighten things up a bit!

Literally every minute that our eyes were open outside provided a sight more unreal than the one before. One of the nastiest and most common obstructions to our path was the "betel juice" splotches, large red blobs of a tobacco substance that resembles blood, located every few feet on the pavement. The human rickshaw drivers spit betel to camouflage the blood they are also throwing up (because of sickness) so they won't lose their livelihood to a more able-bodied person.

The begging never stopped and the methods seemed to get more creative and outrageous all the time. Young children tried to sell themselves in a picture for one rupee: Mothers lay on the ground feigning sleep until they grabbed the leg of a passerby. A man knelt on his knees in a prayer position with his head underground beneath the gravel and his arms crossed behind his back.(No breathing apparatus was anywhere to be found!) Another man sat Indian-style with a third leg draped over his shoulder. We decided to make one large donation at Mother Teresa's house rather than be attacked and followed while trying to satisfy the needs of the literally thousands of beggars on the street.

Amidst the chaos in the streets, some of the children seemed happy and unfazed by the situation they were in, bathing, washing clothes and playing games under the scorching midday sun. Right outside of the Paragon Hotel, we befriended a clean-cut sixteen-year-old entrepreneur selling toilet paper and postcards. He faithfully manned his stand by himself from 7 a.m. until 9 p.m., every single day, always suggestively selling, but never too obnoxiously. He said he works as hard as he does because he wants to be "well-off" financially so his mother will marry him with a "good wife" when he is twenty-two.

We did upgrade our accommodations a bit when we moved across the street to the Modern Lodge on day three. Our room was much cleaner and opened to an outside patio on the fourth floor. The trade-off was the heightened noise and stench levels that had to be endured around the clock. Indian music blared through loud speakers perched on seemingly every building throughout the city. It was a crackly, piercing noise that permeated every cell in our body, begging the questions, why did it have to be so loud? and why did it have to be on period?!

The smell in Calcutta was impossible to put into words, because it changed from street to street and ranged in intensity according to wind direction and speed. Suffice it to say that a lot of bodily functions were taking place in the open air, a lot of people became sick in the open air and bloated animals lay dead or dying all over the place for days on end.

One of the few four-star hotels in the city and certainly the one with the most character is the Fairlawn. It is probably the only establishment in Calcutta to ever win an award and it has chalked up several. Very airy and tastefully decorated, the first step onto its patio immediately transforms a person from the streets of Calcutta present to the posh days of the eighteenth and nineteen century British rule in India. We decided to splurge a whopping 150 rupees for lunch for the two of us and were situated between an English chemistry professor, an English microbiologist, a bearded Swiss guy and a working Indian man from Calcutta. The service was impeccable and the conversation extremely engaging and interesting. Transforming from the extreme budget traveler set to sophisticated, upscale, professional traveler mode from one minute to the next felt like a scene from *Back to the Future*!

After four days of wandering the streets of Calcutta, the small, claustrophobic, yet semi-clean and air-conditioned first class train ride to Varanasi was exactly what we needed to relax and calm our nerves a bit. Except for the continuing stares and a few pesky mice scurrying around at the base of our bunk, it would be one of our most uneventful nights in India.

Ganges, Ghats and Guides

We expected an onslaught as we disembarked at Varanasi station and that's exactly what happened. Flies feasted on the hordes of hopeless beggars and cows that littered the concrete floor. The literate, "upper class" natives slithered through the chaos to try and cut a deal with anyone willing to listen.

With absolutely no preconceived notion about lodging options, we decided to take the advice of a very Western-acting and smooth-talking trishaw (like a big motorized tricycle with a backseat for two passengers) driver named Raj and head over to the 150 rupees a night Veruni Hotel. For the modest fee of 100 rupees, he agreed to be our personal chauffeur throughout the afternoon and evening.

Shortly after check-in, we hopped in the back of his trishaw that would be the standard mode of transport throughout India. Although top speed was only twenty-five miles per hour, the driver was in a much better position to dodge the kids, farm animals and motor scooters on the unmarked, two-lane roads than in a cab, for example. Unlike Calcutta, where cows and dogs ruled the road, donkeys, cats, goats, pigs and even monkeys were everywhere we traveled to, ate or shopped in Varanasi. This is the one country where a video camera would be worth the hassle of carting it around!

Near sunset, we were at the main ghat (steps or landing on a river) area of the Ganges River for which Varanasi is famous. Raj provided the colorful commentary for the evening. A cremation was taking place with four dead bodies wrapped in sheets over several large pieces of wood. Because Varanasi is a pilgrimage center, the ghats are considered to be an auspicious place to die, ensuring an instant route to heaven. Surviving men of the deceased have their heads shaved before the solemn four-hour event. (We were shocked to hear that a quickie electric cremation is now available for ten times the price of this traditional method!) While the cremation was taking place, we were even more alarmed to see several men carrying a much smaller person wrapped in cloth over their heads towards the river. A child of eleven had apparently been hit by a car and died that very afternoon. (since we had arrived there!) The burial custom for children was to take them to the middle of the Ganges, tie a concrete block around their body, throw them over board and scatter flowers over the water. In this extremely chauvinistic society, women were forced to stay at home throughout both types of ceremonies.

We sat on the steps cascading down to the Ganges with Raj and watched the sky turn from blue to orange to black. As advertised, he had the answers to our many questions about the ghats and the Indian customs that never ceased to amaze.

The following morning started about 4:45 a.m. with a cold shower thanks to the power being off all night, again. Raj hooked us up with another rather shady tour operator who specialized in Ganges boat tours. We were beginning to understand the meaning of the term "baksheesh" that we had heard so much about. It was similar to tip money, except it was like a payola to get something done *period* rather than a little something extra. Over the course of any given day throughout India, we'd pop a few rupees in at least ten outstretched hands just to keep things moving and tolerable.

"Mr. Ganges Man" took us for a slow, sunrise glide in his row boat parallel to the entire stretch of ghats. For the better part of 2000 years, natives have journeyed from their tiny sleeping quarters in The Old City to bathe, wash clothes, socialize and pray while standing in or on the banks of the holy river. Generations of laundry were beaten on the rocks on the steps of the Ganges, then laid there to dry in the hot sun afterwards. It was possible to hear the rhythmic splat of the tattered threads from a half mile away. Shortly after our boat slid into the surprisingly clean waters, our guide fell asleep and we were forced to take over the paddling of the wobbly vessel. A few Indian "wannabes," Western travelers who were considering a switch to Buddhism, performed yoga atop ancient buildings along the river.

Susan was now suffering from her own bout of the Delhi belly as a low-grade fever, abdominal cramps, nausea and diarrhea took over her body like an alien. The quality of food seemed to worsen with every passing day and skipping meals was becoming a bad habit. How does someone make a warm milk shake anyway!?

We chased down a trishaw driver to take us to the train station the next morning. Our stomachs already had knots in them from the impending doom of the next eighteen hours—another train station wait followed by the unknown of a *second-class* train berth to New Delhi.

Our train finally pulled up about 4 p.m. We searched for the compartment shown on our tickets for fifteen minutes before coming to the conclusion that it didn't exist. We finally picked one at random and were "assisted" (unsolicited as always) by two little Indian guys who acted like they were trying to clear a spot on a lower bunk for us to sit. They not only failed to do that but they couldn't come close to hoisting my fifty-pound backpack to the top bunk either. To my amazement, they had their hands out nevertheless, muttering "ten rupee sir." Susan gave them two and they were off to find another victim.

The second-class sleeping situation we paid for was on the top of two triple-decker metal bunks lined up like an army barracks on wheels. We weren't informed when we purchased the tickets that the bunk wasn't ours to sit or lay on until 9 p.m., and that was only if we were able to successfully uproot all of the Indian guys sandwiched around our padlocked bags! Chaos started in the early stages of the 2 1/2 hour delay in leaving the station. What started out as a semicomfortable gathering of twenty-one of our closest friends in a six-bunk area the size of a small bathroom swelled to a hundred or so between police interventions. The intruders were dressed like shepherds, carried long pointed sticks, and were extremely unruly. We were kicked, elbowed, stepped on and pushed continually while boot camp-like chanting filled the air. They occupied every nook and cranny of space anywhere and used our knees as steps to crawl like wild moneys onto the top bunks. The whistles and billy clubs of the cops were a temporary deterrent until they left to subdue another skirmish elsewhere. As if we needed more stimuli, vendors pedaled carts of fruit, nuts, betel and tea next to our window, barking through the bars on top of the annoying chants. As the train finally started to move, a victory roar bellowed through the car with an intensity that almost curled our hair. It was thunderously loud and went on for at least ten minutes.

By this time, I had resolved myself to the fact that we weren't going to sleep, eat (to draw even more attention to ourselves) or use the bathroom (if there was one) until we got to New Delhi sometime in the morning. My mission was to keep a close enough eye on our packs to keep from having everything we owned thrown off the moving train. The highlight of each of the numerous train stops was to try and avoid getting grazed by fiery coals underneath the hot tea kettles being drug around by peddlers. We managed a little restless shut-eye despite our bunk mates, and since we slept with our bags chained around our bodies, we didn't lose our few precious belongings. *Eighteen-and-a-half* hours after departure, the train rumbled into New Delhi.

After surviving the train journey from hell, all we wanted to do was to avoid unsolicited bad advice, get our clothes cleaned, have an edible meal and find a clean, comfortable, rodent-free bed. Susan reassured me that the next train or bus ride would *not* be second class if we were to continue traveling together. Following a brief city tour in the capital city, we were on our way to Agra to see the pride of India, the Taj Mahal.

The "Taj"

The considerably calmer, gentler and far less crowded Taj Express transported us to Agra. Before the train had stopped completely in the station, a group of overeager rickshaw drivers climbed aboard and began soliciting! After a visit to the tourist office to locate our lodging for the night, we consumed a very weak attempt (but attempt nonetheless) at an American breakfast, took a brief nap and then made arrangements for driver Peter to scooter us around for the balance of the afternoon for a mere 40 rupees.

Peter was an even-keeled and reasonable guy who we were able to develop a mutual understanding with very quickly. We agreed to listen to his numerous pitches to try and get us into a variety of marble, carpet and jewelry "manufacturers" (he made between 2 percent and 10 percent commission on every sale) as long as he didn't take us into one that we had no interest in visiting. We did consent to go into three in all and ended up making the biggest single purchase of the trip in one of them.

On our tight budget, we certainly didn't plan on shelling out US$300 for a piece of Indian carpet, but everything about it felt right and that's what we ended up doing. We saw the excruciatingly slow process of how a piece is made, a single 2- by 4-foot finished product takes up to four months! We were taking a calculated risk that the rug would never make it to Susan's parents house in Tennessee, but a book of unique testimonials at the store convinced us to do it. Three-and-a-half months later, it arrived intact by sea mail!!

Despite the amazing hype by everyone we met who had seen it, the Taj Mahal was without question the most impressive building I had ever seen. A truly breathtaking piece of work, it took a team of 20,000 men a total of twenty-two years to carry out the vision of Emperor Shah Jahan who had the structure built in memory of and as a burial place for his beloved wife, Mumtaz Majal, the mother of his fourteen children. The neatness and intricate detail of the marble and semiprecious in-laid stones make it look as though it was finished yesterday, whether a person is touching it or standing several hundred yards away. The king was actually planning a second Taj in black marble, a negative image of the first, when his first son overtook him to the throne. In a cruel twist of irony, the Emperor spent his final days deposed in the Agra Fort, looking out across the river at the shrine he built for his wife.

Out of India

After two more lengthy bus jaunts to Jaipur and Udaipur, we made our way back to New Delhi to prepare to exit India. We loaded up on necessities like crackers, peanut butter and oranges that always served us well in times of a crisis, like during mealtime, and frequented Connaught Place, the central trading area in town. We visited the AMEX office there to acquire some money, traded some books at one of the many exchange stores, found a *USA Today International* to get my weekly information fix, and after seven trips to different chemists (drug stores), finally located a single container of dental floss!

The three-day marathon out of India began with a first-class, and therefore, uneventful, train segment to Gorakhpur, where I was startled from a night of unconsciousness by a very anxious Susan. Within sixty seconds, I had awakened, packed and darted off the train to the all-too-familiar clutching and clawing of a dozen skinny guys with a desperate need to lead us somewhere. They followed us like a bunch of tenacious dogs who hadn't been fed in a week, jostling for position to see who could get closest to us, stopping when we stopped and walking when we walked. We were shuttled into an adjoining tourist office and booked on three different buses all the way to Pokhara, Nepal, before we could totally comprehend what was happening. There was an incredible sense of urgency in the air and we were too tired, hungry and anxious to get out of the country to argue at this point. I have no idea if the 990 rupees we paid for sixteen more hours of bus travel was a good deal or not but I did know that our alternatives were nonexistent.

Once we were on the bus to the border, it cost us 40 rupees in "backsheesh," after a lengthy argument with the driver, to be allowed to keep our luggage in the bus within sight rather than on the top with about twenty-five Indians. The travel grapevine told us to pay whatever it took to prevent our luggage from being put on top of any of these buses. Altogether, there were five "backsheesh on the brain," driver aides managing the luggage, passengers and vendor activities. Despite or maybe because of their presence, chaos and disorganization ruled the day.

About 1:30 p.m., we finally arrived near the border. A trishaw driver wanted 50 rupees to take us 100 yards to get our passport stamped to leave. Trudging ahead with our packs, we heard and ignored several familiar "Hey You's" and "Hello's" coming from behind and figured it was either vendors, drivers or somebody else we didn't care to see. Suddenly we were almost tackled by a pair of border guards who came flying out of the woodwork to question us! For some unknown reason, one of the jerks threatened to force us to stay in India. After a lot of babbling, hand gesturing and our last 40 rupees, we were allowed to cross the border.

It didn't take long for us to realize that Nepal was going to be much more amiable than India. As we ventured farther into the country, every bus stop yielded a few more smiles, a few less stares and a renewed semblance of order. Although our experience in India had been a challenging one from the second we set foot in Calcutta, nineteen very long days before, we felt like we were now officially initiated into a very exclusive club of bona fide world travelers. We had met the realities of an extremely poverty-stricken and traveler unfriendly country head-on, with nothing more than a guidebook, a backpack and each other to lean on for support, and had lived to talk and laugh about it.

Nepal: Rhinos and Tigers and Elephants, Oh My!

A very pleasant and knowledgeable twenty-two year-old Napali guy steered his ox cart along a narrow, grassy path from Tidi Bazaar to the Jungle Lodge in Sauraha. He chatted about his country and the upcoming election between the Communist Party and Congress. Most locals felt that a Communist victory would make it easier for people to secure jobs.

Instead of fancy slogans or signs bearing the shiny faces of politicians, party preference was clearly communicated by the symbol drawn on mud huts or other buildings, a sun for the Communist and a tree for Congress. Smiling children waved to us as we sat in the cart, bringing back warm memories of our time spent with the hill tribes near Chiang Mai.

We were shown to a cozy, mud-walled, thatched-roof hut with a mosquito net protecting two single beds for the paltry sum of US$2. Minutes away, a single room at the Tiger Tops Lodge went for a whopping US$430 a night! The only noticeable difference between the two was the presence of electricity and warm showers. A multipurpose, communal, gathering area only fifty feet away from our room contained a small restaurant with hammocks and extremely friendly, laid-back proprietors. It was so nice to be able to relax without looking over our shoulder for a change.

About 4 o'clock in the afternoon, we set out into Royal Chitwan National Park perched with a guide on the back of a huge, leathery elephant. For centuries, the park was used as a hunting ground for British royalty looking for diversion in the area. By 1973, the primary animals pursued, the rhino and tiger, had dwindled in number to a hundred and twenty, respectively. The park was fortunately closed to hunters and transformed into a national sanctuary at that time, allowing the population of rhinos and tigers to quadruple in size over the next two decades.

As promised, Great Indian, one-horned rhinos were easy to spot among the thick elephant grass in the park, as well as sambur deer, peacocks and mongoose. We stayed very quiet, savoring the variety of bird calls and jungle sounds. The scenery around us more than made up for the discomfort of the wooden seats.

After two hours or so in the park, we returned to camp to participate in the daily elephant feeding. About twenty elephants were chained to posts no more than a few feet apart, munching out heartily on a portion of the 600 pounds of food (mostly banana trees and salt and rice packets) and ten gallons of water they consume each day. Between bites, they even bowed when we said "namaste!" (hello) During a leisurely walk back to the lodge, Susan befriended a tame monkey tethered to a tree.

"The Land of Smiles"

Shy, smiling Napalese children seemed to be leaning against a post on every corner, sheepishly following our every move until finally getting up enough courage to interact. They were innocent, nonthreatening and intelligent, more interested in learning about where we came from, why we were in their country and what we did for a living than how much money we could give them. It was a pleasure seeing the joy on their faces as we passed out American coins like Halloween candy to assist with their "educational experience."

After a morning of waiting for the bus and bonding with the kids in Tidi Bazaar, we were off to Pokhara, gateway to the Himalayas. On a typically hazy day, the seven-hour journey followed the length of a grand, green river, about 200 feet below the road on our right. One slip at the wheel along the bumpy, dusty, crowded, half-gravel, half-dirt road and we would have been little more than dental records. Susan clutched her Sacred Heart and said a few "hail Mary's" as we tried not to look out of our window and into the ominous abyss below. Closer to the town of Pokhara, a northern Thailandesque landscape was a welcomed sight with small huts interspersed amongst banana trees, rice paddies and amazing "stair-stepped" hills that ascended skyward. Oxen, donkeys and dozens of people could be seen toiling the fertile ground while machines of any kind were conspicuously absent.

A taxi driver (no rickshaws in town!) at the bus station showed us the way to the Puspa Guest House, an inexpensive 150 Napalese rupee (32 Napalese rupees = US$1) gem of a place that had Susan "playing house" from the second we walked in the door! Clean with carpeted floors, a Western-style toilet that really flushed, a flower garden, electricity and a hot shower, Puspa was a good spot to recover from bout number four of the "Delhi belly" and to prepare ourselves for the much-anticipated, week-long trek in the Himalayas. It was nice to actually bathe and wash our hair standing under a shower head, rather than merely splashing some cold water on assorted body parts.

While on the trip, we tried to call each of our parents and my grandparents every three weeks or so and talk for ten to twenty minutes each time. (at a rate of US$2 to US$4 a minute) This seemingly simple game plan was never easy, especially from a part of the world like Asia. To start with, the time zone had to be synchronized, and then we had to find a place to make the call (usually a designated phone call section of a travel agency of some sort). After trying to decipher country code numbers the size of our national debt, there was usually little to no privacy, and once connected, the line was scratchy and sometimes would go dead without notice. For Susan, waiting three weeks to call her mother was like going through a mild case of alcohol withdrawals constantly. Every other day, her journal entry contained some reference to missing home or wanting to get in touch with her parents. I was sensitive to the fact that it was her single biggest ongoing challenge.

The second major quandary she faced was trying to get as excited as I was about certain adventures, like trekking through mountains and staying in little native villages for a week. Although she thought long and hard about skipping ahead to the alluring beaches of southern Thailand, by herself if necessary, I give her a lot of credit for finally agreeing to tackle the Annapurnas with me. It turned out to be one of the highlights of the entire trip.

One Long Walk

A sleepy, laid-back town with an early 1970's feel to it with a few wandering cows, pigs and roosters thrown in, Pokhara catered to backpackers and was very popular with them. It was a great place to bargain for inexpensive handicrafts, jewelry and handmade clothes and stock up on anything a person might need for a trek in the mountains. There was a large variety of restaurants there to quell our hunger pains, with Western food options from steaks to seafood.

They satisfied our ear drums as well with long-forgotten rock-n-roll tunes thumping through speakers perched above our heads. Although the food was bland and never lived up to taste bud expectations, it was a huge improvement from the repugnant flavor and smell I grew to detest in India. After extending our one-week Nepal visa to three and acquiring trekking permits, (for 180 Napalese rupees apiece), we set out to augment our trekking equipment with wool socks, tie-dyed long pants, Chap Stick, assorted pieces of fruit and health bars, as well as rented "down" sleeping bags and a small knapsack to carry everything. Along with our sweaters, personal toiletries, a pocket knife, a reading book, etc., we brought two pairs of shorts and shirts for daytime wear, with the intention of washing the dirty one each night by hand and drying it on the back of the knapsack the next day as we walked. Since we would be carrying it for ten hours a day while walking on all sorts of terrain, a light pack was critical to preserve our backs and our sanity.

Susan surprised me with a Snickers bar with a candle in it to celebrate my thirtieth birthday on the first day of April. She wrote a wonderful little poem and read it to me before we headed out for a romantic row boat excursion on a placid lake situated at the base of the mountains. After some pizza at a restaurant that night, I was greeted with a delectable serving of apple crumble and chocolate ice cream. It was nice to be spoiled for a change!

After a great deal of indecision and disagreement on exactly how and where we would go on the trek, we left our belongings at the guest house in Pokhara and decided to take a "puddle jumper" up to Jomson at the 8,800 foot mark.(There were probably a dozen viable options varying in length and degree of difficulty.) Although the "town" of Jomson was almost nonexistent, we quickly realized after touching down that strange activity was going on all around us. Donkeys paced about single file with packs of beer, hay, concrete blocks and food supplies strapped to their backs. School children begged for sweets and ink pens, instead of cash. Tibetan jewelry merchants tried to round up a sale (we were about the only potential customers!), and shirtless men, wearing nothing more than a loin cloth, carried up to three long, steel pipes with a huge rubber band strapped to their heads! We quickly met a few fellow trekkers who helped us plot out our path for the day. With desert-looking terrain and snow-capped mountains as our backdrop, we set out on a trail that would take us through a different native village every night for seven days.

As promised, the elements were the biggest obstacle of the initial stretch to Kalopani by way of Morpha and Tukuche. During the first part of the day, sun goggles were an absolute necessity to prevent being blinded by shifting sand propelled by gusty head winds in the thirty to forty miles-per-hour range. By midafternoon, some really nasty clouds appeared to be readying to dump a pre-monsoon shower on us, but fortunately, it turned out to be no more than a chilly, intermittent sprinkle. We found shelter and much-needed food replenishment in the villages en route. Tukuche, a tiny speck on the map today, was once the main trading center of commercial exchange between Nepal and Tibet.

About 5:30 in the afternoon, after close to fifteen miles of steady trudging, we could see smoke spiraling from the rooftops in the village of Kalopani ("cold water"). After some hot chocolate, chicken soup and a tube of Ben Gay to soothe some very achy legs and feet, we found our room for the night, played some chess by candlelight and collapsed.

A likable German girl with a great attitude named Monica joined us at breakfast in Kalopani and stayed alongside us periodically throughout the rest of the trek. While Susan suffered through a particularly trying day two with blisters, sore knees and continuing stomach problems, Monica provided some much-needed diversion from the ailments at hand. There was a lot of up and down walking and a number of precarious areas along the edges of very high mountains with rapidly flowing rivers below. In spots, long, narrow hanging bridges were the only way to stay on the trail.

Between periods of strenuous athletic challenges, it was nice to be able to pause in small towns like Dana and Ghasa to eavesdrop on Napali village life where children played in front of mud-constructed buildings and women openly breast- fed their babies while sewing on nineteenth century-looking machines. Back outside the towns, acres of bright green, barley fields reflected off the beaming sun, and cascading waterfalls dared everyone to go for a soothing dip.

As the shadows lengthened and the muscles started to really tighten up, Monica reminded us that we had reached Tatopani ("hot water") in only two days, when it takes three for most. We made a unanimous decision to "chill out" for a day and enjoy the hot springs only a few hundred feet from our home for the night.

The villages along the trail were famous for their surprisingly tasty and varied food selections and Tatopani was considered the very best. I felt like a defensive lineman at dinner, wolfing down a half pound of roast chicken, a plate of excellent lasagna and eight glasses of fresh- squeezed orange juice. Situated in a beautiful valley and surrounded by mountain peaks on all sides, it's not surprising that the place is called the "French Riviera of the Himalayas!"

After a day of "R & R," we had to climb over one of those mountains starting with a 3500-foot acclivity right out of the chute. The weather cooperated at a cool 65°F with mostly overcast skies and a little drizzle. We passed hundreds of loaded-down donkeys and said "namaste" to dozens of runny-nosed kids. Susan made friends for life in one village passing out candy ("sweets") to the little ones.

Because of their surefootedness and the strengths of their backs, donkeys provide the only means for the villages to transport goods between each other. It seems odd since they look like the slowest and laziest animals known to man.

For the second time in four days, we arrived at our destination, minutes ahead of a torrential downpour. Our guest house for the night was actually the personal home of a native family consisting of a husband, wife and nine-month-old baby girl. Simple pleasures abound when there is no electricity or any other creature comforts like indoor plumbing and toys. The little girl played very contentedly with a plain box and piece of plastic and was spoiled silly by Susan and the Dutch girl who had joined us there along with two other guys. The mother cooked and served every dish one at a time, a great way to keep everyone at the dinner table immersed in conversation. The couple did their best to understand and contribute to our discussion about foods we missed most, politics, and other assorted topics, but eventually gave up to begin preparing our bunks for the night. Tiptoeing outside to go to the bathroom without waking up the chickens, dogs and the baby didn't work out too well.

A red, pink and yellow rhododendron forest engulfed us and our new compatriots within the first hour of the next morning, directly outside of Ghorapani and the purported best views of the entire trek. As I climbed Poon Hill to get a look, it was obvious that haze and clouds would make it a little less than that. The trail from that point on was very slippery and treacherous to navigate with the thick, sticky mud interspersed with the ever-present donkey excrement. Because of yet another rain storm early in the afternoon, we decided to cut our losses short and park it at the Namaste Guest Lodge in Ulleri. While the storm brewed, I bathed on the deck with a warm bucket of water and held the curtain for Susan as she had an even windier version of the same. We collected about six candles after a hot chocolate warm-up and lit them up around the room. It looked like we were having a seance.

By this time in the trek, Susan's ailment list had begun to multiply like randy rabbits, and with a day-and-a-half to go, the "I want this over with now" attitude was officially upon us. I was (and continue to be) amazed at how such a trying day of name-calling and total lack of teamwork could result in us even speaking to each other, much less laughing and joking, but that's precisely what happened on the way to Chandrakot.

The problem stemmed from the fact that around noon we were persuaded by profit-seeking cabbies (who suddenly showed up in the middle of nowhere) to return to Pokhara a full day early. By that time, Susan's knees and ankles were bothering her substantially, we were down to our last 150 rupees (about US$5 that would have to buy a night's lodging, and three or four meals for two!), a very steep climb loomed ahead, and it was as hot as it had been in a few days. For some unknown reason, Susan begrudgingly elected to push onward, moaning and cursing at me every step of the way. Later that night, she summarized her feelings in her journal, "I was in a bad mood all day long. I'm tired of David's adventures, especially those that involve my knees! To top it off, my ankle's twisted and I've got diarrhea. Being sick is not a good thing in a third world country. I laid in bed afraid to move because I didn't want to go back outside."

Another major thunderstorm hit us within seconds of our arrival at the only viable guest house around. We were welcomed by a very friendly and genuine eighteen-year-old manager who gave us a drink of cold water and showed us to our spartan room for the night. It looked and felt like the monsoon season was upon us to stay. The little guy couldn't stop apologizing about the pellets of rain and hail the size of sugar cubes cascading through the makeshift straw roof over our heads! He didn't realize that we were so relieved to just be there, off the trail from hell with our parched throats quenched, that anything short of an avalanche would have been tolerable. When the storm died down a bit, Susan relaxed, read, and tried not to think about her upset stomach while I wandered downstairs to try to negotiate some cheap food with the meager coinage I had remaining. After some vegetable soup and a piece of toast for 15 rupees, our new friend greeted me with a complimentary two-liter bottle of cold water and a delicious, hot plate of spring potatoes, right out of the garden! We talked into the night and when I tiptoed upstairs, my tough little walking partner was sound asleep.

Even though the last stretch to Lumle would have us off our feet and into transportation with wheels by noon, it was a mental and physical test down to the last minute. The gravel road was steep and winding and required tremendous concentration to keep from falling on the slippery, muddy surface. The chilly, gray skies opened up on us for good at the halfway point, so by the time we reached our destination we were simultaneously tired, sore, cold and drenched, quite a combination.

By this point, however, we were dazed, but totally unfazed, by the adversity. A quiet triumph came over us as we slumped into the backseat of the cab, holding hands and listening to the beat of distorted rap coming out of the back speakers. Through wind, rain, heat, twisted ankles and infrequent, cold showers, with no prior trekking experience, no gear-toting porters, and carrying a mere US$70 in our pockets, we had tamed a very long and challenging trail in one of the largest mountain ranges in the world. For Susan, it meant the beaches of Thailand were right around the corner and the last of our physical adventures were behind us at least for awhile. For me, it was the epitome of what this trip was all about—being outside in the great outdoors, taxing the body and the mind, learning about new cultures and building a wonderful relationship with my wife, all for about US$10 a day!

ANALYSIS OF THE JOMSON TREK

	Start	End	Time	Distance	Factors
4/3	Jomson	Kalopani	9 hrs.	15 mi.	wind, distance
4/4	Kalopani	Tatopani	10 hrs	18 mi.	heat, distance
4/6	Tatopani	Chitre	7 hrs.	10 mi.	injuries, hills
4/7	Chitre	Ulleri	6 hrs.	10 mi.	hills, mud
4/8	Ulleri	Chandrakot	7 hrs.	10 mi.	injuries, hail!
4/9	Chandrakot	Suiket	4 hrs.	10 mi.	fatigue, rain, mud

Kathmandu

The last of the amazing bus journeys got off to an auspicious start from Pokhara around 7:20 a.m. the next morning with a competent driver and bus helper and the best scenery we had seen yet in Nepal. By 8 o'clock, we realized it was going to be one long day. The road to Kathmandu, the only way to get to Kathmandu by land, was hardly a road at all, under varying degrees of construction for the full 140 miles. About 11:00 or so, we stopped for lunch in Mugling, a total "hole in the wall," dilapidated town with two times as many hotels as all other types of businesses combined due to the large number of white water rafters making their way down to Chitwan. We parked it there for a solid 3 1/2 hours waiting for a new fuel line to be delivered and installed. Scores of five- to ten-year-old kids swarmed us with coconut slices, bananas and oranges while musicians tempted us with strange Nepali instruments.

Back on the road about 2:30 p.m., the construction scene became almost surreal. Men, boys and women were sprinkled everywhere with rudimentary picks, shovels and jackhammers, and, of course, their bare hands and backs. Some were sweaty and working intently while most were talking or leaning on their tools. Considering that the average Nepali person makes only US$70 a year, I guess it wasn't surprising to see the lack of enthusiasm. We were a blowout in the wrong place away from a harrowing spill into a ravine all day long as the bus hurled itself around corners, over and through divots, mud, water, puddles and small boulders.

By the time we reached Kathmandu after nightfall, we were one hobbling, incoherent group. Never had it taken so long to go such a short distance. We checked into the second place we saw, a rather seedy dive called Ned Kelly's, and collapsed on a bed that felt like a work bench with a sheet over it.

While Susan laid around in a pain pill stupor with her still-swollen foot wrapped in a bandage, my primary concern was to find a travel agent and confirm our upcoming flights to Bangkok and beyond. After that task was accomplished I set out for a day of meandering exploration.

The scene in and around Durbar Square and Freak Street looked like an odd cross-section of Bangkok and several haunts from sister country India. The thing that stood out the most was the sheer number of temples (called stupas in Nepal) of all sizes and descriptions built in virtually every nook and cranny imaginable. People slept on them, dried their clothes on them and bathed around them, and their revered animals were caged up in them. The temples were as much of a fixture of their everyday lives as a supermarket or a ball field would be for Americans.

I was approached incessantly to buy Tiger Balm, change money (U.S. dollars were like gold), take rides in rickshaws, sell my sunglasses!, look at carpet and purchase weird Napali voodoo-looking brass decorations. Although a bit monotonous after a while, the onslaught was much friendlier and less intimidating than in India.

Most people smiled and appeared well-fed and happy, especially the children who still viewed us as a curiosity worth following a few hundred feet behind. The native adults were very busy as well, spinning yarn, washing clothes or carrying heavy items on their heads from place to place. Around midday, I walked down to the river and witnessed a neighborhood of kids and pigs digging together harmoniously in a continuous garbage dump a half-mile long. It was virtually impossible to identify anything remotely edible or usable out of the dozens of plastic bags being filled and brought back to parents for a thorough examination!

Back at "the ranch" later that afternoon, we treated ourselves with a rare mid-trip look at a roll of film and a quick call to our parents. Susan felt rested enough to hobble to a nearby shopping bazaar and help me bargain for some colorful carry bags and tee shirts for loved ones back home. While relaxing in our "infirmary" throughout the day, she compiled a heartfelt list of "Things I Miss a Lot":

- Home (family and friends)
- Good food of any kind (especially Mexican, Doritoes, cheese, cereal, the grill, popcorn with Parmesan cheese, green salads, etc.)
- Clothes washed in a washer and dryer
- Talking on the telephone (with no time limit!)
- Car/interstate travel
- My choice of music
- Comfortable double bed mattress
- My pillow
- Time alone
- Receiving mail
- A good haircut/shampoo
- Dressing up
- Going barefoot
- Carpet
- Going to church
- Seeing all of our pictures
- Grocery stores
- Clean, indoor, flush toilets
- Cooking/baking
- Unleaded gas/emission control

A change of venue to the clean Holy Lodge gave us a little more room to sort through our belongings and prepare for the next major segment of the trip—the beaches of southern Thailand! The "temple tour" was rapidly drawing to a close and not a minute too soon.

Departure day from every country was memorable in its own right but throw in language barriers and conniving bureaucracy and the likelihood of conflict increases exponentially. We started sensing that trouble might be on the horizon when we met a couple from California who had been waiting two days to leave on Royal Nepal Airlines because of "visa problems."

While in line to get our final passport stamps for departure, the three people in front of us encountered difficulties of their own. Only after lengthy discussions were they allowed to leave the country. As usual, three guys were standing at the immigration counter to do the job of one. After stamping my passport, they muttered something between themselves before looking up, shaking their heads and handing Susan's back to us! Apparently, the immigration office in Pokhara had forgotten to stamp hers with the proper departure date. We tried to explain that we were obviously together, and that we entrusted *their* government to get the stamp date right, but they replied that it was *our* responsibility to make sure it was recorded correctly! They tried to bribe us into paying US$60 to be allowed to leave the country, knowing that the only flight of the day to Bangkok was scheduled to leave in thirty-five minutes. We decided that the only way to win the battle was to give them a dose of their own medicine and try to overcome them with paperwork. We brought out ragged trekking permits, as well as proof of every rupee that we got converted from dollars while in the country. Somehow, some way, after yet another huddle, they were begrudgingly satisfied that we were telling the truth about the length of our stay and that we had spent an appropriate amount of rupees to substantiate our claim. With a final glare and a quick, messy stamp of approval, we were on our way.

Back in Thailand: Civilized Heat

Six weeks in India and Nepal gave us a renewed appreciation for our long lost, suddenly very civilized- feeling friend called Bangkok. Of all the major cities we had visited in the Far East, Bangkok had a certain charm that put it a notch above the rest in our minds, despite the pollution, the noise and the masses of humanity therein. Perhaps it was the delicious and cheap food from the Koh San Road street vendors, the innocent, helpful smiles of the locals, or the breezy rides in the river taxis up and down the Phrya River. Whatever the attraction, we knew that by heading south, we were retaining most of the good qualities and relinquishing some of the bad. The time had finally come to head for the beach!

Three bus segments and a two-hour boat ride through the calm waters of the Gulf of Thailand brought us to the entry dock of Koh Samui, an island renowned for its easygoing, relaxing atmosphere and white beaches. We opted to catch a songthaew to the more quiet of the two primary tourist areas, Lamai Beach, and found the Weekender bungalow with cold shower, double bed and native lizards in abundance for 150 baht (US$6). The sandy "boardwalk," located between the bungalow and the beach, was replete with restaurants, discos and bathing suit shops. After locating Susan a salmon-colored one-piece, it was only a matter of minutes before my sun goddess would step into action.

April was among the hottest months, as well as the slowest, tourist-wise, on the island. We benefited greatly on the first night at Noy's, our restaurant of choice, where we got incredibly delicious food and impeccable service. With a candlelight setting under the stars and great music as a backdrop, we were coddled from start to finish in a scene befitting of royalty. Generous portions of squid cocktail, grilled prawn, salad, fresh fruit, bread and surprisingly tasty iced tea set us back a mere US$15!

The primary escape from the blazing rays was also the only indigenous money maker on the island, the coconut tree, which yielded over two million coconuts a month for shipment to Bangkok. We were told that most of them were plucked by trained monkeys! Since the beach was relatively uninhabited, we became quite familiar with the large and muscular Thai masseuse ladies that roamed the hot sand looking for anyone who wanted to become a human pretzel. Broken bones and sprained ligaments were the first thing that came to mind when I saw them ply their trade on fellow beachcombers. A root canal suddenly seemed enticing by comparison! While Susan laid on her stomach, deep-frying her buns, I traversed the length of the white, sandy shore and unexpectedly stumbled on beach hut paradisimo supremo at the end of a rocky cove. Sunrise Bungalows would become our second home on the island.

One of the countless advantages of traveling one- backpack-apiece-light was the ease of changing lodging arrangements in a matter of minutes. Sunrise was only a fifteen-minute walk away and fit the description of the type of place we were dreaming about whenever we felt sorry for ourselves in India.

We were shown to a tiny, quaint, A-frame cottage within fifty giant steps of the ocean and about ten steps from a roomy, open-air restaurant/reading area with ceiling fans, a rare and wonderful commodity in the ultrasticky climate. Our hobbies for the two days there, skinny dipping, sunset watching, star gazing and squid cocktail consuming, helped us forget the hot, sweaty, restless nights very quickly. In a semiconscious stupor on the last night, I stumbled onto our tiny porch in search of an elusive breeze, and actually fell asleep, awaking just in time to see the bungalow's namesake emerge over the deep blue gulf.

Despite the laid-back charm of the areas we visited, I left the island of Koh Samui with an uneasy feeling about its future. A recently completed airport would almost certainly escalate the magnitude of tourist activity and the entry/ departure port city of Nathon was already a garbage dump. It seemed very strange to be admiring the afternoon sun, as it melted between two almost perfectly-symmetrical islands in the distance, while huge rats scurried on the polluted, garbage-strewn beach at low tide in the foreground. Inundated with the revving engines of motorcycles and motor scooters and a seedy, underbelly feel reminiscent of Tijuana, Nathon did the island no favors in the final impression department.

A four-hour bus ride due west to Krabi offered some excellent views of the trademark geological feature of the area, rock formations known as karsts. We caught another songhaew to a recommended, secluded bungalow in the coastal community of Ao Tang Villa, a very quiet beach community with no more than ten bungalows, a few restaurants and one small television screen outside of a bar to watch videos. With almost nonexistent entertainment options, it was definitely a place to downshift another full gear.

The restaurants were fairly populated with older-looking Western men and their quiet, demure, Thai "girlfriends" who looked longingly into their eyes across the tables. It is very common for prostitutes to offer "companionship junkets" to secluded areas like Krabi or Koh Samui for up to a week at a time for unbelievably low prices in the 1000 baht range.(about US$50) The highlight of our abbreviated stay in Krabi was a longtail (long, narrow boats resembling canoes that are popular in southern Thailand) boat excursion into the Phangnga Bay.

After a day of Frisbee-tossing, shell-searching and lotion-lathering at Ao Tang, we packed our bags again and set out for the third segment of our search for the perfect beach. After wading into waist-deep water to board an anchored longtail about 8:30 in the morning, we stepped out across a slippery, bouncy plank onto a bigger boat for the one-and-a-half hour journey to Koh Phi Phi (pronounced Pee Pee). Koh, we figured out, means island, and this very recently inhabited one had a decidedly tropical, Caribbean feel. After walking through an extremely overcrowded, trashy-looking "downtown" area of bamboo hut shops, restaurants, food stalls and travel agents, we settled into a comparatively overpriced (300 baht), unattractive, concrete bungalow. We were told that the high price was reflective of our close proximity to ultra-touristy Phuket.

We immediately befriended a loquacious and very interesting forty-four year-old Dutch woman who had been working in the travel business for twenty-five years and knew six languages fluently. It was wonderful getting travel tips from someone else for a change and she invited us to visit her when we were in the Amsterdam area.

Another boat tour, for only 150 baht apiece, featuring a cave visit, an edible lunch of fried rice and cucumbers, water, snorkel equipment and four, fun companions, followed the next day. My primary motivation for taking this tour was to get reacquainted with snorkeling, an activity that we came to enjoy thoroughly on The Great Barrier Reef. The cloudless, sunny sky helped to improve visibility in the already crystal clear waters, and we stopped on three different occasions to admire the incredible variety of unusual, colorful fish. For the first time, I felt really comfortable being tossed out into fifty feet of water.

The next day's boat ride to wonderfully desolate Koh Lanta was breezy and very comfortable, the perfect setting for an extended daydream peering out over the horizon. We were determined to find at least one place devoid of an onslaught of travelers, virtually untouched by modern civilization, and this was it. In fact, there were no more than a hundred people, natives and travelers combined, on the entire island.

The Lanta port area, built entirely on stilts, was extremely rudimentary in comparison to Koh Samui and Phi Phi's over-development. We listened to the sales pitches of several bungalow operators around the dock, and decided on one, appropriately-coined Paradise, on the far side of the island. An exhilarating thirty-minute lift in the back of a pickup truck, through mud puddles and potholes the size of industrial kitchen sinks, reminded us of Chitwan in Nepal, and the glimpses of coconut trees and virgin coast were the image of southern Thailand we had envisioned months before. We picked out a hut close enough to the water to be lulled asleep by the crashing waves.

Reading, postcard writing and card playing were our primary inside activities over the next two days, sandwiched between many, hot, sticky hours of frolicking beach time. Susan posed in and around the crashing surf in her one piece as I did my best to impersonate a *Sports Illustrated Swimsuit Edition* photographer! The lighting was perfect and I was amazed at the quality of the shots when we got them developed.

The last day in Thailand saw us abruptly turn off the final episode of *Fantasy Island* and resume another segment of the ongoing series, "Boats, Buses and Trains." The country ended up being one of the most pleasant surprises of the entire trip, as our original plan to stay two weeks there quickly stretched to six. For the budget traveler with diverse interests and a sense of adventure, it is close to utopia.

"Please God, help me stay thin. You can fade the tan."
—*Susan on the way to Malaysia*

Malay Peninsula

Although we had met many people who chose to view Malaysia as no more than an inconvenient speed bump between Thailand and Singapore, I was attracted by the very fact that few people found it worthy of a look. Since it was eleven days until we had to fly out of Singapore for points west, it seemed like a great place to explore and say a few prayers after surviving the last near-disastrous bus ride in Thailand.

Malaysia is a polyglot of cultures with large segments of Moslems, Chinese and Indians among its populace. A relatively prosperous country making an elongated, but smooth transition into Westernization, it is very easy to enter, get around in and converse in. Almost every person we met there spoke fluent English.

During original trip preparation, travel agent Arthur Mills had whet my appetite about the so-called "jungle train" into Malaysia and we were far from disappointed. Verdant rain forests glistened with recently dampened leaves on both sides of the chugging locomotive as we made our way towards Tapah, at the base of the Cameron Highlands. Mist from a drenching rain shower covered our faces through the half-closed windows of our third-class berth.

By the time we reached the train station in Tapah, it was late in the afternoon and almost dark, and we missed the last bus to the Highlands by fifteen minutes. A businessman/ traveler from Paris shared our situation, so we decided to split cab fare for the fifty-mile trip that would feature over 500 curves on the way to the precipice. We had our pick of several taxi driver prospects and chose the cleanest cut and most Western-acting of the group. It was definitely our lucky day as our chauffeur turned out to be not only an expert driver (extremely unusual in this part of the world!), but a great tour guide and a versatile conversationalist as well. We were informed about a recent reduction in school holidays for children to help the country better compete academically with other cultures (most notably Singapore), the rapid industrialization that the country was going through, the amazing number of species of butterflies in the Highlands, and the fact that the country had been free of Communist rule for twenty years. Our chat was tantamount to listening to a welcome video, and set the stage for a really enjoyable six days there.

Although situated in the heart of Asia, the Cameron Highlands and the surrounding area could easily be mistaken for the United Kingdom, thanks to its roots as a resort community for British colonists seeking cool refuge from the heat found elsewhere in the country. The number one tourist attraction in the area, as well as the primary source of employment, are the vast expanse of tea plantations with up to 2000 acres of tea bush. We took a guided tour of the Boh Tea Estates where over 200 workers make about M$30 a day (3 Malaysian Dollars = US$1), but have their housing, schooling, etc. paid for by their company. An elaborate process of picking, fermenting, drying and packing is completed before the final product is shipped off to Kuala Lumpur, the largest city in Malaysia.

The combination of cool, misty weather and green, rolling hills was extremely invigorating to me after three months in much warmer climates. While Susan had visions of curling up with a good book on the bed dancing in her head, I was immediately drawn to the miles of weaving trails throughout the woods around us and the prospect of getting a week's worth of exercise in a single day. Shortly after lunch on our last full day in the Highlands, I set out to do just that.

My naive infatuation for the woods quickly turned into "I hope I get out of here alive" reality the deeper I walked along the damp, foggy, sloshy, muck of a trail. Fallen branches lay in my path around every bend and strange, jungle sounds permeated the grayness. Halfway through the ten-mile trek, I noticed my heart rate and pace quicken as my fear of leeches and snakes, (at least for that day), and realization that I was helplessly alone, intersected for the first time. After close to an hour in a cold sweat, the trail mercifully started to widen and overhanging branches became fewer and farther between. Fields of flowers that I had heard so much about suddenly came into view about the same time I spotted three other humans ahead of me. I don't think I've ever been more relieved to see people before.

A farewell picnic on our bed featuring peanut butter and fresh strawberry jam sandwiches, whole wheat bread, oranges and Dramamine set us in motion for yet another lengthy bus trip to Kuala Lumpur. The humidity seemed to rise at a rate of 10 percent an hour on the way there and by the time we reached our destination at nightfall, it felt like we were in a greenhouse.

A German girl whom we had met on the bus showed us the way to our first lodging choice, but unfortunately it was full. Seemingly hours later, sweating like pigs and extremely testy, with loaded backpacks and a thirty-pound carry bag (full of gifts we had accumulated to ship home from Singapore), we finally settled on a youth hostel. Any thought of staying in Kuala Lumpur longer than twelve hours was quickly dispelled as we settled into the prison-like surroundings that would be our home for the night.

We stopped at Mickey D's that night and promised to make it our last stop at one until August. Just to make sure we weren't going to miss anything by not staying in K.L., we walked the streets for a while to relieve some tension. The scene reminded me of a low-scale Hong Kong with food stalls everywhere, the familiar smell of Indian/Chinese food, tacky souvenir stands, book shops and guys doing caricatures. After watching a solo musician in front of the hostel performing a sad imitation of Mick Jagger, I took a cold shower to wash off the sweat and called it a night.

Bright and early the next morning, we were headed for the historic port city of Malacca. Originally a humble fishing village, the area grew into a powerful trading center for gold, silk, tea, opium and perfume between the East and West. For 500 years, it was a site of constant turmoil between greedy suitors from Portugal, the Netherlands and England. After the last British rule ended in 1957, the town declared its independence. It now thrives on showing off the artifacts of an exciting past.

We were greeted by the happy faces of several guest house owners, all bearing pictures of the accommodations they were pitching to us. Amy Guest House, owned and operated by a long-haired, Malaysian guy named Amy, looked cozy and clean with a dining and lounging area, perfect for mingling with fellow guests, catching up on some magazine reading and cooking our own food. We even caught a glimpse of CNN, our first exposure to television since Tokyo, 4 1/2 months before!

Before heading out for a leisurely, self-styled walking tour of the city, we did our first load of laundry in almost a month and Susan got a haircut from a Malaysian beautician student for a whopping fifty cents! We primarily visited fortresses and churches built by the Portuguese and Dutch during the sixteenth through eighteenth centuries.

Around 10 p.m. that night, a British couple from the guest house joined us at a Light and Sound Show, a first for Asia, and apparently very similar to a performance shown at the Egyptian pyramids. The light and sound was "shaped to the environmental time frames from 1511 to the present" in a very entertaining and intense fashion.

The Clean City

After the hassles we had experienced leaving chaotic and unorganized India and Nepal, the fact that the checkpoint into Singapore set us back only ten seconds seemed very strange. We were expecting something closer to a full body and bag search from an incomparable monitoring machine like Singapore. Once inside the independent city-state limits, we found the streets adorned with nicely manicured trees and flowers. "Strictly enforced" signs were everywhere, ranging from littering (S$500, which equated to about US$300), to gum chewing, to failure to flush a toilet. Drug trafficking is punishable by death and no fewer than seventy-five hangings have taken place over the past two decades to prove it! The pristine environment, tough stance on crime and misdemeanors and obsession with prosperity is the culmination of three decades of vision by one man, Prime Minister Lee Kuan Yew, who brought Singapore back from the ashes of despair. Once settled by Malaysians and then the Brits, today it is a tiny independent republic that over three million people call home.

Although it was a bit stuffy for our tastes, Singapore nevertheless had a lot to offer two vagabonds in need of services and a respite from practicing survival techniques. It was our first designated mail point since Bangkok and we made quite a haul with eighteen letters and five packages! The highlights were definitely the four pairs of underwear that Susan got from her parents and the sports magazines sent by my parents. The tallest hotel in the world, the Stamford Westin, was only a few blocks away so we paid the obligatory visit to add it to our list of superlative sights.

Getting "rained out" of a day's activities was almost unheard of on our trip, but thanks to a rather noisy electrical storm, it did happen one of the days in Singapore. Feeling a need to release some creative expression, we constructed a fake ransom note to Susan's parents (the keepers of our worldly possessions back home) using letters cut out one by one from newspapers, Burger King wrappers, tourist brochures and a Quaker Chewy granola box! It read like this:

"Dear Parent, We have your children. We, the members of the FTG (Friendly Terrorist Group), demand one batch of chocolate-chip oatmeal cookies sent to the GPO in Zurich, Switzerland by mid-June. Their release depends on it. If you fail to comply, they will be issued continuous around-the-world tickets with no stops! If we were you, we'd send the package...

Sincerely,
The FTG

Singapore is meticulously designed and planned, from the roads and subways to the airport, buildings and beautifully manicured lawns, medians and store fronts. It was like somebody said, "Okay, let's start today with a clean slate," and an extremely organized committee mapped the whole thing out. No other city that I had ever seen even came close in cleanliness and efficiency.

In addition to being tidy and well-kept, the city-state is also one of the most prosperous as well. The level of middle-class prosperity is underscored by the fact that nearly 90 percent of Singaporean adults own their own homes and the work force is rated the best in the world in terms of productivity, skill and attitude by the Business Environment Risk Intelligence service. A well-noted downside is that the people have very little freedom.

It was raining again on our last day in Singapore and since Susan was in one of those "I'm content right here nestled up with my book" moods, I decided to solo it to the highly-acclaimed zoo and bird parks. If time was not a major issue, I always enjoyed taking the city bus wherever we were to get a real authentic feel of the ebb and flow of life among the locals. It was also inexpensive and allowed me to be more spontaneous and get off if something out of the window looked appealing.

The zoo was aesthetically pleasing in terms of its physical layout and natural setting, but after seeing many of the same animals in the wild over the past year, the captivity thing really bothered me. It just didn't seem unpredictable or interesting enough, not to mention the animal freedom part. I can see paying a visit again with kids in tow, but not before.

It took several different bus connections and a lengthy walk to get there from the zoo, but the Jurang Bird Park was really worth the trouble. Condors, pelicans, flamingos and ostrich were among the 350 species and over 8000 birds in the beautifully landscaped park, built for Singaporeans who are known to revere their feathered friends the way Americans adore dogs and cats.

The time had finally come to bid farewell to a Southeast Asia that we had come to enjoy immensely. The only regret we had was not having any more time to explore Vietnam, Burma, Indonesia or China, but it's always great to have an excuse for a return visit! Our long-awaited summer in Europe was only a plane ride away.

"A border is always a temptation."
—*Larry McMurtry*

"...travel is more than the seeing of sights; it is a change
that goes on, deep and permanent, in the ideas of living."
—*Miriam Beard*

"A journey is a person in itself; no two are alike. And all the plans,
safeguards, policies and coercion are fruitless. We find after years
of struggle that we do not take a trip; a trip takes us."
—*John Steinbeck*

Europe

There is not another continent in the world that Americans are more attracted to than Europe. The lure of being able to visit a variety of countries and customs whose histories date back centuries instead of decades, even for a meager two-week stay, is simply irresistible. Guidebooks abound for the time-impaired tourist, with explicitly detailed descriptions of every restaurant, castle, hotel and church within the borders of every major city, and even some noteworthy smaller towns as well. We were blessed to have exactly three months from our May 10th arrival to explore the soon to be frontierless Europe, and made a pact with ourselves to use one of those heavy "everything you ever needed to know" guidebooks as sparingly as possible. Our mission while in Europe was very simple: to plan our itinerary no more than three days in advance, to try and stay with friends or acquaintances whenever possible and to see their corner of the world through their eyes, to continue to seek the unusual or rarely sought, and to eat, sleep, and travel on the cheap while never compromising for adventurous or once-in-a-lifetime experiences.

Claudia

The only lodging that we had prearranged before leaving the States was at the Nitz residence in Bingen, Germany. The sole daughter of the family, Claudia was a twenty-three year- old, quadralingual "interpreter in training" who had attended Middle Tennessee State University as an exchange student the year before. We had met her as she worked as a beautician's assistant for Peggy Hollandsworth, a good friend of ours in the Murfreesboro area. Warm, friendly and extremely mature for her age, Claudia seemed genuinely excited to have us visit for a few days to show off her little corner of Germany.

After a very comfortable 11 1/2 hour flight on Qantas Air, we arrived at the Frankfurt Airport, the busiest in Central Europe, at 5:05 a.m. Susan immediately called her family to tell them we were "practically next door," only an ocean away! After some airport browsing, we called our friend Claudia to get instructions on how to get to her quaint little village along the Rhine River.

After several months of trial and error, we were starting to become extremely adept at handling the bombardment of new languages, signs, symbols, money and transportation systems we encountered in every new country. Susan had a knack for picking up bits and pieces of each language, especially the local niceties like "thank-you," "please," and "excuse me." That talent came in handy many times daily when we were asking for directions or a favor. My specialties were coordinating the myriad of transportation selections and schedules, navigating around to check out lodging options and tabulating currency conversions at every purchase.

After a subway ride to Mainz, we walked over to board one of the ultrapunctual, comfortable trains for our much-anticipated entree into the chilly, but sunny, European countryside, dotted with Tudor-style homes and flowery meadows. Claudia was waiting for us in Bingen about noon and chauffeured us to her parents house less than three miles away. Lunch is the main meal of the day in Germany so we were definitely getting into town at exactly the right time! Mother Nitz had a feast of fresh fish, green peas and rice waiting with five kinds of ice cream on deck for desert. It was the first time we had seen the inside of someone's private residence in several months and the around-the-clock availability of a bath, toilet, books, food and personal tour guides was almost overwhelming!

It was refreshing to be able to discard the stereotypical notion of cold, insensitive German people that had somehow gotten lodged in our heads. Time and again throughout our three-day stay, we were amazed at the generous, unselfish hospitality shown by Claudia and her family. We could not have imagined a better way to be introduced to the continent we would call home for the majority of the summer.

The Rhine (Rhein in German) River flows approximately 900 miles through the western half of Germany. We inspected several areas by foot and took a wonderful four-hour cruise up the primary trade artery of the Middle Ages near Bingen. Centuries-old castles, built as fortresses so their owners could defend their towns, were scattered along the thickly wooded shore of the venerable river. Under a canopy of misty, gloomy skies, it was easy to imagine the Romans and barbaric German tribes fighting it out along the terraced banks that were now home to souvenir shops and wineries.

Germans are very fond of eating and drinking and we were introduced to some wonderful home-prepared meals and neighborhood bars during our stay with the Nitz'. Among many other delectable spreads and jams, I was welcomed into the incredible world of Nutella, a chocolate concoction that turns a plain hard roll into a delicacy. It would become a staple in our backpack the rest of the time we were in Europe.

The entire family joined us at a beer garden and neighborhood wine bar on our final night in the area. The owner at Straubwirtschaft Eidt served his own wine and sat down to enjoy it along with the chattering patrons. Like most German meals, an assortment of meats (salamis, hams, bratwurst, etc.), cheeses and breads was the centerpiece. We were surprised to learn at the beer garden that Germans despise ice cold beer, preferring to drink it at room temperature or barely cool. Taste seemed to be the primary purpose of consumption ahead of effect and refreshment. After a wonderful evening of merriment, we thanked our generous hosts for their wonderful hospitality and packed for Frankfurt.

With over 100,000 miles of passenger tracks in Western Europe alone, stretching from the Arctic Circle in Scandinavia to the Mediterranean beaches of Spain, the Eurrail train system offered the perfect primary means of transportation for our kind of journey. With a ninety-day price tag of US$900 apiece that included unlimited train travel plus bonus boat and ferry rides in certain locales, the pass was the easiest and most enjoyable way to bounce from country to country. In addition to being a great place to mingle with fellow travelers, it was also the transportation mode of choice for a good percentage of locals as well.

We were instructed by our travel agent back home to pick up Eurrail passes at the AMEX office in Frankfurt, but unfortunately our tickets to freedom and flexibility had not yet arrived. A succession of calls to Susan's mom and our travel agent revealed that the passes were actually in a "holding pattern," in customs of all places because of their high value! We were instructed to be back at the AMEX office the next day around noon.

We were rightfully nervous that our Eurrail problem was threatening to cause a longer visit in Frankfurt than we had hoped. The day of reckoning arrived and we observed the mandatory 8:30 a.m. check-out at our hostel, taking our backpacks to the train station to store in a locker. The tickets were to be sent FedEx from the customs office to the AMEX office, but 12 o'clock rolled around and they were no where to be found. I started calling FedEx about 1 p.m., and finally got through about 2:15. In the meantime, we impatiently stood near the door of the AMEX office, hoping the package would arrive in time to allow us to catch the last train of the day to Berlin at 3:26. (Somehow I found the fact that both of these companies names ended with EXPRESS very ironic!) After thirty minutes of checking and call backs, I was told that it would be there in five minutes! Tick...tick... at 3:05 it arrived, and we immediately sprinted from the AMEX office to the subway and onward to Hauptbahnhof, the main station. At 3:20, we had luggage in hand, finagled our way to the front of the line to get our passes validated, and made the 3:26 train with three minutes to spare!!

Although the unification of Germany had officially taken place two years before, the train journey to Berlin revealed the noticeable difference between West and East Germany. While the West was modern and affluent-looking in appearance, the Eastern side was almost eerie, with empty streets and houses lit up like a haunted house where no one dares to enter. Cars were very rare and even the land looked unproductive with no apparent agricultural progress.

Berlin

Common sense dictates that it's not a particularly good idea to invade a world-renowned, punker-party capital like Berlin at 11 o'clock at night with no reservations, however, the uncertainty of the day left us with no choice. We were very, very fortunate to avoid spending the night in its very seedy train station.

I immediately sensed that we were in a serious dilemma when every single phone in the station was occupied by young people of one description or another. Due to a major women's tennis tournament, there were literally no youth hostel or hotel rooms available. After a lot of calling and a lot of comparing notes with others around us, we befriended a couple from Atlanta who had seen a hunchback old man outside holding up a sign that said "room." Since he spoke no English and looked rather suspicious, he could find no "takers," even in this desperate situation. The four of us huddled for a minute and decided to take a chance with the guy, figuring we could outrun him up if he tried anything. He beamed a big smile when we gave him the thumbs up signal, and helped us cram our four backpacks and four large bodies into his matchbox-sized Yugo!

I was in the front seat with a backpack in my lap and tried my best to appear interested in his gibberish. The number of streetlights seemed to decrease with every minute that passed and a twinge of paranoia pierced through all of us. I would've bet money we were being driven to Poland to be sold for blue jeans! At long last, we entered a *subdivision*, and moments later "Hunchy" pulled out an *electric garage door opener* of all things. To our amazement, the house was impeccably clean and tidy, and the rooms he gave us had double beds with dunna comforters! We almost felt guilty that we had talked him down to DM25 (25 German deutsche marks = US$15) a night per person...

We were still shaking our heads in amazement as we joined several other guests for a complimentary breakfast of assorted meats, cheeses, bread and coffee. There was even a big screen television with CNN on it in English! Our newfound friends from Atlanta, Christy and Terrence, decided to join us for a day of exploring in East and West Berlin.

It had been eighteen months since the fall of the ninety-three mile long Berlin Wall, and it was fascinating to be able to see remnants of the past and a prelude to the future at the same time. Checkpoint Charlie was the name of the border crossing separating the formerly divided city. Today, it is a museum housing real-life re-creations of successful and unsuccessful escapes, and photographs of people crawling out of car trunks, hoods, undersides and fenders. No warning was given to the inhabitants of East Berlin the night the wall was built and an amazing 50,000 guards kept people from leaving!

A few sections of the original wall remain, with graffiti making its mark on almost every square inch. A thriving industry exists in the Brandenburg Gate area with relics of communism, from East German army uniforms to Russian-style winter hats, binoculars and observation telescopes, sold to the highest bidder. Chunks of the wall (or a piece of brick that looked like it) could be bought for a *very* negotiated price.

An observation floor of a television tower thirty feet taller than the Eiffel Tower gave us a great view of both sides of the Gate. The contrast in color and style was amazing, just like the train ride into Berlin. A huge, luscious green park made up one-third of the West Berlin side with a huge avenue dissecting it. The east was drab with colorless shades of gray and brown. All of the buildings were about the same height and seemed run-down, the result of years of neglect by the socialist government. The chilly, rainy weather seemed very appropriate.

"Bohemian Rhapsody"

The price of the Eurrail permits unlimited segments as long as a person sits in a seat, not on a bed. We were beginning to figure out that an uncomfortable night slumped in a seat was usually compounded by hourly interruptions by ticket collectors and border patrols. Oh well, nobody said that budget travel was supposed to be comfortable. By the time the seven-hour trip to Prague was history, we were cumulatively cramped, groggy and cold, not a particularly good way to start the day in a city for which you have no guidebook, no clue about the money or exchange rate, and no knowledge of the language.

We benefited from Czechoslovakia's newfound freedom from communist control at the very onset. While trading in some deutsche marks for Czech koruna at the exchange counter, I noticed a small sign in the window advertising a room for the night for US$15. It turned out to be the exchange lady herself who had the room and she even knew a little English! She gave us directions to the place and even apologized for having to make us lounge in the hallway until the present tenants could check out. At 5:30 in the morning, we hardly expected to be able to just climb into bed anyway.

A series of rectangular, eight-story, apartment complexes stood at the end of a twenty-minute subway trip. It looked like a government housing project and it was. The communist party constructed the "panelaks" throughout the late 1960's and early 1970's to house the workers that toiled in their system. The original intent was to accompany the planned housing with nearby schools, parks, shopping and community centers and other amenities, but they were so busy creating housing that they sort of forgot about the amenities. What's left is a daily reminder and legacy of the former regime.

Since the end of communist control, the ancient city of Prague has become a magnet for foreign travelers in search of an inexpensive overseas living experience and a good time. Unlike many other European cities like Frankfurt, Prague was spared most of the bombing suffered during the two world wars. Today's combination of old-world charm, a laid-back atmosphere, and the golden opportunities inherent with economic reform is certainly an intoxicating attraction. It'll be interesting to see how this great social experiment and clash of nationalities plays out over the next few years. For now, everyone seems to be adjusting fairly well and some are prospering a lot.

Prague is built on seven hills, providing an array of incredible views of church steeples and picturesque statues from many vantage points. The Charles Bridge, regarded as one of the best in all of Europe, is the nucleus of activity in the city, a sort of international meeting place populated with musicians, entertainers, souvenir stands and vendors. The variety of performances was inspiring, from a little eight-year-old kid playing a flute while sitting on a statue (one of thirty Baroque statues of various saints and sinners that line the sides of the bridge) under reconstruction to hilarious puppet acts and full-scale, five-piece bands. In a hundred-square-foot area, we saw all sorts of combinations of cellos, violins, pianos, drums, bagpipes, clarinets and trumpets being played! Artists busily sketched drawings of the variety of castles and other buildings in the distance, while simultaneously trying to sell what they had already done.

The thousand-year-old Prague Castle has always been the official seat and place of coronation of Czech sovereigns, and since 1918, it has been the seat of the Presidents of the Czech Republic. Perched in royal splendor atop a high bluff, it looks like it was created for Walt Disney's magic kingdom. The nearby Cathedral of St. Vitrus was an impressive church with towering stained-glass windows pulchritudinously illuminated by the morning sun.

While it wasn't really a conscious decision on our part, the aimless, mapless, wide-eyed, open-minded approach is really the only way to experience Prague. Almost every small, winding street has a surprise, from random beautiful statues on rooftops and windowsills, to ancient paintings gracing the sides of many buildings. It is one of the few, true, walking cities that rewards the curious, every hour of the day.

Susan felt a special affinity for Czechoslovakia since her dad's ancestors came from the country and her maiden name, Klika, while fairly rare in the United States, was listed in the Prague phone book *sixty-five* times! She saved the page for her father as a souvenir and picked up a few other bits of memorabilia as well.

Whenever possible, we tried to make Mondays our "travel day," since most museums and other attractions in Europe were closed. A 4:30 a.m. wake-up call was required to allow us to make it to Budapest by way of Vienna, Austria in a single day.

Sixteen hours of yellow mustard fields and eight passport checkpoints after "lift-off," we arrived at a filthy train station in Budapest, teeming with bums and gypsies. With an immediate bombardment of "change money mister" and "good room for you" mutterings, it felt like we had arrived in Varanasi, India all over again. Just in time to save our wavering sanity, a nicely dressed, nonthreatening woman in her mid-twenties swam through the throngs and stood before us. She told us that she would pay for our bus ticket if we accompanied her to check out a room located in the back of her house.

We were shown a spacious "flat" with kitchen, bathroom, huge living room and four beds to choose from for US$15 a night! Having our own bathroom was a luxury we only dreamed about. The talkative lady spoke six languages, English, Hungarian, Russian, Polish, German and French, and provided us with a thoughtful dialogue of "must sees and dos" in her city. She spoke openly of her elation about the recent liberation because of the free-lance job opportunities it created, but said that it was harder in many ways because there were no longer any guarantees. Shedding some light on the dozens of gypsies (mostly middle-aged ladies) populating the train station, she informed us that they were from Romania, in search of a better life outside of their repressed country. We became extremely fond of our new friend and were happy to be supplementing her husband's paltry US$150-a-month plumber earnings.

Budapest's elaborate subway system was efficient and easy to use, and best of all, free! We got on and off at our leisure and never saw an attendant over two days. The focal point of the city is Deak Square, where twenty-first century shopping flash and frenzy collide with lines of sad-looking Romanian ladies standing outside hawking scarves, rugs and embroidered, cloth, table mats. It was obvious from the brand-conscious feel of the crowd why Budapest had earned the title of the "Paris of the East." Susan found a silk scarf to her liking and we picked up a perfect homemade apron from one of the Romanian ladies for our Grandma.

Mozartville

Vienna was one of the places that we were advised to make reservations in before arriving, but the local youth hostel inexplicably canceled our advance booking and for the second time in two weeks, we were in real danger of not finding a room. Ninety minutes of persistent phone calls finally resulted in success in the form of a 420 shilling (12 shilling = US$1) a night motel about fifteen minutes from town. Considering the unacceptable US$60+ alternatives in the priciest city we had encountered since Tokyo, I guess we should have felt pretty lucky.

Susan's love of the piano after years of lessons and her appreciation of classical music made Vienna a special destination for her. The primary reason for the rush on rooms was a lot of hoopla centered around the 200-year anniversary of Wolfgang Mozart's death. Before our three-day visit was finished, we were convinced that the city should be renamed Mozartville! Without trying especially hard, we saw the house he grew up in, a special exhibit set up in his honor, a headstone honoring him, and an opera that featured his music. Ironically, Mozart was actually appreciated little while he was living and playing in the social and political circles of Vienna. He died at a young age, totally broke, and was buried in a mass grave because a more appropriate one could not be afforded!

We walked around dodging cold rain drops for three solid days. The State Opera House (Staatsoper) was the most impressive-looking building in town as well as the focal point of Viennese social life. Marble statues of Beethoven, Hadyn, and of course Mozart, are displayed prominently in the enormous building that has been almost entirely rebuilt since being bombed in World War II. We watched a large team of construction guys set up the massive and complex stage for the evening show where seats would go for as much as US$250 in the first six rows of the Emperor's Box. After an afternoon trip to the cemetery, a bus dropped us off at Staatsoper again, and although we were attired in jeans and a sweater and were dripping wet, I insisted that we take a shot at getting a standing-room-only ticket. There were 500 standing slots in total and due to the inclement weather, a few of those tickets were still available. Since we were far removed and not visible to the paying, tuxedoed patrons, the dress code was surprisingly unenforced. All we really wanted was a taste of it anyway, and at US$1.50 apiece, it was worth every mouthful!

A 334-step, spiraling staircase at St. Stephens church gave us an added bolt of aerobic exercise before we went down into the twelfth-century Gothic cathedral for a look around. The view from the top was worth the effort even though the dreary cloud cover didn't do the skyline any favors. While Susan called her parents to get the Singapore ransom note reaction, I engaged in a lively conversation with a middle- aged couple and their daughter from Ohio. After a half hour of filling them in on our travels and comparing notes on places seen and to be seen, I guess they felt pretty comfortable with me. When Susan walked up, the lady blurted out, "you need a haircut honey!" Another forty-five minutes later, we had some great lodging tips and the women were all hugging each other good-bye. Another man we met shortly afterwards said he saw the picture of "the Freedom Riders" (our bike group from the previous summer) in the Cleveland paper—very small world.

Salt, Hitler and Julie Andrews?!

Seasoned travelers themselves, Heinz and Trude Poppenberger boarded back-packers in their comfortable little house in Salzburg. In addition to offering a spotlessly clean room and standard bread and jam-style breakfast, they took more than a casual interest in their guest's sightseeing plans and overall well-being while in the area, arranging bus tours, maps, books and even a pick up at the train station. Despite the fact that it was late in the afternoon when we arrived, they were able to get us squeezed into the ultra-popular *Sound of Music* bus tour for the very next morning.

Although I hadn't seen the movie in twenty-five years and had little remembrance of it at all, the perfect synchronization of tour guide humor, interesting tidbits, beautiful scenery and sunshine made for a memorable day. Songs from the movie were thoughtfully interspersed into the running commentary as we passed landmark buildings and sites from it, such as the primary living quarters, the Wedding Chapel, Marabellas Garden and Utesburg Mountain. On the way back to Salzburg in the afternoon, we took a pit stop at a ski resort that was operating a toboggan course in the off-season. After a pulley ride to the top of the mountain, we slid back down along a narrow, winding path in a brakeless bolt of speed that was pure exhilaration!

Although beer drinking is the favorite pastime in Salzburg, Mozart was born there and Hitler hung out near there, the city actually got its name from the abundance of salt mines in the area. To help foster an authentic experience in the mines, all participants in the underground tour are dressed in coal miner-looking outfits, overalls and cloth jackets. The best part of the tour was an austere German guide who led us around with his nonchalant, deadpan humor. To take a jab at us "yanks," he simply banged the English signs with his hand and said "English" instead of going through the explanation of a topic like he did in German. He talked in a totally unexcited monotone that sounded like it would end in zzzzz after each thrilling sentence.

Next on the agenda was a visit to Eagle's Nest, Hitler's hideout on top of a mountain near Salzburg. The panoramic view from the front yard of his week-end home was unparalleled and awe-inspiring, the only time I have ever felt like I was standing on top of the world. The road to the top, series of tunnels around the area and house itself were amazingly constructed in a single year leading up to a surprise fiftieth birthday party on April 20, 1939. The guys who worked on it were highly skilled, highly motivated and well-paid Germans who got generous benefits the rest of their lives for taking part in the colossal effort.

Blasted out of the mountain, the most fascinating parts of the structure were the nine-foot-tall tunnels and a 124-foot elevator shaft with green leather seats and brass mirrors. It was obviously a safe haven and the house was never damaged during an air raid (unlike his primary house and compound in Obersalzburg which were destroyed). Hitler lived at Eagle's Nest with Eva Braun for several years before "tying the knot" with her on April 28, 1945, just forty hours before they committed double suicide. It was confiscated by American occupation troops shortly afterward and kept under surveillance until 1952, then reopened for tourists. After a timely visit to a 5000-seat beer garden to digest and discuss the thought-provoking events of the day, we strolled hand and hand along the rushing Salzach river that separates the old and new towns of Salzburg. A sudden burst of warmer, breezy, springlike weather was the perfect finale to our short stint in Austria.

Trude's parting gesture of cordiality was to arrange for us to stay with her son Heinz and daughter-in-law Chrissy in Munich, where they were in the experimental stages of the lodging business. We set up camp in their living room area, and were provided with our own eating table, bowl of fruit, drinks and walking-around munchies. The couple had been married for five months and had a month-old daughter, Natalie. Chrissy was still adjusting to life in Germany, as she had just moved over from Boston two years before. Our new hosts were extremely accommodating, even to the point of preparing a very unGerman-like breakfast treat of scrambled eggs to go with the mouth-watering Nutella on bread. After a great, relaxing meal, we decided to embark on our conscious-raising trip to Dachau, Hitler's very first concentration camp.

A total of 200,000 prisoners, predominantly Jews, gypsies, religious types and others who were caught speaking against Hitler's regime, passed through the gates of the camp between 1933 and 1945. Dachau was one of the most important ammunition factory sites for the Germans and many of the "fortunate" prisoners were allowed to work in the ammo product facility throughout the war. Those less fortunate were subjected to horrendous conditions with frequent episodes of torture, no dignity or privacy at all and barely enough food to keep themselves alive.

We walked around the camp area where two reconstructed barracks still remain with 400 beds cramped into a space big enough for about sixty. Inspections of the bunks that found the slightest remnant of dirt or perception of untidiness could result in some form of torture. All visitors whispered out of respect—if you closed your eyes, you could almost hear and see it as it was sixty years before. The absolute worst section we saw had to be the baking ovens where the emaciated bodies were tossed in together and cremated. Unlike Auchwitz, the gas chamber was never used.

An afternoon stroll around the meticulously landscaped, tulip-inundated Marianplatz area yielded a trio of hand- crafted beer steins for Grandma, Uncle Bobby and Dad. With beer on the brain, we decided it was only fitting to pay Hofbrauhaus, arguably the most famous suds hall in the world, a visit.

The last night at the Poppenberger residence was a good one for both of us— I played a few games of chess and male-bonded with Heinz, and Susan engaged in some long overdue, girl talk with Chrissy. It was the culmination night of an extremely fortunate string of lodging choices. Italy would jolt us back into reality for awhile.

"Da Boot"

We arrived in Venice on the cusp of the peak visitor season when over 100,000 outsiders a day clog the alley ways and waterways of one of the most popular cities in Europe. It actually feels more like a Disney amusement park than a real- life city, making it hard to imagine anyone actually working there, except in shops, museums or restaurants catering to tourists.

At its zenith in the fifteenth century, Venice was much, much more than a place to walk around in shorts and sneakers and look at things. Magnificent palaces and churches, a renowned school of arts, and its charmed watery setting made it a living city, a rich and powerful entity that ruled a vast maritime empire. The ravages of nature and the unrelenting tourist invasion have taken their toll on a place built on wooden piles driven into the center of a crescent-shaped lagoon. Tides and floods regularly leave parts of it underwater and the cost of living is exorbitant because of the expense of bringing everything in by boat and on foot. Despite its immense character and uniqueness, Venice is tragically sinking, albeit very slowly, into the Adriatic Sea.

The most noticeable attribute of Venice is its conspicuous lack of cars or air pollution. Canal ferries (vaporetti) are the primary means of transport since the popularized, stud-paddled gondolas are too pricey for the average traveler. Dozens of the water buses can be seen in the sloshing waters throughout the day, carting people back and forth to St. Mark's Square, as well as outlying islands.

We divided our time equally between St. Mark's Square, getting lost on purpose in the narrow cobblestone alleyways, and sitting in cafes sipping cappuccino and eating cheap spaghetti. The Square had a spacious open spot in its interior, surrounded by the most famous and impressive landmarks in the city, St. Mark's Cathedral, Palazzo Ducale, and a bell tower. The pigeons outnumbered the throngs of people and had no problem staying satisfied with all the eateries around. I'm sure we would have felt differently about the caliber of the cuisine had we decided to "break the bank" and splurge in a nice restaurant or two. The unimaginative fare at the "pay double to sit down" places we frequented was still expensive by our budget travel standards, but at least we enjoyed the people watching.

When names like Julius Caesar and Michelangelo become a regular part of a day's conversation, you know you're either playing trivial pursuit too long or the train has just arrived somewhere in Italy. Welcome to Florence, the birthplace of the Italian Renaissance and the home to more museums and sculptures per square foot than any other city in the world.

Not being particularly scholarly or a connoisseur of the arts, the primary concerns for the duration of our stay in Italy were to keep from getting robbed, to see David, the sculpture, to see the Leaning Tower, and to try and find the Pope. All other deviations and distractions were merely build-ups or afterthoughts to the primary goals.

It seemed like the longer we stayed in Europe, the more expensive eating and sleeping were becoming. A clean, but unimpressive room set us back 59,000 lira (that's about US$48) and cafeteria-caliber food was running close to US$8 a head. We were definitely getting a very strong impression that this was the land of the "loot," and he who didn't have it or didn't want to spend it was left "in the cold." We were wondering out loud how so many college students could afford to "live it up" in a country like this.

We only had to wait in line for thirty minutes or so to see my statuesque namesake and I'll have to admit that it was pretty impressive. It was given an entire, dome-shaped room to itself, so that no one would be left wondering if they had actually seen it. Our 10,000 lira donation also allowed us to peek at seven other Michaelangelo pieces and a whole room of sculptured heads. There's something about the three-dimensional effect of sculpture that makes it much more appealing than a piece of art on a wall.

Gypsy bandits were all over the place as we had read and heard they would be. Even the churches weren't spared! In fact, they were an extremely popular place for the pickpockets to work their magic, since they were dimly lit and people were praying and not paying attention.

The town of Pisa was a convenient, two-hour side trip from Florence. The Tower, and two government buildings next to it, looked almost surreal with the magnificently manicured lawns and sleazy sunglass and bag salesman. It was hard picturing what the surroundings would have looked like when it was built 800 years before. Today, it's fifteen feet off center, and climbing to the top is no longer allowed.

Amidst all of the line standing and speed walking from church to statue to museum to church in Florence, Susan and I were trying to work our way through an emotional tough spot in the trip. There was no one else around that we could escape to or confide in and the constant togetherness sometimes got the best of us. It would be a relief to get back into the youth hostel scene in Switzerland, where we could connect more readily with fellow backpackers.

A bag of rolls and a full liter of orange juice were the perfect send-off from a very nice manager at the Florence pensione (one-star hotel). What we really needed was a tranquilizer after accidentally heading north on the wrong train in the morning, and then experiencing some four-star "pensione tension" upon arrival in Rome. Although locating a room by phone wasn't the problem this time, tracking it down through the maze of motorbike-infested alleys was no easy chore. Once at our destination, we were led through a series of dimly lit hallways and narrow staircases barely wide enough to fit our bodies and ever-expanding backpacks. Although we were certain that it was an actual dungeon, the room was seemingly rodentfree and safe.

Steeped in political, religious and literary history, the Spanish Steps were a great place to unwind and peruse an extremely diverse crowd of artists, vendors, punkers, gypsies, business people and budget travelers. The native women were a pretentious-looking lot, very well-groomed with an air of turned-up-nose cockiness about them. Maybe "Swank Avenue" across the street, with the likes of Cartier, Hermés and Bulgari on every storefront, had something to do with it. The place was so fashion conscious that even the meter maids wore Gucci!

Spending a day in Rome is like living a chapter of one of your sixth grade history books. To think that a building is 2000 years old and still standing is almost incomprehensible to a generation of Americans that never live in a house long enough to pay off a thirty-year mortgage! The oldest and one of the best preserved monuments was the Pantheon, built in the reign of Augustus Caesar as a temple to all the gods. Throughout its 2018 year life span, the only light that has illuminated the interior is from the sun, shining through a hole in the center of the dome.

If you're not paying attention striding up Via dei Fori Imperiali on the way to the Colosseum, you'd think that you were on your way to a modern-day, sporting event. The wide boulevard was created by Benito Mussolini as a place to hold military parades, and the entire facade of the Colosseum facing it is intact and has the general shape of an American football stadium. As you get closer, it looks more like a 50,000 seat arena that just got incinerated by an atomic bomb. The Colosseum is probably the single most recognizable icon in the city of Rome. In the first century A.D., it was a seat of commerce and government where all business, imperial and mercantile, was conducted. The original "floor" is gone, exposing an intricate labyrinth where lions, prisoners and general provisions were kept. After stopping to observe a group of archaeologists digging in the area, we continued walking towards Circus Maximus, a big, open, grassy field that was the site of the ancient chariot races.

The ruins, fountains and outdoor statues were as much a part of daily city life in Rome as temples were for the Nepali people in Kathmandu. It was not uncommon to see laundry draped across the outstretched arm of an artistic treasure while scores of passersby lounged in its shadows. Many of the structures were located in great squares called piazzas, where solo musicians, as well as five-piece bands, entertained throughout the evenings for no charge.

Susan was in her glory in what has to be the most Catholic city on the face of the earth. Religious book stores and jewelry stores can be found everywhere and she wasted no time finding the perfect little silver cross for her mom. Selecting a cross in Rome is pretty special, but having it blessed at St. Peters Basilica is the "icing on the cake."

The design of St. Peters in its present form drew from the genius of the architectural wizards of its day and took 200 years to finish. Completed in 1626 with a big assist from Michaelangelo before his death, the interior of the building is simply overwhelming in its enormity and unparalleled detail. Marble sculptures sit atop the marble floors of the massive room, at least seven masses take place simultaneously, and confession booths in at least seven languages never miss a beat. It was the most intensely religious feeling place I had ever seen. Susan struck gold by finding two priests that agreed to bless her beloved

cross, one from her home state of Wisconsin and another from Rome!
Postcard stands, featuring X-rated renditions of the David statue as well as
countless variations of Venice party masks, carved out a winding path from the
Basilica to Vatican City. Looking far into the distance, about a football field
away, we spotted a small, high-perched balcony against the wall of a massive
fortress-looking complex. As we were staring intently, several people walked
out on the balcony for a breath of fresh air, including a white-haired, older man
in a white cape and white hat. To this day, I know it was the Pope, even though
the local paper said he was traveling in Eastern Europe!

Museum-whipped, rain soaked and devoid of lira, we waited for several hours
in our hotel lobby, anticipating the notoriously thief-ridden, night train to Lucerne
by way of Milan. I guess we looked pretty pathetic sitting there, writing in our
journals and plotting out future plans, because the lady owner brought us over a
pair of hot zucchini omelets, two pieces of bread and a cookie!

Despite the fact that the pensione gave us a wonderful gesture of kindness, I
instinctively felt uneasy, unsafe and on guard in Rome from the minute we
stepped onto its noisy, bustling streets. Whether it was the "horror stories" we
had heard, the warnings we had read, the gypsies we had seen, or all of the
above, I found myself extremely suspicious and paranoid the entire time we
were there. If you think people are up to something, after awhile they start
looking guilty. Despite the paranoia and the precautions we took, it didn't do us
any good—we *still* got robbed on the train.

Moved up to the first-class section for no apparent reason, I was thrilled
because I thought we would be more protected from potential trouble there. As
we found out later, that's the *worst* place to be on a train in Europe, since it is
assumed that you have the most money and valuables. We were alone in a six-
seat cabin, and since our seats folded down, we made a makeshift bed out of
them. Our primary backpacks were locked and secured on the top of the compartment and we carried our most valuable possessions in our money pouches
and in a smaller daypack.

The pouches, located inside our shirts, contained money, passports, International Driver's Licenses and credit cards, while the knapsack housed our guidebook, Susan's spare set of contacts, the cross she had purchased for her mom,
sunglasses, a Swiss Army knife and the Eurrail passes. We slept with the knapsack in our sleeping bags because of the ridiculous frequency of Eurrail Pass
inspections throughout the night.

Susan is an especially light sleeper and it is very rare for both of us to remain
sound asleep past 6 o'clock in the morning. The morning after our Rome departure, we were startled by bright sunlight piercing through our window at 7:30
a.m. We immediately commented on how unusual it was for us to sleep through
the early hours of the morning without having to use the bathroom. When I
reached down to look for my toothbrush in the knapsack, I realized that it was
gone.

The cold reality that we had been victimized *again*, despite the conscious effort to avoid it, was very hard to accept. Angry with the train system for failing to install locks on the doors, place curtains on the windows or turn the overhead light out, we knew we were "sitting ducks" for a professional rip-off artist or artists. The only thing we could've done was to take turns staying awake like we were in a battle zone.

Despite the fact that we had traveled far into Switzerland, we decided to change trains and return to the Milan station to look around in trash bins and file a police report. The long line at the police counter suggested a serial bandit and our "how" hypothesis was later confirmed—we had been gassed, most likely while the train was loading and unloading passengers in the Milan station! While we were standing in another line to pay 66,000 lira (US$55) for replacement Eurrail passes, another backpacker came up to us in search of some information. When we told him that our guidebook had been pilfered, he responded that his "fanny pack," with guidebook inside, had been *cut* from his body just a few minutes before!

Unfortunately, it was hard to get excited about the gorgeous mountain scenery en route to Lucerne. While I tried to mope and daydream in silence, Susan was incessant with her "is this really worth it commentary." With no back-up contacts and that sickening, violated feeling, I tried my best to console her. We needed some fresh air, sunshine and open spaces to clear our heads—Switzerland turned out to be "just what the doctor ordered."

Land of the Watch and the Knife

Perfectly situated in the heart of Europe, with enough lakes, waterfalls, lush green meadows and mountain vistas to keep a nature lover happy for a lifetime, Switzerland was our ticket out of the city and back into the sunny, breezy, pollution-free, fresh air. We decided to target youth hostels as our primary accommodation choice in an effort to get back into the "backpacker circuit" and away from the staid, anonymity of the one-star hotel routine. With a network of hundreds throughout Europe, the hostels typically offered dormitory-style housing in rooms accommodating from two to twenty people. Men and women were usually assigned segregated wings or floors and provided with a bed, blanket, pillow and breakfast consisting of toast and coffee for between US$7 and US$12 a night.

On our second and final night in Lucerne, Susan felt like "world traveler celebrity of the month" as a dorm room full of recently graduated, college students surrounded her bed to hear a few tidbits of our story. The "people therapy" she received from chats like these paid big dividends for her, as well as our relationship later.

Before leaving Perth in December, Trixie arranged for us to pay her parents a visit in the tiny Swiss community of Mellington, despite the fact that she was going to be in Canada herself. The Halter elders were just as bubbly as their daughter when we called about seeing them, inviting us to stay as long as we liked. They picked us up at the train station and had a delicious meal of spaghetti, fresh salad, homemade bread and peppermint tea from the garden waiting at home. Within minutes, it felt like we had known them for years. Mr. Halter owned his own trucking company but his wife basically ran the business. She was also quite involved in the local community schools and political scene with a number of plaques rewarding her for not missing a vote on a Mellington issue in over *ten years*! No other democracy in the world allows its citizens to exert such a direct influence on their national and local legislation, with quarterly ballots to vote on laws. Any Swiss citizen can request an amendment to the constitution provided he can find 99,999 other voters who share the same opinion!

The Halters lived in a quiet farm house within earshot of the town clock tower that rang its bell every thirty minutes. It was a modern place by Swiss standards with a refrigerator and dishwasher inside a wooden cabinet in the kitchen, a washer and no dryer. Like in most parts of Europe, a trip to the store was actually a trip to the *stores*. Cheese, meat, vegetables, bread and deserts were all purchased at different places, although they were all within a block of each other, in an area the size of one superstore in the States.

Susan was invited to attend Mrs. Halter's English class one night and ended up doing a "Q and A" session on life in America. Afterwards, the group took their "guest teacher" out for a salad and bottle of wine.

After a filling breakfast of Corn Flakes, lots of bread, butter, fresh strawberry jam and coffee, Trixie's sister, Susie, drove us to nearby Baden to catch the 9:15 a.m. train to Dachsen, home of the largest waterfall in Europe. After a long walk with packs, we found that the youth hostel near the falls was full, but the area was beautiful, with wild flowers in bloom all over the place. After the coldest May on record, summer had finally arrived! Trying to avoid making another long excursion for naught, we called ahead to book a room for the night in OberWinterthur.

A vine-covered, thirteenth-century castle was our lodging choice by happenstance, a half-museum, half-hostel conglomeration unlike anything we had ever seen. The stern, inhospitable warden who demanded three pieces of identification despite our reservation, should have been asking about a vet license or proof of a rabies vaccine instead of picture ID's. Peacocks, donkeys and horses roamed the patio and the roof in numbers far exceeding the patrons.

It was my turn to stay up all night and chat, this time with an interesting chap from London who had a Swiss birth certificate and had lived in Toronto and Detroit. We conversed about everything from politics to women to economics to the European Community to America versus Switzerland, etc. before dozing off in mid-sentence. . .

On the same day that we were to go and pick up the "ransom-dictated," chocolate chip, oatmeal cookies in Zurich, we decided to send another wacky flare in the direction of the keepers of our bank account, car and worldly possessions—an invitation to our own "Welcome Home" party! The note read like this:

> It is with great pleasure and festive anticipation that we announce a huge, elaborate, costly, ostentatious, two-day Welcome Home Bash for Susan and David Klika-Wooten to be given by her parents, Mr. and Mrs. Darwin William Klika, in our own home.
>
> The immense love for our children has brought this momentous occasion into being. It is not necessary to bring anything but gifts or cash, as we will provide the rest.
>
> Some recommended gifts include:
> - A king-sized bed
> - A used '83-'87 Mazda RX7
> - A Queen Anne dining set
> - A 5 1/2 foot baby grand piano
> - Etc.
>
> If by chance you have out-of-state, city or county guests, feel free to bring them (and a gift) along.
>
> We look forward to (hopefully) seeing you, if we can find you amongst the thousands.
>
> Sincerely,
> Bud and Rita Klika
>
> P.S. Don't forget your overnight luggage.
> P.P.S. Just park on the lawn next to or in front of the house.

(Bud hated it when we drove on the lawn.)

Zurich rewarded us with our fourth and final mail stop. The deeply-appreciated letters and magazines from friends and family were a godsend since the phone calls were extremely expensive and all too few and far between. The letters made the afternoon train ride to Liechtenstein, a country that proclaims its post office as its biggest attraction, go by very quickly. Although it was truly a stamp collector's haven, the main reason most people made the trip was to get another stamp in their passport.

One very important segment of our "land of the watch and the knife" tour remained, a journey into the Alps! From Oberwinterthur to Grindelwald, by way of Winterthur, Zurich and Interladen, the trip was a five-hour, visual feast of wild flowers, rock faces and sun-kissed valleys. The closer we got, the better the views got, all the way up to the entrance of the hardest to reach, but most perfectly situated youth hostel we had been to yet. Nestled into the side of a mountain overlooking the North Face of the Eiger, this piece of property would be worth a million dollars in America.

Grindelwald itself was a quaint, expensive, touristy little city with a friendly, easygoing attitude. We arrived during set-up day for a weekend country music festival and saw over 5,000 Swiss, German and French people playing cowboys and Indian dress-up. Black leather pants, halter tops, boots of all shapes and sizes and license plates from the Western United States were the rave amongst the "take this job and shove it" crowd.

While the country music was echoing through the glacier fields, we set out to explore the natural wonder of the area. After a short claustrophobic walk into an unusual ice cave, we rented mountain bikes to traverse the hilly countryside and found rushing streams overflowing with the residue of winter.

The Coast of France

An unsavory, stationary, cold front quickly convinced us to abort a planned overnight stay in Geneva in favor of a night train to Nice. Hours before the sun would pierce through the window to welcome us to the Mediterranean, the flashlight of a train security guard was pointing towards my face. Although I had been sleeping in fifteen-minute intervals, jumping to attention at the slightest noise or train movement, the sudden glare, coupled with a garbled French message on the loudspeaker, was enough to make our spines tingle. Was it a war, earthquake, murder, robbery, or ... strike?! at 4:30 in the morning?! Sure enough, the employees had chosen this inhumane hour of the night to make a point. Forty minutes later, to our relief, we were traveling in another train that apparently was not on strike.

The heavy scent of perfume and dogs in the turnstiles told us we must have gotten on the right train. With a pet population of thirty-five million in France, more than twice the number of children, dogs and cats throughout the country and in the Cote d'Azur in particular, get the royal treatment. Whether it's the twenty-four hour clinics, animal ambulances, bone and muscle treatments or canine taxis, these animals are pampered, fussed over and spoiled unlike any furry creatures anywhere outside of a zoo.

Thank goodness they couldn't check themselves into a hotel or the last beds at the Hotel Belle Meuniere would not have been ours. Unlike more conservative Switzerland and Germany, the dormitory accommodations in France were usually co-ed throughout, greatly increasing the odds of an entertaining slumber party. We had a total of fifteen different roommates during our three-night stay in Nice and really enjoyed the diversity of meal partners and travel strategists. We arranged to visit a hilarious Swedish girl named Ulwa later in the summer at her flat in Belgium.

We constantly challenged ourselves to find out-of-the-way gems, whether it was a cemetery, museum, beach or even a town. Walking up a precariously steep and rugged back road to the village of Eze, a short train trip from Nice, we felt like Lewis and Clark discovering a new settlement in the wild. The half-mile jaunt was so elevated that it felt like our heads were going to touch the ground in front of us! We could see the outline of what appeared to be an old fortress at the top, but the real spectacle was the "take your breath away," ever-changing view of the expansive shoreline and blue Mediterranean Sea behind us. Hot and sweaty and absolutely exhausted, we clawed and scratched to reach the pinnacle. . .only to find that a swarm of dressed-up, made-up, fresh smelling tourists had already beat us to it, *on tour buses*!

Within minutes, we had blended into the crowd with the quiet satisfaction that we had been touched and inspired by this place like nobody else there. (A few years later, a painting depicting this memory would be a heartfelt birthday present from me to Susan.)

Since perfume appeared to be such a big deal on the Cote d'Azur, we thought it would be educational to visit a perfume manufacturing facility that featured its wares at prices 50 percent cheaper than the stores. Our cute little Irish tour guide explained that there are only fifty professional perfume "smellers" in the world, forty-eight men and two women. Because of the superior nose genes that are passed on, most jobs stay in the family throughout the generations!

From Eze, we headed east to Cap d'Ail where a shoreline boardwalk mean-dered all the way to the ritzy principality of Monaco. The sudden and tragic death of Princess Grace in the early 1980's still pervades over every step that is taken in this part of the world. An immaculately-maintained, memorial rose garden in her honor stands at the base of the "rock," the site of the Royal Palace, her former home. A life-size portrait of the royal family, all dressed in white, welcomes visitors who choose to tour sections of the Palace that are open to the public. Very few places anywhere exude wealth like Monaco. From the look of the scenic harbor, they buy yachts like most people purchase telephones.

Heading back towards Nice and beyond, we stopped in Cannes, home of the world-renowned International Film Festival, as snooty and stuck-up as you imagine it would be. Every one of the opulent, gaudy, US$500 a night hotels along the promenade had their own little private section of perfectly manicured sand. It reminded me of the logo indentions left in hotel lobby ashtrays in America, except for the fact that they were the size of a bedroom!

Every "room" was identified with its own pastel-colored umbrella and chairs, with Speedo-adorned waiters catering to the every whim of their guests. Full-scale restaurants with menus duplicating the selections found inside the hotel drove my rather ordinary smelling equipment crazy. Thank goodness the loaves of French bread were filling at least, or I would have chewed off my right arm! The sun-bathing section for the commoners like us was about the size of a Twister board. I laid there in the only athletic supporter-looking suit I had ever worn, and probably would ever wear again, for three hours.

"Don't you guys have a reservation. . ." are definitely not the first words you want to hear in the morning when you need to catch a 6:38 train. Thankfully, one of our roommates at our hotel in Nice woke us up in time to speed pack, speed walk and dive into our cozy first class cabin for points due west. The ongoing, train strike forced us to change trains again in Marseilles, but at least it was daytime.

Instead of heading all the way to Barcelona in one day, being forced to get acclimated to a new country and finding shelter after nightfall, we decided to check out a medieval, fortress city called La Cite within the town limits of Carcassone, France. The place was like a life-sized, toy castle perched high on a hilltop with double walls and pointed turrets. The exterior wall was completed under Louis IX in the early thirteenth century in an unsuccessful attempt to declare independence from northern France. Restored to its original condition in the mid-1800's, La Cite is presently considered to be the world's most impressive medieval town.

That evening, we met up with a pair of spunky girls from New Zealand and Canada who would help us consume a few bottles of wine, sitting on a grassy embankment overlooking the fantasy-land castle. In a matter of minutes, we were talking about the most intimate details of our lives and everyone else's as well! Upon our return to the castle hostel, we found that our fellow bunkmates were also rocking until 3:00 in the morning! The people we met, again, had helped make a memory of a place something very, very special.

Olympic Fever

From the size of the adjoining train station and airport, it was obvious that we were entering the big city, big leagues again in Barcelona, Spain. The typical first steps—find a map, change money, directions to hostel, etc., —were simple enough, however, what we hadn't expected was a language barrier worse than anything we had experienced since Japan. A youth hostel scavenger hunt with a pair of Irish travelers that should have taken an hour at the most, quickly turned into four despite the fact that we had long given up on talking and had resorted to pointing to our map! Between the San Francisco-type hills, heavy pack weight and thirst, I really thought the four of us were going to lose it this time. I eventually left the others and went out to look for myself, minus the backpack, and found our elusive Holy Grail. The others were walking away by the time I made it back. . .

After a lot of whining, we decided to celebrate Ian and Polly's first day in Europe with a round of cold beers, some pizza and a night on the town. The choice of entertainment, at least, was made easy for us since it was the initial celebration of the Days of Juan, a national mega-party that was like New Year's, St. Patrick's Day and July 4th combined. Primary attractions at the event included the typical rides and food stalls associated with fairs or carnivals in America, but the location of the action in and around monuments and towering fountains made it very unique. Despite the presence of countless infants and young children of all ages, the prevalence of reckless fireworks became really scary, especially as the night got longer and the users got more inebriated. The huge explosions within inches of monument pillars sounded like an air-raid strike in the Gulf War! Bottle rockets and cherry bombs bounced out of control on the ground as the sirens of ambulances billowed in the distance. This was definitely an accident waiting for a place to happen.

With marble pillars, a grand piano, stained glass windows and candles throughout, the entrance foyer of our very unique youth hostel had a charmingly haunted look. It had the appearance of a castle from a distance and was elevated high on a hill with a panoramic view of the Barcelona environs, including the harbor area where the members of the 1992 Olympic Team would be staying in another year or so. Although the harbor looked enticing from a distance, up close it was crowded, dirty, hot and sticky with an Olympic-sized construction project going on all around.

After picking up an ace bandage and a super-sized bottle of Advil to try and reduce the pain of Susan's reoccurring knee injury, we boarded the metro subway en route to the Sunday bull fight at Arenes Monumental. Although we had been amply forewarned about the absurd brutality of the "fights," I was very interested in going for the cultural value alone since it was such as institution in the country.

Matadors are at the absolute top of the Spanish sports adulation food chain, akin to the American quarterback, the Japanese suma wrestler or the Brazilian soccer player. It is the only major sport, however, that focuses on man versus animal, instead of man versus man, and the only one where death is encouraged, cheered and expected to occur. In fact, one of the measures of a good matador is the speed at which he brings a bull to its knees. Taking "too long" to get the job done is booed like a dropped pass or a three-second violation.

Perhaps the most significant architectural contributions to the buildings of Barcelona came from a man named Gaudi who was opposed to 90° angles and flat surfaces. Until his accidental death in 1926, he designed an amazing collection of modern art edifices in the city, most notably the wildly unconventional cathedral, Sagrada Familia.

The structure of the building gives only a hint of Gaudi's original vision and it is still a work-in-progress, despite the fact that it is 103 years-old already. I climbed over 500 steps to the pinnacle of one of the cone-shaped cylinders while Susan rested her weary knees in the church. After a casual stroll along Rambles, a long, popular, tree-lined boulevard that is considered to be the city's focal point, we set out to locate the largest Picasso museum in Europe. The collection ranged from his early childhood sketches done in Malaga, Spain (his birthplace), to exhibition posters done in Paris shortly before his death.

Although the start of the Olympics was only a year away, there was a lot of work that was yet to be done on Montjuic, the area where many of the events would take place. Dozens of armed tanks and foot police protected the area from terrorist activity or foul play of any sort. Not overly enamored by the city ourselves, we wondered how Barcelona was able to convince the Olympic Committee to allow them to stage the games.

With a blazing sun directly overhead already, Seville, the fourth largest city in Spain, was in full gear when our train pulled into a brand-new train station at 9:30 a.m. the next morning. Just as Barcelona metamorphosed in the wake of the Games, Seville was in the midst of a wholesale make-over all its own in anticipation of the World's Fair. Because of the impending scarcity of accommodations, the state-of-the-art train station was built to allow people to commute from as far away as Madrid, three hours north, for the daily activities.

Although ruled by the Romans, Moors and Catholic kings over the centuries, Seville is perhaps best known as the place Christopher Columbus returned to after discovering America. His remains are entombed at the dark and gloomy Cathedral, the world's third largest church after St. Peter's in Rome and St. Paul's in London. The rather nondescript-looking Golden Tower, along the Guadalquivir River, was the point of arrival for ships returning from the West Indies.

Although the narrow streets, sun-bleached buildings and ever-present, flower-boxed balconies were quaint, the noise and sheer volume of construction projects really diminished the ambiance in the city. It was a great place, however, to get caught up on sixteen days worth of dirty laundry, trip planning and postcard writing and to experiment with some of the national culinary favorites. Store and restaurant owners were apparently already in the practice mode for the summer of 1992 price gouge throughout a country once considered the cheapest in Europe.

Perhaps if our budget and lifestyle had permitted us to "do as the Spaniards do," drinking-wise, we would have left with a more favorable impression of the country. With stifling heat and humidity rivaling the Australian outback, throats were definitely parched a lot and alcohol seemed to be the solution of choice. It is a country of night people because of the mandatory mid-afternoon siesta (we found it very difficult to adapt to that), oppressive heat, and extremely long daylight hours. Dinner time is typically after 10 p.m., and the bars don't start hopping until 1:00 or 2:00 o'clock in the morning.

We left Seville for a town named Ronda in search of fresh air, few cars and a taste of rural Espana. The countless acres of olive plantations, sunflower fields and vineyards outside the window of our speeding train offered a wonderful change of scenery in one of the least densely populated areas in all of Europe.

The Muslim conquerors who occupied Spain in the Middle Ages are given credit for white washing their "pueblos" to ward off the intense, almost year-round heat in the area. Aside from the dramatic ravine, El Tajo, the ancient houses and other buildings in and around Ronda proved to be its most endearing attractions. After a leisurely afternoon of meandering through the charming cobblestone streets, we found a relatively inconspicuous pizzeria in a white house overlooking a magnificent gorge, bridge, river and surrounding valley.

Canadian Invasion

Five years earlier in Ft. Lauderdale, I thought for sure that I had experienced the eternal rite of passage into adulthood for the third and last time. Never again would I stay out until 4 o'clock in the morning doing kamikaze shots with teenagers and college students while smelling the sweet, intoxicating smell of the ocean. Never again would I be in the company of a bunch of guys living minute to minute with nothing more than a credit card advance and their galloping hormones. Never again would innocent, young, impressionable co-eds spill their guts to me while I nursed brewski numero double-digit until I could hardly see, much less talk. Never again, until. . . O'Canada weekend in the Algarve!

By the time we arrived in Lagos, Portugal, we were a close-knit family of eleven—two male college students from Cincinnati, two party-hungry Dutch guys, a quintet of eighteen, going on thirty-five year-old lasses from Canada who had just graduated from a prestigious Swiss high school, a laid-back, twenty-something, surfer dude from San Diego, Susan and I. The first beer run took place around noon, after we missed a train about halfway there. Last call was a street vendor hot dog just before sunrise.

After bargaining an apartment from a lady about to fall out of her tube top at the train station, the clan convened for a swordfish dinner at a restaurant/pub televising a Portuguese soccer match. While I spent the rest of night one playing Dr. Ruth with my curious, Midwestern pals, Dave and Mike (I was an instant expert to them because of the fact that my relationship with Susan had survived and actually prospered despite the consecutive number of days together, almost joined at the hip.), Susan was lassoed into a slam-dancing session with the intermittently worldly and naive teenybopper contingency. To the dismay of some of the "munchie"-possessed taste buds in the group, the little hot dog vendor outside the bar actually got arrested by the hot dog police for failure to get his cart registered!

The two-for-one (or better) enticements offered at every bar in town insured everyone a mind-splitting hangover, at the very least. Susan fed me breakfast in bed at 1 p.m. the next day and my feet finally hit the floor about 2 1/2 hours later. Not since the Midnight Oil concert in October had I felt so utterly worthless.

Since it was actually Canada Day (July 1)—the second year in a row we were in the presence of Canadians to celebrate a fine holiday I had never even heard of before—there was definitely no rest for the weary. The girls painted their faces with maple leaves and everyone put Canada pins and stickers all over themselves. In a scene reminiscent of the old "strip" in Lauderdale, it felt like all eighteen million of our northern brethren were crammed into five hole-in-the-wall bars with local favorites Rush and Bryan Adams blaring at 130 decibels.

The persistently clear blue skies, steady breezes, splendid beaches, secluded coves and comparatively inexpensive prices make the Algarve one of the most popular vacation spots for Europeans outside of the French Riviera. The jagged Lagos coastline was absolutely filled with sun worshipers in search of the almost total body tan. San Diego Joe talked us into taking a two-mile walk to an amazingly peaceful *total* body tanning nook he had found the day before. Fifteen middle-aged bare-buffers strolled and stretched out along a 200-foot private shoreline at the bottom of a steep, treacherous embankment. An eighty-year-old man who looked like he had been there every day of his life molded tiny mud sculptures on the protruding rocks. Only the sound of an occasional family of sea gulls passing overhead and the crashing waves of the sea interrupted the serenity of the soothing sun.

While the kiddie corps were running into friends and acquaintances of their own during our last evening together, Ma and Pa Wooten decided to "lay low" and give the brain cells a much-deserved break from the booze. The three-day, nonstop, laugh-a-thon ended with a huge group hug, a promise from us to keep our romantic flame burning and a vow from them to never miss a single party. They swept into our lives like a hundred-yard sprint at the tail end of an ultra-marathon giving us an infusion of energy at just the right time.

"Castles in the Air"

Thanks to its mild climate, fertile landscape and lush greenery, the Loire Valley is known as the Garden of France. Although a bicycle is definitely the preferred way to visit the string of castles, museums and other points of interest along the Loire River, demand always exceeds supply at rental sites during the summer and we were left doing the familiar "hoof it and chug it" shuffle. Tours was a typical European city with an abundance of flower boxes, fountains, well-manicured lawns, dogs on leashes and specialty shops of every description. People carried around baguettes (loaves of bread) like personal accessories, under their arms, over their shoulders, in their backpacks, even strapped to the back of their no-speed bikes! With a busy youth hostel shuttling kids to and from camps and tours all over the country, it was an ideal hub for a two- to three-day exploration of the Valley.

Castle-hopping turned out to be a lot more tolerable to me than church, museum or temple sightseeing with their distinctively different styles and unique reasons for being built in the first place. Chateaux Blois, just up the river from Tours, was constructed over a period of four centuries with Feudal, Gothic-Renaissance, Renaissance and Classical influences. It is full of intrigue with hidden panels operated by foot pedals, doors concealed by tapestries and stories of murder and assassination for almost every room. After tackling its long and spiraling staircase, we sampled some wine to quench our thirst.

Neighboring Chambord is the Taj Mahal of the castle world. Resting in splendid isolation in the middle of a several-hundred-acre forest and game park, the mega-mansion was originally built by Francis I as a hunting lodge. Huge tapestries adorn the walls along with countless deer antlers and stuffed boar. While visitors enjoyed the enormous, double-helix staircase (one person can ascend and the other descend without seeing each other) designed by Leonardo da Vinci, three young ladies resonated atmospheric symphony music throughout the main foyer area. Horses tap-danced at every entrance with riders dressed in Renaissance-style clothing.

As we shared our loaf of French bread with a cute dog on a leash outside, a group of fifteen guys, with packs fully loaded on eighteen-speed Cannondales and Peugeots, pulled up to a post. It was the first serious flashback to the summer before that I had experienced in a while and for an hour or so I felt a serious pang of sadness and envy. Despite the fact that we were still "roughing it" by most people's standards, I knew that there is absolutely no better way to get a flavor for a place than to see, feel and smell it from a bicycle. I know that feeling will never go away and it really hit me just how much I missed it.

Although much smaller than cousin Chambord, the castle at Chenonceau was our personal favorite, and getting there was more than half the fun. Following a thirty-minute train ride, we loaded up our packs with wine, bread, cheese, apples and meusli bars and walked three miles down a sun-blazed, blacktop road towards our destination. We intentionally kept our conversation to a minimum in order to fully enjoy the cacophony of chirping birds, buzzing crickets and quishing Reeboks that permeated the air. The sweet smell of red poppy flowers blooming on both sides of the narrow road only heightened the ambiance.

Eating lunch outside on a blanket or in a park was one of those unexpected treasures of the trip throughout. This particular setting was special because of the perfectly temperate conditions and the romantic feeling that France seems to automatically bring out of people.

With stomachs satiated, we strolled through a *Hansel and Gretel* forest en route to the majestic Chenonceau. Gorgeous gardens with every flower imaginable surrounded the castle, in addition to dozens of "bush animals." Although the structure was constructed during Henri II's era almost 500 years ago, the river around it marked the division between free and occupied France during World War II and it served as an escape passageway for thousands of refugees fleeing the Nazis.

Le Tour de France

Based on comments from fellow travelers about the lack of inexpensive lodging availability in Paris, we felt extremely fortunate to snag a pair of dorm beds at Europe's largest youth hostel on the very first phone call. (Except for Switzerland, very few hostels in Europe accept advance reservations.) With 431 beds available, it was obviously going to be a zoo, but the location was perfect, and at 84 francs each (about US$14), it would have been impossible to beat the price anywhere else.

With city map and metro ticket book in hand, we were off and running in one of the few places that I was really looking forward to visiting tourist attractions. Over the next few days, the sights, the city, as well as the ease of interaction with the people, would all surpass my expectations.

Criticizing French people is an automatic response for many Americans. We made a pact in France, and in every other country for that matter, to put all preconceived notions out of our minds and just make an effort to be as friendly as possible and to attempt to address people, order food, order tickets, ask directions, etc. in their language. Compared to the outright rude, or unemotional, mechanical French response we saw levied on others who didn't try, people actually smiled at us and usually started speaking in English! It was amazing how the slightest bit of forethought and sincere respect made such a major difference.

French people seem to take time to really enjoy their surroundings, the fruits of their labor, and the people around them. From the double peck-on-the-cheek kiss (I really like this custom but every time I do it I worry about starting on the wrong side and ending up in the middle!), to the patience to sit and sip a two-ounce cup of cappuccino and look vacantly into the street for a half hour, to the works of art arduously prepared in shop windows throughout the city, they are a society that savors the daily rituals of life instead of racing past them. We could all learn a lot from this attitude, a relatively foreign notion in most major American cities and for the corporate climber set.

Our tour le grand through Paris kicked off at arguably the most famous church in the world, the Notre-Dame Cathedral. Located on an island in the middle of the Seine, it's been a place of worship for over 2000 years, although the building itself was actually built between 1163 and 1345. From there, we passed St. Chapelle and The Conciergerie, where thousands of prisoners, including Marie Antoinette, were condemned to die during the French Revolution.

A few blocks farther down the Seine stood the surprisingly modernistic Louvre, sporting a transparent glass pyramid at its entrance. Originally a fortress built in the twelfth century by Philippe Auguste to defend Paris from Saxon intrusions, it was knocked down during the Middle Ages and resurrected in a design more in keeping with Renaissance tastes. Virtually abandoned in the early 1700's as the royal court moved to Versailles, Napoleon opened it to the public in 1793 as the art gallery and museum it is today. He even demanded a tribute in the form of works of art from the nations he conquered!

Mona Lisa, probably the best known piece in the building, stands behind a thick, bulletproof glass window due to a break-in that occurred eighty years ago. With fifteen layers of gawking expressions reflecting in the glass, it was rather difficult to examine the intricacies of the treasured painting.

The scene outside the storied confines of the Louvre resembled a college campus the week before graduation. No less than a hundred guys and girls in various stages of undress basked in the sun, on the rim of a huge reflection pool. Statues were everywhere as we exited down a gravel path to the start of the Champ-Elysees.

While the French would never dream of striking up a conservation with a total stranger at a grocery check-out line or asking someone their profession unless the context of the conversation called for it, they appear to have far less sexual hang-ups than Americans do. Most bathrooms and hostel dorm rooms are totally co-ed and dressing and undressing in front of members of the opposite sex is no big deal at all. It's not surprising that the French have such a hard time getting along with their stodgy, ultra-conservative neighbors across the channel.

Our July 24th ferry sailing to Ireland (thirteen days away) had to be booked in person in the coastal city of Le Havre, two hours west of Paris. We were incredibly fortunate to be able to time our visit there to catch the final sprint of the fifth stage of the Tour de France! Since many people organize their vacations to Europe for the purpose of following the world's most challenging bike race, we felt privileged to experience a taste of it on a spontaneous, "side" trip.

An otherwise quiet little town was abuzz with activity all day long in anticipation of one of its biggest happenings of the year. Trucks, cars, signs, roadblocks, speakers and chairs were slowly put into position as spectators jockeyed for the best view and race officials fortified safety precautions along the route. We hurried down for a so-so standing spot along the final 200-foot stretch and waited for the lead biker to appear in the distance. Led by a car and motorcycle escort, the cyclist accelerated in front of us at no less than forty miles per hour on a pancake-flat, asphalt surface! Ninety seconds later, the crowd roared as a cluster of thirty others burst into the open and motored past the finish line. It was amazing to me that after 150 miles of pedaling in a single day, all bikers finished within five minutes of each other. . .

Since the 24th would be our third wedding anniversary and we were given separate sleeping quarters on the ferry crossing for that night, we decided to advance book an "up-scale" one-star accommodation in the 150 franc range (US$20-$25) for the 23rd. Despite some initial trepidation on the manager's part to allow two foreign backpackers to reserve a room, we finally found what we were looking for at the Le Green Hotel. As soon as I said a few words in French, the "dolled up" proprietor softened up, and within minutes she was sharing marital secrets with Susan. She obviously loved the idea that we had chosen her humble sleeping quarters as our anniversary suite!

Back in Paris, hundreds of flags were arched over the sidewalks of the immaculate, café-lined Champ Elysees in anticipation of Bastille Day. It is one of the twelve streets emanating from the towering Arc de Triomphe, like giant spokes in a wheel. Napoleon ordered that the Arc be built in 1806 as a memorial to the Grand Army, but he died before it was completed thirty years later. The view from the top on a very clear day was breathtaking.

The most recognizable structure that we saw and maybe the most recognizable structure in the entire world is the Effiel Tower, built in 1889 for the World Exhibition. Like any other icon that you hear about all your life and that practically symbolizes a country or a continent (the Taj, the Leaning Tower of Pisa and Ayers Rock also come to mind), the Effiel Tower is hard to take your eyes off of at first.

The architectural marvel actually looks like a massive erector set up close. We were allowed to climb 337 of its 899 feet in height and were entertained by some interesting information displayed on placards on every floor. Over the years, it has been used as a radio and communications tower, weather station, landing lights for the trans-Atlantic Charles Lindbergh flight, and a tee box for an Arnold Palmer golf shot. Restorations have been frequent and it is painted every seven years.

After yet another picnic at the base of the Tower, we began the long walk back to the train station for our afternoon train excursion to Reims, the champagne capital of France. With incredible weather on our side and an array of delicious, inexpensive, carry-along food to choose from, we had now gone ten days in a row without setting foot in a restaurant!

With absolutely no information on Reims at our disposal and the tourist center closed upon our arrival, I decided to just walk around and ask people for a lodging recommendation. After several failed attempts, I finally ran into a helpful, English-speaking bar owner who even offered to call the local youth hostel to reserve a spot for us! It turned out to be one of the most clean and quiet places we would frequent anywhere. We borrowed some blankets and stretched out on the grass in the back, basking in the glow of a midsummer night under the stars.

Bastille Day

Since Reims was the home of champagne, naturally we set out to learn as much as we could about the subject while keeping an eye out for sampling opportunities along the way! The two largest champagne producers in the Reims area were Tattinger and Mums, well-known for their great products and interesting tours. The Tattinger facility was actually a cave, originally dug out by the Romans who used the rocks for building materials. Century-old sculptures of painted faces and even a statue of John the Baptist could be seen in the nooks and crannies of its cavernous storage area.

An enlightening tour in English at Mumm's ended with a steady round of samples around happy hour. We rewarded their generosity with the purchase of a bottle that we vowed to save until our anniversary night.

After a visit to the local French Car Museum, we walked back through town where the locals were busy preparing for Bastille Day-eve festivities. Back at the hostel, I phoned and finally connected with Kristin, an American college student studying in Paris whom we had met while on the train near Geneva. She invited us to stay at her flat, located only minutes from the Effiel Tower, and excitedly informed us about a fireworks display we would be seeing.

An uncharacteristically chilly and overcast mid-July Parisian day was a perfect backdrop for a very somber Bastille Day parade. Unlike the boisterous celebration bestowed on the American troops upon their return home, the French quietly reflected on a war recently ended, as stoic men and women in tanks, trucks and jeeps slowly inched along the Champs-Elysees and helicopters roared overhead. Very few people amongst the orderly throngs clapped and even fewer smiled. It would have been impossible to deduce that we had "won."

Kristin's tiny pad was a welcomed taste of home. She treated us to a delicious meal of chicken and mushrooms over rice while we chatted nonstop for four hours! Our faces hurting from laughter, we trotted to the Effiel Tower around midnight to watch the grand fireworks finale. Only the glow of the explosive display illuminated the landmark while we laid in awe in the cool summer grass. It would have been impossible to come up with a more fitting way to climax our stay in this amazing city.

About the size of Rhode Island and located squarely in the heart of Western Europe, Luxembourg has always had to fight for an identity of its own amidst much larger, more powerful neighbors. Saturated with fortresses and citadels from wars gone by, it is a neutral country today and known as one of the world's most prominent financial centers as well as a peaceful stopover of flowery rolling hills between France, Germany, Belgium and Holland. Evidence of the merging cultural influences of neighboring countries was found in a nearby McDonald's where the menu was in German and the trash can lids in French!

Since the city was tiny in comparison to Paris or Barcelona, it was easy to map out a half-day walking tour that would cover most of the "hot spots." Like Ronda, Spain, the gorges and towering bridges were its most physically striking and impressive attributes. The elevated, main portion of the city contained a variety of war relics, including the underground Casemates Bock with fifteen miles of passageways and tunnels that were used to shelter 35,000 people from the bombs of World War II. At the bottom of rue Wilthelm, one of the most picturesque, century-old, cobblestone streets, was perched the Three Towers, the site of guillotine activity during the French Republic.

Freedomville

At the very top of our "most anxiously anticipated" city list was Amsterdam, Holland, a place rivaling New York and San Francisco for the variety and entertainment per square foot award. We arrived at its infamous train station about 6:00 in the afternoon, and were greeted by an unbelievable mixture of humanity that ranged from "musicians" to beggars to individuals who had simply consumed one too many psychedelic suppers and had no place to go for desert. Makeshift "garage bands" jammed all over the place, totally oblivious to crowd gawking and boos. It was not uncommon to see guitarists with matted, unwashed hair walk away in mid-chorus, only to be replaced by someone else ambling about "looking for a gig." The beggars were actually more like scavengers, spastically searching through garbage cans for something, then looking for a match to set the entire receptacle ablaze! Small circles of multi-body pierced, skin heads chanted undecipherable verses of indiscernible songs while passing around enough dope and assorted "change agents" to keep William Bennett on edge for a lifetime.

In between this megadose of people watching, I attempted to phone one of the three locals that we had met while in Thailand and India. About two hours after arrival, we successfully connected with Wilhelm and Jimmy, roommates from nearby Apeldoorn, whom we had befriended on the Chiang Mai trek some five months before.

Wilhelm, a gardener at the Apeldoorn Royal Palace, picked us up at his local train station, an incredibly sedate contrast to what we had witnessed in Amsterdam only an hour before. He led us through the sleepy little town of 140,000 or so to his quaint renovated pad, tastefully adorned with a combination of antique and modern furniture and auction-purchased art. Jimmy prepared us a dinner of liverwurst, cheese and egg on bread with pickles (I must have been starving!) and a bottle of German wine while we exchanged travel stories and reminisced over their Thailand photos. Since the paid lodging options were virtually nonexistent at the time of our arrival, we felt very fortunate to hook up with a pair of familiar faces.

Midsummer meant peak hostel season in Europe and it was dicey trying to find a room since most didn't accept advance reservations. At Jimmy's suggestion, we decided to try and locate a bed in the "authentic" Dutch community of Haarlem, until we could explore our options in Amsterdam a bit more in person. He informed us that the Haarlem we were heading to was actually the sister city of Harlem, New York, originally settled by the Dutch along with neighboring Brooklyn!

After successfully checking into the bucolic, barracks-like accommodations in Haarlem, we were back to perversive Amsterdam for another visual-stimulation fix. The first stop, less than a mile from our favorite train station, was the one and only Sex Museum, filled with enough plastic models, paintings, videos and assorted paraphernalia to enlighten, stun or repulse almost anyone.

Other than sex, drugs, rock-n-roll, wooden shoes, canals and tall skinny houses, Amsterdam is perhaps best known as the home of Anne Frank, the young Jewish girl who wrote a diary about the two years her family and friends were in hiding from the Nazi police. More than half a million people a year come to see the tiny house and a chilling reminder of the horrors of World War II. No one knows who revealed the hiding place to the authorities that eventually led to the concentration camp deaths of her close-knit family.

Since we had slept in a half dozen places in as many days, we needed an anchor for a while and made an executive decision to rise at the crack of dawn to stand in line at the extremely crowded and popular Amsterdam hostel. Although it was 11 a.m. before we were assured of a bed, we were offered a complimentary breakfast and lunch for our trouble, which I thought was quite amazing for such an institutional kind of place.

One of the many reasons that Amsterdam is such a popular city for tourists is its compactness and walkability. Spacious sidewalks and bike lanes are on most roads already, and a movement is afoot to virtually banish the car from its confines. Karien Maas, the Dutch travel guide and part-time police interpreter we had met in Koh Phi Phi, Thailand, was very involved in environmental issues affecting her lifelong home. We spent a fascinating evening with her learning about the unusual housing laws, the genesis of the liberalization of sex and marijuana, and her very interesting occupations.

The four-story building that Karien lives in was built in the 1700's and has been occupied by someone almost every year since. Although it is now one of the 7,000 houses in the city with protected "monument preservation" status, when Karien found it in 1970 the dilapidated place was on the verge of being destroyed. She negotiated a 43 gilder (2 gilders = US$1) per month mortgage, with a fixed 6 percent payment increase every year. That works out to about US$60 a month today! The price of houses two centuries ago was determined by their *width*, which helps explain why most abodes in Amsterdam are so long and narrow. The steep, spiraling staircases were so difficult for a person to maneuver through, it was hard to imagine transporting anything else up them. We were told that the large hooks at the base of the A-frame top of the buildings served as hoists for large items like couches and pianos, but I couldn't envision how they actually worked.

Karien had a dream employment situation made possible by the fact that she was fluent in six languages. She spent four to five months a year traversing the globe as a travel guide while moonlighting as a police interpreter locally. Most of her free time was spent on the adventure travel circuit.

The Amsterdam "open" drug use scene began in the early 1970's when recreational use of up to three grams of pot, hash, etc. became decriminalized to the point of really being legal. As long as a person consumes within the confines of one of the dozens of designated "coffee shops" or in private, they are never hassled. Karien felt that if all countries had done this at the same time that "soft" drug use as we know it today would be very different, with the dealers out of business, crime reduced dramatically, and the general population happier, yet no more stoned. Instead, Amsterdam has become a magnet for hardcore drug dealers, and combined with the centuries-old sex trade has managed to attract among the most outrageous characters on the planet.

Fully satiated after our wine and cheese dinner party, we left with Karien for the most intensive pub crawl we had ever experienced. Her typically rusty three-speed bike was padlocked behind a fence near the front door with a lock the size of Fort Knox. The reason that almost all of the 555,000 bikes (almost one per person!) in the city are so basic and cheap is because of the incredibly flat terrain and the high incidence of drug-related theft. She's gotten to the point now that she buys used ones from the junkies instead of bike shops. One of these days, she may buy back her own bike!

Karien informed us that there were over a hundred pubs within a five minute radius of her house. From yuppie-type bars to "sand on the floor to absorb the spill" type of establishments to a tiny six-seater the size of a large van, we ventured in and out of at least a dozen of them, but never finished a single beer. Our colorful hostess knew at least one person in every watering hole, flirtatiously engaging in small talk while treating us like her long-lost niece and nephew.

The final stop of the evening felt like the wind down after a four-hour exercise marathon. Although only a few hundred feet from the noise and commotion of pubdom, we were led into an unusually serene area that seemed to be completely shut off from the world around it. It is called the beguinage, a convent-like housing triangle, originally constructed for women whose husband's were off fighting wars. Although a church adjoins the living quarters and beautifully manicured common lawn, it is not religiously oriented. Men are not permitted to live there, but can visit and even stay overnight if they are discreet. Karien is on the waiting list to live there, but will be lucky to be awarded a flat before she's seventy.

Although biking and walking are the easiest ways to get around Amsterdam and the surrounding area, a boat cruise along the seemingly endless network of canals offers probably the best view of the thousands of old homes that give the city a lot of it's charm. Surprisingly, all of the waterways except one were man-made, constructed during the 1700's in a massive project that spanned a fifty-year period. Guard rails were only recently installed on bridges arching over them, saving thirty or forty cars per week from tasting "the drink," according to our boat guide and operator. People who choose to live in one of the many floating bungalows and old cargo boats that lined the borders of the canal were charged 500 gilders (about US$250) a year for the "water space." One of the advantages of being a "boatperson" was the fact that friends and relatives could ice skate right up to your living room window in the winter time!

After several weeks of anxious anticipation to get "back in the saddle" on a bicycle seat in Holland, the weather and rental availability finally cooperated with us on our last day there. We opted for a lazy, countryside ride towards the coastal community of Zanvoodt instead of a hectic, car- dodging experience in Amsterdam, and our bright, shiny zero-speeds set us back a whooping 7 gilders for eight, fun-filled hours. The blustery winds kept our gearless pursuit of the Atlantic more challenging than we had anticipated, especially when we ventured through a scarcely-inhabited national park of scrubland, sand dunes and a single lake. By midafternoon, we made it to our ultimate destination, relishing the salty spray of the gray and agitated North Sea while nibbling on yet another cheese and bread smorgasbord.

In a country sometimes criticized for its liberal ways and perceived indifference to the well-being of its people, I was extremely impressed by the unwavering respect shown to cyclists and to the ubiquitous pursuit of exercise and health by the general population. They are a tolerant and modernistic people and yet a very simple one at the same time, proudly and steadfastly clinging to centuries-old traditions and to the unique heritage of their forebears while constantly seeking to find new commonsensical and practical ways of doing things. One of the easiest places to be and one of the hardest places to leave, we vowed to make a return trip some day.

Ulwa

Heading south for the first time in almost a month, we maintained our hyperactive pace with an abbreviated stopover in Belgium, highlighted by a visit to the summer apartment of a vivacious friend we had met in Nice, Ulwa. (pronounced Ulva) Although born in Sweden, Ulwa spoke fluent English and could easily have been mistaken for an American because of her mannerisms, speech pattern and attitude. She had a seasonal job in Brussels, the capital of Europe and headquarters of the EEC (European Economic Community) and NATO, and energetically relayed her plans for us on the way back from the train station.

We were fortunate to arrive in Brussels on the beloved king's sixtieth birthday, fortieth anniversary as king and thirtieth anniversary to his wife. The locals celebrated by making it a national holiday and throwing one huge party. Ulwa guided us and two of her friends to the site of the 1958 World's Fair where a 200 million times larger than life replication of a molecule served as the central landmark and backdrop to the evening festivities. A throng of no fewer than 100,000 people burrowed and pushed their way around a huge field while a symphony performed classical music in the distant background. Climaxed in typical fashion by a barrage of fireworks activity, it was the fourth Independence Day type of gathering we had witnessed in the past thirty days!

While Ulwa went off to work the next morning, Susan and I ventured over to Brugge, a living, breathing, medieval town, considered by many to be the prettiest in all of Europe. Thanks to strict preservation laws, the cobblestone streets, canals, flower boxes, rounded doorways, humpbacked bridges and majestic churches have hardly changed since the Middle Ages. While Susan visited a museum featuring the works of Salvador Dali, one of our newfound favorite artists, I sat on a park bench enjoying the breezy sunshine and feeding the ducks. After a late afternoon laundry marathon, Ulwa returned from her vocational obligations and introduced us to the Grand Palace, one of the most ornate market squares in Europe. The intricate sculptures and exterior work were artfully brought to life by the ambient lighting as bands entertained the outdoor cafe crowd. After a delicious burger feast at the very Bennigan's-like, Henry Beans, Ulwa took us back to her abode to help us pack our newly washed clothes. We bid her a tearful farewell the next morning and boarded the train en route to Le Havre, the predetermined destination of our anniversary celebration, and the departure point for le cruise to Ireland.

Le Havre

The proprietor at the Hotel Green, who had taken our reservation during the Tour de France visit, checked us in with a complimentary bottle of champagne and a warm smile of remembrance that we didn't expect to see. She was the perfect French hostess, prim and proper, and definitely in need of a bigger hotel to showcase her infectious hospitality. We felt like a king and queen as we perused the double bed with dunna, color TV, bathroom and shower, all our own! With no curfew and a complimentary private breakfast to look forward to, we happily indulged ourselves a bit and reflected on our 2 1/2 months in continental Europe.

Although the English Channel tunnel or "Chunnel" was to be completed in 1994, the only options for crossing over to the British Isles or Ireland at the time of our trip were by ferry service or plane. Since the ferry was included as part of our summer-long Eurrail package (saving us US$85 apiece), the method of travel was an easy decision to make. The Le Havre ferry station was crawling with money-conscious backpackers, including an unusually high percentage of the hard-core, "haven't showered in over a week and proud of it" variety.

The St. Killian II was comparable to a very low-budget cruise ship, minus the live entertainment, sports activity options and continuous food replenishment. I was shown to a microscopic four-man cabin and shared a bunk with a lonely, twenty-two year-old Frenchman who had taken English in school for ten years, yet comprehended about 10 percent of what I said. He followed Susan and I around like a surveillance camera on wheels. We had a feeling that the ride was unusually bumpy, judging by the bouncing mug of Robert DeNiro at the ferry cinema. We wouldn't find out until the end of the ride, however, that we had survived the worst weather conditions of any crossing in the past two years. I guess we weren't as wimpy as we first thought.

With all the Dramamine, nocturnal interruptions and the pitch-black cabins, neither of us woke up until 11:30 the next morning! As soon as Susan tried to brush her teeth, she knew the Dramamine hadn't worked! After some bread and crackers to try and soothe our stomachs, we lounged around and plotted a game plan for the next few days in Ireland. Susan had mixed feelings about the visit since her mom was Irish and has always dreamed of making the trip to her native land. She missed her dearly, and was sad that they couldn't experience it for the first time, together.

Ireland

"A hard life, sure, but a good life, with plenty of fresh air, fresh food, earth, wind and water. He had nothing, but he needed nothing".
—*Home to Ireland by Michael Walsh*

The seven hours after touchdown in Rosslare were a blur as we journeyed by foot, bus, train and taxi from Waterford (home of the crystal!) to Limmerick Junction to Cork. As expected, the local Irish folks were a joy to be around, never missing an opportunity to tell a quick joke or to relate a story about their homeland. Our cute, little, old, bus driver taking us to Waterford stopped his vehicle in mid-sentence, shut it off in the middle of the road, tipped his hat with a "good-bye now" and walked over to another bus in the adjoining lane doing the same thing! Imagine that happening in Los Angeles. . .

Although renting a car is definitely the easiest and quickest way to traverse the narrow, two-lane thoroughfares of Ireland, as usual, we opted for the less expensive and more adventurous travel options available, buses, trains and thumbs. Since Ireland is such a small island, with less than two hour's drive to the sea from any point, it really wasn't that much of an inconvenience at all.

The Kinley House in Cork offered bunk-bed accommodations and a hearty complimentary breakfast, right across the street from the Shandon Steeple, the bell tower of St. Anne's Church. It's also only a ten-minute walk to the bus station and shuttle service over to the Blarney Castle, the primary reason why anyone makes a stopover in the area in the first place.

Right outside the castle and cardigan shops (we donated our share to the local economy there!) is an enchanting, woodsy area with Grimm's fairy tale-looking trees, neatly- lined, pebble footpaths and centuries-old rock formations with names like Witches' Kitchen, Witches' Stone, Wishing Steps and Druid's Cove. Along with the luscious greenery and flowers closer to the castle, it is truly a magical setting for an experience as unique as "kissing the blarney stone."

The reason the Blarney Castle looks so old is because it is—dating back to the fifteenth century—and the fact that it has never been restored. Along with a steady stream of tourists, we climbed the twisting, narrow steps past fireplaces and trap doors used at one time to drop things like boulders on unsuspecting guests! The real action takes place in the battlement lookout area at the top where a line is formed to kiss the blessed rock. To accomplish the act and be assured of "silver tongued loquaciousness" forever, one must perform a small acrobatic feat, leaning upside down over the parapet wall before touching the stone with your lips. Strangely enough, nobody knows for sure how this rather odd tradition originated.

Back to the crowded streets of Cork to acquire a few odds and ends, like camera batteries, food and travelers checks, I spotted a tattered concert announcement on a telephone pole that really got my attention, ROD STEWART LIVE IN KILLARNEY. Ever since we had seen Midnight Oil in Aussieland, I longed to catch at least one more mega-show somewhere else along the way, and until now did not have the opportunity. Within minutes, we were on our way to see Rod on his home turf. (actually it's Scotland, but close enough!)

Stewart was playing the last performance of his summer-long tour and the first concert ever in Killarney. Threatening clouds teased the audience throughout the warm-up acts and finally opened up on the second song of the main event. With rain and inclement weather such an integral part of the heritage of the British Isles, it was actually the perfect compliment to the evening if the band could somehow play through. Rod was like a chameleon, changing outfits on numerous occasions as they became saturated from the dousing and stage-long slides through the watery mess. The audience hung onto every word and sang along on most songs, particularly the many that made reference to the rain we were all experiencing.

After a final round of phone calls before our return home in twelve days, we opted to go the tour bus route, in favor of the three-day bike tour route, to see the popular Ring of Kerry. Even I was able to concede that without some essential bike gear (spare tubes, rain jackets, padded riding shorts, etc.), more than a one-day ride just didn't make sense at this point in the trip.

Dero Tours was the recommended guide company in the area and bus driver/resident expert Mr. McCarthy made sure we got our 8 Irish pounds worth (about US$13). The 110-mile, circular trek was incredibly crowded from start to finish as cars, buses, cyclists, horse-drawn carriages and sheep shared a very narrow piece of asphalt. Our guide chatted nonstop, providing as much commentary as anyone cared to hear. The first town of note along the way was Killorylin, with 1280 people and fifty-two bars! It sounds a little outrageous, but supposedly each bar makes enough money to survive all year long from a single drunken festival during the month of August. Now that's a lot of drinking.

Despite the low-lying, cumulonimbus clouds looming everywhere, the unique combination of tiny villages, mountains, valleys, coves and winding roads along the seascape offered breathtaking views. Almost every Irish person we met, especially the older ones, were extremely concerned and even borderline obsessed with the clouds, rain and the weather in general. Mr. McCarthy explained how the sheep helped everyone predict the onset of precipitation, moving to high ground when the conditions were going to be favorable and back down the mountain when trouble was looming. We passed a weather station and everyone that worked there was out looking for the sheep! I guess Doppler radar won't be coming to this area anytime soon.

We got up at the crack of dawn the next day, to the dismay of our seven roommates, and caught a series of buses northwest to the Dingle Peninsula. Susan was able to slip in a fifteen-minute Irish Catholic Mass in the town of Tralee along the way while I stayed back at the local bus depot and "guarded the goods."

Shortly after noon, we were met at the Dingle station by an American named Mike in search of people to stay at his "in the process of being renovated" youth hostel, a few minutes away. He and his girlfriend Tina, from California, were in the midst of a worldwide trip of their own when they were persuaded to stay for awhile and help run the place. The 290- year-old mansion was recently sold by an eighty-four year-old lady who originally wanted to make it a posh hotel.

Dingle was basically a seaside community, tolerably touristy with a wealth of B & B's and plenty of cyclists on rentals touring the nearby peninsula. We stumbled across a Dillon's Bed & Breakfast (Susan's mom's maiden name) without any problem, and stopped to see if there was any connection with her extended family. The 109-year-old lady that ran the place conversed with Susan for a while, but apparently this wasn't the "needle in the haystack."

Ireland didn't become one of the friendliest and most hospitable countries in the world by accident. They continue to take it seriously and to work at it, as evidenced by the thousands of bed and breakfast signs in resident front yards all over the great green land. Since we had grown immediately attached to the Dingle area, it was an easy decision to try and find a B & B to our liking for the last night and morning there. Although I'm sure there were dozens that we would have been perfectly happy with, we were very fortunate to find the cozy, ocean view Seaside Farmhouse within walking distance of the hostel. We dropped off our bags in the morning and hitched a ride the few miles into town.

Unlike the Ring of Kerry, cycling the Dingle Peninsula was a very reasonable endeavor of thirty, somewhat hilly but scenic miles. We rented brand-new, fifteen- speed, mountain bikes (neither of us had ever been on a mountain bike before) from a shop in Dingle, and crossed our fingers that the intense car and tour bus companionship we had been forewarned about would not materialize. Fortunately, the narrow, curvy roads were relatively clear all day. Although the day was mostly hazy, at times the sun would shine through the clouds like the lights of an air traffic controller watch tower, casting a sparkling glow on the deep blue waters to our left. In the stop and gaze in awe per mile department, only the cliff-hugging Road to Hana in Maui and California's majestic Highway 1 could compare in my book.

About halfway through the morning, a pair of ancient rock formations in the shape of bee hives caught our attention across the street from a cliff that carried down to the sea. A little, grandmotherly woman in her seventies called us over to take a closer look at the mounds that were actually 2000 year-old Celtic ruins. Although we were pretty impressed, our talkative little tour guide was a lot more interested in hearing the details of how we got caught in the storm the night before. (There's that weather theme again.)

After stopping off at Sleighhead Beach for a few moments to look out over the Blasket Islands, we found a quaint little village of three stores and a post office. Although the postmaster tried to converse with us in broken English, it was obvious that he primarily spoke Gaelic, the original language of the country. Actively suppressed and considered a barbaric tongue at the time of the English conquests in the 1840's, today its use is encouraged and Irish children must demonstrate proficiency in the language as a high school graduation requirement. We wrapped up a long, memorable day with a delicious crab and fish dinner at Long's Seafood House, then took the beachcombing trek back to Seaside.

Besides the impeccably clean and comfortable accommodations and the opportunity for enlightening conversation with fellow travelers, the best part of staying at a B & B was that first smell of an all-you-can-eat, home-cooked meal in the morning. Irish innkeepers, in particular, are known for being especially conscientious about making sure that their guests don't leave hungry, and Mary was certainly no exception. Upon entry into the breakfast nook, we were greeted with grapefruit slices, cereal, coffee, juice and toast. I would have been perfectly happy to stop right there, but as we were to quickly find out, that was merely the appetizer. While exchanging travel stories with a friendly Irish family of three across the table, Mary brought out an assortment of meaty specimens that drove our cholesterol fifty points higher on sight. Looking in disbelief in a counterclockwise motion on my plate, I was introduced to a clump of sheep's blood, big gamy-tasting sausage links, a couple of pieces of Canadian bacon and a sunny-side up egg with a stuffed tomato! After completion of the first course, I plodded gingerly through the new selection until it was obvious that there would be leftovers that Mary didn't need to see. I could always count on my wife to come through in a crisis and this time she outdid herself. As Mary stepped up to go to the kitchen for the coffee pot, Susan adroitly napkined the scraps, brought them under the table and handed them off to me in one fluid motion. Without hesitation, I instinctively resorted to a long-forgotten childhood prank and raced to the bathroom for a surreptitious flushing away of the evidence! We all bid Mary farewell shortly afterwards and our newfound friends across the table graciously offered to take us to the bus station.

The ride to Limmerick wasn't that far distance-wise, but the narrow, curvy roads en route made it close to a full day journey. We checked into a stale and gloomy youth hostel in the drizzly late afternoon, and quickly decided that a beer at the Olde Tom Pub, and *Thelma and Louise* on the big screen, was just the tonic we needed to cure a slight twinge of motion sickness. From what we were told, it rains in this city at the mouth of the Shannon River all the time.

The culmination of our far-too-abbreviated stint in Ireland was the cosmopolitan city of Dublin, home of the Guinness Brewery and our Aussie outback pal, Kevin. Since Kevin was working upon our arrival in midmorning, we immediately ventured over to sample some of the world famous, dark, frothy Guinness suds and take a tour of an extremely aromatic facility. Although over ten million pints a day are produced for consumption around the globe, it was interesting to learn that 99 percent of the barley, hops, yeast, etc. used to make the beer are actually imported! Every year, contests are held to encourage people to try and make the ingredients domestically (in Ireland), but thus far no one has succeeded.

Kevin got home around 8 o'clock in the evening and after a late dinner with some of his friends, we retreated to his modest apartment for a trip down memory lane. In addition to checking out photos of the travels we undertook together throughout Australia, he also showed us some of the highlights of subsequent trips to Bali and other places. His flexible engineering contract work allows for at least three months of adventure travel a year when he's not living in another country on assignment. With a great temperament and laid-back style, he is perfectly suited for the "Lonely Planet" trail.

A litany of famous poets and authors, including Jonathan Swift, William Butler Keets, Oscar Wilde and James Joyce hailed from Dublin, and nowhere is the legacy of their work more proudly displayed than at Trinity College. Until recently a Catholics-only institution, Trinity is the Irish equivalent to the American Ivy League. The highlight of the school is the library, which according to our tour guide, was supposed to be large enough to house every book published in the world! It undertakes a rigorous restoration program every year to insure the preservation of the centuries-old books within its hallowed walls.

We escaped, thankfully, without getting a quiz, and began our search for one of the many surname historical computer banks around town. Names are a big deal to Irish people, probably even bigger than the weather, so they make it easy for someone to find out all about their heritage. Susan already knew that her maiden name was part Czech, part Polish, but I really wasn't sure about mine. As it turned out, I'm part Dutch, part Irish and mostly English (as in England). No earthshaking revelation there.

By day, we sought the sights and by night we slurped up the suds. With the smell of Guinness pervading the humid evening air everywhere we walked, it wasn't hard to get in the mood. While we enjoyed the beer at O'Dwyer's and O' Malley's and O'Donnaghues and o'the rest, what we really enjoyed the most was the ambiance of the Irish music, the boisterous camaraderie and the unrelenting chatter. This was part of the essence of Ireland, a big part, and it was wonderful seeing people have so much unbridled, unpretentious fun.

The hardest part was saying good-bye for the second time because we didn't know if we'd ever see our kind and generous "friends from the road" again. As Kevin drove us to the Dublin docks for our 3 1/2 hour crossing over to Wales, he assured us that we would be able to pay him back because he would be paying us a visit someday, somehow, for some reason. Coming from a true vagabond like him, I knew it would happen.

Susan had been battling an aching, sneezing, congesting cold for close to a week now and lay curled up with her head on my lap trying her best to fall asleep. We sat in the main room of the Sea Link ferry, surrounded by Irish and British merrymakers, whooping it up on a Saturday night. Children everywhere were hollering, totally unhappy with the unusual and confining sleeping arrangements while a man wailed an indecipherable tune to no one in particular. Others just snoozed with an assist from a token Guinness, while a few browsed through the ever-popular British gossip mags. Finally, as the clock approached the hour of midnight, the shuffling of bags indicated that our destination was near. We were on the verge of disembarking into Great Britain, the final country on our worldwide itinerary.

Lindsay

Nothing is ever as easy in reality as it looks on paper, and our scheduled train ride from Holyhead, Wales across to London was certainly no exception. While we waited out a three-hour delay in our uncomfortable assigned seats, two Italian guys with about forty-five beers in their system came into our no-smoking section right across from us and immediately lit one up. When we politely asked them to refrain from smoking because of Susan's cold, you would have thought we had just declared war on their country! Within milliseconds, Italian expletives and hand gestures were flying and one particular four-letter English word was used about twelve times for emphasis and clarity. Not especially happy about the prospects of getting an ice pick in the head, we decided that it was best to keep our response to ourselves and hope that they would eventually get bored and leave. As other people started filling in around us, they quietly disappeared into the darkness.

It was already halfway through the night by this time and with the best chance for an en route robbery in weeks, I didn't really even try to go to sleep. Watching the magnificent sunrise of lavender and purple emerge through my first English fog made it all worthwhile. With less than a week left before the final departure, there would be plenty of time to catch up on sleep.

Like Kevin, we originally met Lindsay on the outback trip back in November. We got 'on "famously" with her from the very beginning and had been looking forward to reuniting ever since we got word that she was back home in London. A lawyer by trade, but perfectly suited for the adventure travel circuit as well, Lindsay was one of the wittiest people I had ever met. She picked us up at the Victoria Train Station near her rented flat and asked us if we'd like to visit with her sisters and parents at their "country cottage," an hour or so out of town. Of course the answer was a resounding "yes!"

The "cottage," she modestly referred to, was actually a big, richly decorated brick home with a swimming pool, elaborate gardens and expansive view of the surrounding valleys. After a great summer lunch of salads and breads and a quick dip with her sisters, Mr. and Mrs. Cliff returned from a day of shopping with a few of their friends, primed and ready for their "afternoon tea." The father was characteristically conservative and reserved, yet spontaneous and funny at the same time, practically interviewing us about our trip and the way we planned to use it to better ourselves after it was over. The British are so proper at times, it seems almost choreographed. Susan and I smiled across the table at each other through the whole conversation. The degree of formality was epitomized by the actions of one of their friends who left, cranked up his car, then shut it off and walked thirty steps back to the conversation area to say good-bye to Mrs. Cliff, thank her for tea and give her a peck on the cheek!

In the midst of sightseeing in London over the next few days, we also managed to connect over the phone and visit with a variety of other individuals that we had met in Australia. Over a thirty-six hour span, we traveled south to Haywards Heath to see James Purvis (from the Southwest Australia trip) and his live-in girlfriend Judy, to Arundel to visit Andy Kendall (from the outback safari), and had lunch with Bridgette (SW trip) back in London. Although it was great to see some familiar faces after such a long period away from home, each one of our friends was having a great deal of difficulty adjusting to the "real world" again after months of freedom and discovery. They had "settled" for jobs because of the horrendous employment market and seemed to be counting down the days again until their next adventure. We couldn't help but wonder if we were seeing our future. . . two spots, up front and center, in the unhappiness line. It was all too depressing to think about.

With twelve million people spread throughout a massive geographic area, London is one of the largest cities in the world. Due to the fact that the English Channel has kept its shores free from invasion for more than 900 years and British people intuitively prefer the old to the new, it is also one of the most preserved, and consequently, one of the most visited.

We supplemented leg power with the economical and easy-to-use, underground subway system ("the tube") and the bright red, double-decker buses whenever possible. The frenzied pace of the city was closer to New York than Paris or Amsterdam, and for the first time in over a year I found myself paying more attention to guys in white button-downs than the nose ring and a knapsack set. Although I could never welcome the end to a trip like ours, knowing that it was inevitable, I was glad to be winding up in a place like London. Although not a conscious decision, our minds were ensuring our sanity later by "transitioning" a little early.

By the time a person is thirty years old, he's seen and heard about the "sights" of London so many times that he feels like he's already been there. Lindsay was well-aware of this fact, and offered to take us on a slightly different, personalized, commentary tour of the famous landmarks at *night*, when traffic and crowds

were at a minimum. The Tower Bridge, Westminster Abbey and St. Paul's Cathedral were illuminated like a fairy tale, and thanks to Lindsay, we were almost completely by ourselves to savor them.

The absolute best bargain in London is the quality and affordability of theater. For only US$65 between us, we were able to get reasonably good tickets
with only a day's notice to two of the most popular musicals around, *Miss Saigon*
and *Les Miserables*. With its great acting, realistic and easy-to- follow plot,
wonderful music and special effects, I absolutely loved *Miss Saigon* from start
to finish. *Les Miz* was a lot harder to follow if you weren't familiar with the
historical time line of the action.

At long last, after more than 400 incredible days on the road, it was time for
one grand, farewell get-together. To help us celebrate, we invited Jac and Derek
(also Australian safari alumni) who had moved in together about an hour or so
north of London, and one of Lindsays' friends, an around-the-world traveler
himself a couple of years back. Susan helped Lindsay prepare an exquisite dinner of chicken with mushrooms, rice, fried bananas, and lots and lots of wine.
We toasted the love we all shared for the open road, the challenge of always
finding a place in our lives for adventure and to friends—brought together in
the most unlikely of places. We never gave ourselves time to think about the
fact that the end was so near and suddenly with a single toast, we realized it was
really upon us—the bittersweet conclusion to a dream of a lifetime.

"To be sure that your friend is a friend, you must go with her on a journey, travel with her day and night, go with her near and far."
—*Angolan Proverb*

"...once you have traveled, the voyage never ends, but it is played out over and over again in the quietest chambers. The mind can never break off from the journey."
—*Pat Conroy*

"The real voyage of discovery consists not in seeing new landscapes, but in having new eyes."
—*Marcel Proust*

"Each of us is the accumulation of our memories."
—*Allan Loy McGinnis*

"Your travel life has the essence of a dream. It is something outside of normal, yet you are in it. It is peopled with characters you have never seen before and in all probability will never see again. It brings occasional homesickness and loneliness, and pangs of longing. . . But you are like the Vikings or the master mariners of the Elizabethan Age, who have gone into a world of adventure, and home is not home until you return."
—*Agatha Christie*

"Measure wealth not by the things you have, but by the things you have for which you would not take money."
—*Anonymous*

Epilogue

It has now been five years since our re-entry onto American soil. In reflection, Susan and I both feel that the extended period of around-the-clock togetherness has had a positive impact on our marriage and on how we see the world in general. Susan summarizes her feelings on the matter, "What seemed like an insurmountable chore at the beginning, now feels like a distant but vivid part of me. Now we have memories to last a lifetime that will bond us forever. The trip has changed my perspective on everything."

After a few weeks of visiting friends and relatives upon our return, we immersed ourselves in the task of re-entering the working world and were very fortunate to succeed within three short months. We owe a huge debt of gratitude to Susan's parents for allowing us to use their home as an office and a bedroom during my interview process and to Mr. Ron Balsbaugh of the Quaker Oats Company for giving me a chance despite the fact that I had been out of work for nineteen months. He was one of the very few people who truly understood that a lifetime of experiences was worth more than a year and a half of working.

Within a year of our subsequent move to Chicago and Quaker, Sarah Nicole came into our lives. Three short years later, Rachel Elizabeth was born. Susan said the bike trip was even harder than giving birth! We are blessed to have two healthy, energetic girls who also happen to be extremely acclimated to travel. Sarah joined us on twenty-four round trip flights by the time she was 2 years old and both of them absolutely love being carried around in our "kid backpack carrier"! While I was busy rebuilding my career with Quaker, Susan worked part-time at a local hospital and doctor's office. Four years and three positions after moving to Chicago, I accepted a new assignment with H.T. Marketing, the largest domestic distributor for Hawaiian Tropic suncare products, in Murray, KY. We moved into our new home in May '96.

As much as I miss the freedom and spontaneity of "life on the road", I honestly embrace the challenges of my career with the same fervor. Traveling is and always will be an extremely important facet of my life and I am fortunate that it is an essential element of my chosen field of sales management.

Although the trip itself is a distant memory, Susan and I are constantly amazed at the number of times every week that it touches our lives. Whether it happens while watching television, reading the newspaper, dining in a restaurant, talking with friends or playing a game, the recollections are vivid and intense and remind us that we share a common bond that is truly special. We now feel a quiet confidence to take on challenges together or individually that may have seemed overwhelming before. "Stuff" doesn't mean as much to us now as we are much more cognizant of buying what we really need rather than everything we might want. Hopefully, a morsel of that restraint will rub off on our children! We continue to seek and embrace the "off-the-beaten-path" destination when on vacation and to make every effort to mingle with other travelers. The world really has become a smaller and more accessible place.

A heavy dose of foresight and planning, some saved up cash, an open mind, self-confidence and a lot of determination are the only ingredients one needs to accomplish an achievement of a lifetime. Thanks for allowing us to share our story with you. May it inspire you to tackle the dream you have never given a chance to happen.

Appendix

Various and Sundry Travel Tips

- Travel at night whenever possible to save money, either on planes, buses or trains, but BE CAREFUL—strap your backpack to your body or chain it to a storage rack.
- Public transportation (how the majority of the locals get around) is almost always the best way to go. It's cheap, cultural and sometimes quite exciting. (i.e. Bangkok!)
- Don't forget to write down traveler's check numbers whenever you turn an AMEX advance into them.
- To add substance to your diary, include current event information about the country you are visiting at the time
- Buy Christmas gifts along the way and ship them home via sea mail—it takes about three months, but it is cheap and very reliable.
- Don't forget to bring spare eye glasses or contacts!
- Buy contact lens cleaner whenever you see it, it is very hard to find.
- Start Eurorail Pass within six months of issuance. (Observe issue date or risk losing prepaid amount if not used within allotted time)
- Get Japan Rail Pass in hand before entering Japan to maximize time on it.
- Trade books at hostels, guest houses, bookstores, etc. with fellow travelers instead of buying them.
- Watch free movies at many bars, especially in Thailand.
- Keep track of all expenses, you'll spend less if you do.
- Iodine is the only thing that kills everything in water—Pur-a-Tabs don't touch ghiardia.
- Make sure to check stamps made by government officials going into and out of a country, especially with double entry visas—"it's your responsibility."
- Carry no more than 25 percent of your body weight in your backpack to avoid back anguish.
- Hostels are full of notices from people looking to sell rides, cars, backpack gear, etc. Less advance planning is needed than you might think.
- Set up an account with a local camera store before you leave home to get a 50 percent discount on all developing. Send *film* home first class mail instead of sea mail to be extra safe.
- Try to arrive in cities as early as possible in the morning to secure reservations. If you need help, go to the tourist hotel information desk. With rare exceptions, advance reservations aren't necessary.
- Eat outside as often as possible. Food seems to taste better and you're usually eating for less money. Bread is almost always cheap, and it's filling and good for you.
- Always keep an eye on your bags!

- Always carry an extra roll of toilet paper.
- Bring an inflatable soft pillow—they are fairly comfortable (with a towel wrapped around it especially) and perfect to use on buses, trains, in hostels or whatever.
- Always keep a small stash of bread, fruit, peanut butter and museli bars in your backpack, just in case you have a delay, can't find a restaurant or everything is closed.
- Find lodging close to train stations on short visits—the places are usually cheaper and not as backbreaking to get to.

Accolades: The Good, the Bad, & the Ugly

Best Restaurant View: Pizzeria in Ronda, Spain
Bridge Most Similar to Golden Gate: Lisbon
Liveliest Bridge Scene: Charles River, Prague
Best Place to Buy Hummels: Germany
Cheapest, Most Accessible Wine: France
Pay to Use the Toilet!?: Germany
Surprisingly Entertaining Tours: "Sound of Music," Salzburg; City Tour of New Delhi
Most Breathtakingly Scenic Youth Hostel: Grindelwald, Switzerland
Most Overrated Cities: Vienna, Lisbon, Barcelona, Melbourne
Things I Missed: Ice in drinks, availability of orange juice and cold cereal, "bottomless" cups of coffee
Biggest Rip-off: Paying double for a table vs. standing at restaurants in Italy
Sleaziest Train Stations: Milan, Lisbon, Calcutta, Varanasi
Most Beautiful Ocean Walk: Eze, France to Monaco; Kangaroo Island, Australia
Bargains: Carpet in India (it made it home!); Le Havre, France to Rosslare, Ireland Ferry (included with Eurrail Pass); buy theater tickets in London at 6 a.m. the day of the show; clothes and cassettes in Thailand
Least English Speaking Countries: Japan, Spain
Hardiest Native Party Goers: Spain, Australia
Most Suited for Cycling: Holland, France
Cleanest City/Country: Singapore
Biggest Buddha: Lantau Island (Hong Kong); Kamakura (outside Tokyo)
Coldest: Nikko, Japan
Most Scenic Ocean Point: Southwest tip of Australia (where Indian and Southern oceans converge)
Worst Road: "Highway" from Pokhara to Katmandu, Nepal
Steepest Tram: Hong Kong
Most Redundant Food: Nepal Trek (porridge, soup, noodles, water)
Most Animals in the Wild: Kangaroo Island, Australia
Drunkest Night: Midnight Oil Concert outside of Karanda, Australia
Best Beachcombing: Ao Nang Beach, Krabi, Thailand
Worst Food: India
Most Staring: India

Worst Odor: India
Most Consistent Hassle: India
Most Expensive Meal: McDonalds, Hiroshima
Longest Day: Nepal Trek-Kalopani to Tatopani
Cutest Kids: Nepal
Most Unusual Sleeping Place: Sunya's Raft Trip, Kanchanaburi, Thailand
Best Snorkeling: Great Barrier Reef; Koh Pee Pee, Thailand
Best Street Food: Thailand
Favorite Countries Overall: Australia, Thailand, Holland, France
Peskiest Insect: Australian outback fly

What You REALLY Need To Bring

- Small flashlight
- Thongs (sandals) for showers
- Diary or journal
- Sunglasses (wrap-around best), not too expensive-looking
- A paperback or two
- Walkman/tapes (optional), I prefer to absorb myself in my surroundings
- Small toiletry bag
- Basic first aid kit
- Shots/pills depending on country visiting
- Sunscreen, lip balm
- Plastic bags
- Ziplock bags
- X-Ray proof film container
- Locks for bags/room/train
- Small towel
- Inflatable pillow
- Wash cloth (optional)
- Small calendar/note pad/pen
- Lightweight sleeping bag
- Sleep sheet (a must to stay at many youth hostels)
- Swiss Army Knife
- Address book
- *Lonely Planet Guide* of the first country you are visiting (pick up others right before visiting them)
- Deck of cards (optional)
- Miniature backgammon/chess board (optional)
- Dramamine (air/boat sickness pills)
- Bathing suit
- Extra eye glasses/contacts/solution
- A roll of toilet paper
- AMEX card
- Telephone calling card number
- Health insurance

- Money pouch
- Day pack
- Trip supply of dental floss (almost impossible to find)
- Pur-a-Tabs/iodine (for water purification)
- Watch (optional)
- Small alarm clock/(radio part optional)
- Calculator (for currency conversions)
- Camera that can shoot quickly and zoom when necessary
- Contraceptives
- Rain gear in stuff sack
- Extra camera batteries
- Passport
- International driver's license
- Mini foreign language dictionaries
- Comfortable walking shoes
- Small umbrella (optional)
- Youth hostel card
- "Fanny pack"
- Less than half the clothes you think you'll need (you can always buy them cheap along the way). Here is a summary of what we brought:
- 3-4 pairs of underwear
- 1 pair of blue jeans
- 1 pair of casual pants (guys and girls)
- 2-3 dresses (girls)
- 3-4 tee shirts
- 1 sweatshirt
- 1 sweater
- 1 belt
- 3 pairs of shorts
- 2-3 casual shirts
- Leave nice jewelry at home! Susan brought an inexpensive gold wedding band.
- 1 pair of walking shoes
- 1 pair of slightly dressier shoes
- 3-4 pairs of socks
- Sleepshirt (optional)

References and Inspirations for Our Journey

1. *Transitions Abroad*; Newsletter-style composition with tips on working, traveling, studying and living abroad.

2. *Travel Smart, Enjoy More, Pay Less*; Brief, informative tidbits for people of all ages about travel.

3. *USA Today*; numerous articles over the past five years.

4. *The Day Man Lost, Hiroshima, 6 August 1945*, by the Pacific War Research Society.

5. *Learning Vacations*; "From campus to campground and Kansas to Kathmandu, more than 400 opportunities to relax, have fun and learn at the same time," by Gerson Eisenberg.

6. *Adventure Travel Abroad*; Reliable information on worldwide adventures, by Pat Dickerman.

7. *Survival Kit For Overseas Living*; For Americans planning to live and work abroad, by Robert Kohls.

8. *Vagabond Globetrotting: State of the Art*; How to get started and keep going with a low-cost adventure, by M.L. Endicott.

9. *Budget Asia: Southeast Asia and the Far East*; Concise, to the point guide book, by Dan Spitzer.

10. *Made in Japan, the Story of Sony*, by Akio Morita.

11. *Europe for Free*, "Thousands of free things to do all over Europe," by Brian Butker.

12. *Europe: Where the Fun Is*, by Rollin Riggs and Bruce Jacobsen.

13. *Beat the High Cost of Travel*, by Tom Brosnaham.

14. *City of Joy*, "An epic of love, heroism and hope in the India of Mother Teresa," by Dominique Lapierre.

15. *Six Months Off*, "An American family's Australian adventure," by Lamar Alexander.

16. *Miles From Nowhere*, "A round-the-world bicycle adventure," by the late Barbara Savage.

17. *World Walk*, "One man's four-year journey around the world," by Steven M. Newman.

18. *Frommer's New World of Travel* (1991), "A guide to alternative vacations in America and throughout the world," by Arthur Frommer.

19. *Outside Magazine*, in my opinion, one of the best monthly publications available on all outdoor activity.

20. Any *Lonely Planet Guide* in the countries we visited.

Guidebooks We Used

1. *A Bantam Travel Guide to Australia*, 1990 edition, several contributors, published by Bantam Books.

2. *Frommer's Australia on $30 A Day*, by John Godwin, published by Simon and Schuster, Inc.

3. *International Youth Hostels: The Guide to Budget Accommodation*, published by International Youth Hostel Federation.

4. *Budget Asia: Southeast Asia and the Far East*, by Dan Spitzer, published by William Morrow and Company, Inc.

5. *Illustrated Today's Japan*, by the Japan Travel Bureau.

6. *Lonely Planet*, "the best," we used it throughout Asia.

7. *Fodor's '90 Europe*, "a guide to the best of 32 countries," by Fodor's Travel Publications, Inc.

8. *Let's Go Europe*, St. Martin's Press.

Conversion Table By Country
Approximate Rates in 1990-91

Country	Currency	US$1 Equals
Australia	Dollar	A$1.25
Japan	Yen	130 Yen
Hong Kong	Dollar	HK$7.70
Thailand	Baht	25 Baht
India	Rupee	19 Indian Rupees
Nepal	Rupee	32 Nepalese Rupees
Malaysia	Dollar	M$2.70
Singapore	Dollar	S$1.75
Germany	Deutsche Mark	1.7 Deutsche Marks
Czechoslovakia	Krona	27 Krona
Hungary	Forints	72 Forints
Austria	Schilling	11.7 Schilling
Italy	Lira	1230 Lira
Switzerland	Franc	1.47 Swiss Franc
France	Franc	5.9 French Francs
Spain	Peseta	108 Pesetas
Portugal	Escudo	148 Escdos
Holland	Gilder	1.92 Gilders
Belgium	Franc	33 Belgian Francs
Ireland	Pound	.63 Irish Pounds
England	Pound	.57 British Pounds

David Wooten

Trip Spending Grid
Total Expenditures by Country in Total and by Day

Biking Across America	# of Days	David Bikecentennial Fee	Susan Bikecentennial Fee	Bikes	Bike Accessories	Bike Repairs	Other Trip Expenses	Airfare to Seattle	(U.S. Dollars) Total Spent	(U.S. Dollars) Avg. Spent/Day
Seattle to Maine	90	$ 2,000	$ 2,000	$ 1,130	$ 657	$ 280	$ 1,365	$ 478	$ 7,910	$ 88

(fee covered all lodging, meals and maps—$22/day per person)

Backpacking Around the World

Country	# of Days	Lodging	Food	Transportation	Necessities	Entertainment	Postage	Souvenirs/Gifts	(U.S. Dollars) Total Spent	(U.S. Dollars) Avg. Spent/Day
California	11	$ 119	$ 260	$ 365	$ 128	$ 145	$ 15	$ 24	$ 1,067	$ 97
Australia	72	$ 834	$ 1,205	$ 1,458	$ 704	$ 1,280	$ 93	$ 298	$ 5,944	$ 83
Japan	38	$ 1,669	$ 892	$ 938	$ 646	$ 326	$ 111	$ 204	$ 4,824	$ 127
Hong Kong	5	$ 71	$ 100	$ 20	$ 132	$ 10	$ -	$ 116	$ 454	$ 91
Thailand	39	$ 159	$ 511	$ 265	$ 287	$ 292	$ 141	$ 301	$ 1,995	$ 51
India	18	$ 89	$ 171	$ 212	$ 9	$ 76	$ 6	$ 376	$ 957	$ 53
Nepal	20	$ 52	$ 211	$ 146	$ 69	$ 137	$ 7	$ 78	$ 720	$ 36
Malaysia	6	$ 47	$ 113	$ 44	$ 16	$ 27	$ 3	$ -	$ 256	$ 43
Singapore	5	$ 46	$ 105	$ 19	$ 114	$ 58	$ 63	$ 51	$ 461	$ 92
Asia Total	131	$ 2,133	$ 2,103	$ 1,644	$ 1,273	$ 926	$ 331	$ 1,126	$ 9,667	$ 74
Germany	10	$ 161	$ 145	$ 90	$ 25	$ 73	$ 33	$ 230	$ 767	$ 77
Czech.	3	$ 56	$ 34	$ 9	$ 7	$ 12	$ 1	$ 14	$ 136	$ 45
Hungary	3	$ 50	$ 48	$ 2	$ 6	$ 20	$ 7	$ 28	$ 164	$ 55
Austria	6	$ 220	$ 230	$ 29	$ 24	$ 204	$ 36	$ 78	$ 827	$ 138
Italy	7	$ 217	$ 244	$ 10	$ 56	$ 88	$ 50	$ 133	$ 805	$ 115
Switz./Liecht.	10	$ 168	$ 198	$ 35	$ 88	$ 73	$ 77	$ 140	$ 789	$ 79
France/Monaco	15	$ 309	$ 406	$ 88	$ 41	$ 158	$ 42	$ 140	$ 1,199	$ 80
Spain/Gib	7	$ 130	$ 198	$ 45	$ 75	$ 52	$ 48	$ 43	$ 598	$ 85
Portugal	7	$ 100	$ 168	$ 21	$ 59	$ 34	$ 36	$ 14	$ 439	$ 63
Luxembourg	1	$ 19	$ 26	$ -	$ 21	$ -	$ 3	$ 7	$ 77	$ 77
Holland	5	$ 87	$ 124	$ 24	$ 18	$ 135	$ 29	$ 39	$ 461	$ 92
Belgium	2	$ -	$ 56	$ 2	$ 8	$ 9	$ 4	$ 18	$ 99	$ 50
Ireland	10	$ 152	$ 264	$ 209	$ 47	$ 200	$ 22	$ 216	$ 1,120	$ 112
England	6	$ -	$ 126	$ 104	$ 32	$ 103	$ 5	$ 46	$ 422	$ 70
Eurrail				$ 1,860					$ 1,860	
Europe Total	92	$ 1,669	$ 2,267	$ 2,528	$ 507	$ 1,161	$ 393	$ 1,146	$ 9,763	$ 106
Overseas Airfare				$ 7,400					$ 7,400	
Overseas Grand Total	306	$ 4,755	$ 5,835	$ 13,395	$ 2,612	$ 3,512	$ 832	$ 2,594	$ 33,841	$ 111
Cost Per Day By Segment		$ 15.54	$ 19.07	$ 43.77	$ 8.54	$ 11.48	$ 2.72	$ 8.48	$ 110.59	
Overseas % Breakdown		14%	17%	40%	8%	10%	2%	8%	100%	

| **Total Trip** | | | | | | | | | $ 41,751 | |

About the Author

David Wooten grew up in the Carolinas and received a degree in journalism from the University of South Carolina. A fast-track sales management career with Pepsico and the Quaker Oats Company has led to his current position of Vice-President of Sales at HT Marketing, Inc., the largest distributor of Hawaiian Tropic in the world. His passions are his family, travel, bicycling, work, golf and baseball. He and Susan now reside in Murray, Kentucky.

Order Form

Use this form to order additional copies of
We're Outta Here for your friends or family members.

Name:_____

Address:_____

City:_____State:_____Zip:_____

Daytime phone: (___)_____

If gift, message that you would like enclosed:

_____

_____

If gift, ship to:

Name:_____

Address:_____

City:_____State:_____Zip:_____

Method of payment: *(Make checks payable to Creative Pursuits)*

❏ Check   ❏ Money order   ❏ VISA

Card #_____Exp._____

Signature:_____

(required for credit card purchases)

Quantity: _____ x $14.95 = $_____

Shipping & Handling Quantity: _____ x $3.00 = $_____

Subtotal: $_____

KY residents add 6% sales tax: $_____

TOTAL: $_____

Please return form and payment to
Creative Pursuits
P.O. Box 977
Murray, KY 42071

Thank you! Your order will shipped within 1–3 weeks from receipt.